In accordance with the latest syllabus prescribed by the Council for the Indian Certificate of Secondary Education Examination, New Delhi.

A TEXT BOOK OF
ENVIRONMENTAL SCIENCE
CLASS IX

Manasa Sampat Hegde
M. Sc., Chemistry
PGDESD

OSWAL PUBLISHERS
1/12 Sahitya Kunj, M. G. Road, Agra-282 002

No part of this book can be reproduced in any form or by any means without the prior written permission of the publisher.

Edition : 2020

ISBN : 978-93-89937-06-0

OSWAL PUBLISHERS

Head office : 1/12, Sahitya Kunj, M. G. Road, Agra-282 002
Phone : (0562) 2527771-4, +91 75340 77222
E-mail : contact@oswalpublishers.com
Website : www.oswalpublishers.com
Printed at

Preface

In order to order to understand the various aspects and challenges of the environment, there is a need for a resource that aids in a holistic understanding of Environmental Education.

Oswal's 'A Textbook of Environmental Science' for class IX successfully meets this requirement and is equipped with essential and relevant information. It is composed in strict adherence to the latest syllabus prescribed by the ICSE board.

The title also introduces the concept of sustainable development. Through the activities and exercises that are provided in this book, learners can explore more on the topics of environmental conservation and sustainable development.

The chapters and exercises are written in accordance with the syllabus. Some significant latest advancements in the field of environmental science have also been incorporated in the form of examples and facts. Each chapter in this book has been composed and assembled in a way that helps the learners to understand the topics in an effective manner.

We hope this book will enable the readers to strengthen their understanding of the concepts of environmental science.

All suggestions regarding the book are welcome.

Publisher

SYLLABUS CLASS IX
ENVIRONMENT SCIENCE

(Candidates offering Environmental Applications are not eligible to offer Environmental Science.)

There will be one paper of two hours duration carrying 80 marks and Internal Assessment of 20 marks.

The paper will have two Sections :

Section A (Compulsory) will contain short answer questions covering the entire syllabus.

Section B will contain six questions. Candidates will be required to answer any four questions from this section.

1. **Understanding our Environment**

    (a) What is Environmental Science?

    What do we understand by 'Environment'? What does the study of Environmental Science involve?

    (b) What are our main environmental problems?

    Environmental problems to be studied in terms of resource depletion, pollution and extinction of species.

    (c) A global perspective of environmental problems.

    To be studied with reference to the developed and developing countries.

    (d) The root of environmental problems.

    Population crisis and consumption crisis should be covered.

    (e) A sustainable world.

    Concept of sustainability to be explained; sustainable societies to be discussed.

2. **Living things in Ecosystems**

    (a) What is an ecosystem?

    Concept of ecosystems to be explained; biotic and abiotic structures, organisms and species; populations, communities.

    (b) Habitat and ecological niche.

    To be discussed in terms of address and function.

    (c) How species interact with each other.

    Interaction of species should be covered in terms of - predation, competition, parasitism, mutualism and commensalism. Law of Limiting Factors; synergisms.

    (d) Adapting to the environment.

    Evolution by natural selection; co-evolution, extinction.

3. **How Ecosystems work**

    (a) Energy flow in ecosystems.

    An explanation of how life depends on the sun; who eats what; respiration: burning the fuel. Energy transfer: food chains, food webs and trophic levels.

    (b) The cycling of materials.

    *The water cycle, the carbon cycle (how humans are affecting the carbon cycle) and the nitrogen cycle; **Not to be tested, for knowledge and understanding only.***

    Interdependence of natural cycles.

    (c) How ecosystems change.

    Succession- secondary and primary.

4. **Kinds of Ecosystems**

    (a) Forests.

    Tropical rainforests and threats to rainforests; temperate rainforests; temperate deciduous forests; Taiga.

    (b) Grasslands, Deserts and Tundra.

    Tropical savannas; temperate grasslands: prairies, steppes and pampas; deserts; Tundra. Threats to the temperate grasslands, deserts and Tundra.

    (c) Freshwater ecosystems.

    The study to cover - lakes and ponds; wetlands - marshes and swamps; rivers. Threats to wetlands and rivers must also be highlighted.

    (d) Marine ecosystems.

    Estuaries, coral reefs, oceans and how each is threatened should be discussed. Polar ecosystems of the Arctic and the Antarctic and the threats to them must also be covered.

    Only threats to the specifically mentioned ecosystems will be tested for the purpose of the examination. The rest are for knowledge and understanding.

    (e) Biogeographic zones of India.

    The different biogeographic zones/regions of India and predominant wildlife in these zones/regions.

5. **Water**

    (a) Our water resources.

    Water resource in the form of frozen solid in polar ice caps, surface water (rivers of controversy, dams), groundwater (aquifers running low). Solutions to water shortages must be covered in terms of desalting the sea, towing water, water conservation and water harvesting.

    (b) Freshwater pollution.

    Point pollution and non-point pollution; wastewater treatment plants, pathogens. The manner in which water pollution affects ecosystems; artificial eutrophication, thermal pollution. Cleaning up water pollution. The special problem of groundwater pollution; bottled water.

    (c) Ocean pollution.

    How pollutants get into oceans; preventing ocean pollution; who owns the oceans?

6. **Air**

    (a) What causes air pollution?

    Air pollution due to - natural disasters; domestic combustion; air pollution on wheels; industrial air pollution.

    Major air pollutants - carbon monoxide, oxides of nitrogen, oxides of sulphur, ozone, lead, hydrocarbons, benzene and particulates - their sources, health effects and the environmental effects must be studied.

    Classification of air pollutants based on composition - gaseous pollutants and particulate matter (grit, dust, smoke and lead oxide); broader classification - primary and secondary pollutants.

    Aerosols (smog), sources – natural (continental, oceanic and anthropogenic); their effect on our lives.

    Air pollution episode - the Bhopal gas tragedy.

    (b) Thermal inversions, photochemical smog and acid precipitation.

Thermal inversions (Los Angeles), Photochemical Smog (Mexico City) and Acid Precipitation (Mumbai) - how acid precipitation affects ecosystems.

(c) Impact of air pollution.

Impact of air pollution should be covered in terms of economic losses, lowered agricultural productivity and health problems.

7. **Atmosphere and Climate**

   (a) The atmosphere.

   Balance between photosynthesis and respiration; layers of the atmosphere. **Not to be tested, for knowledge and understanding only.**

   (b) Climate.

   What determines climate (latitude, atmospheric circulation patterns, ocean circulation patterns, local geography, seasonal changes in climate). **Not to be tested, for knowledge and understanding only.**

   (c) Greenhouse earth.

   The Greenhouse Effect, rising carbon dioxide levels, GHGs and the earth's temperature (global warming); effect on weather, agriculture and sea-levels; slowing the temperature change.

   (D) The Ozone layer

   Ozone in the troposphere, ozone in the stratosphere; detection of the damage to the ozone layer; causes and consequences of ozone thinning; alternatives to CFCs.

8. **Soil and Land**

   (a) Deforestation.

   Causes and consequences of rapid and progressive deforestation in the developing world - fuel crisis, competition for land, land exploited for cash and food crops, population pressures, increasing demand for timber to meet the needs of the developed world, grazing and its link with desertification.

   Effects of deforestation on climate, atmosphere and soil process.

   (b) Soil erosion and desertification.

   Causes and consequences of soil erosion and desertification - removal of vegetation, overgrazing, overculture, clearance of slopes, drought, heavy rainfall, bad farming practices.

   (c) Land pollution.

   Causes and consequences of land pollution - salinization, fertilizers, pesticides, toxic wastes, nuclear wastes, domestic wastes, ground water contamination.

9. **People**

   (a) World poverty and gap between developed and developing countries.

   Dimensions of world poverty and gap between developed and developing countries using development indicators such as per-capita incomes, housing, levels of disease and nutrition.

   (b) Poverty in developed countries, poverty in developing countries.

   Rural poverty and urban poverty.

(c) The implications of poverty trap for the environment in developing countries.

Self-explanatory.

10. **Urbanisation**

    (a) Causes of urbanisation.

    The push-pull factors to be discussed.

    (b) Manifestations of urbanisation.

    Growth of slums, growth of informal sector, pressure on civic amenities; degradation of human resources; growing sense of despair.

    (c) Social, economic and environmental problems.

    Problems of housing, congestion, pollution, loss of agricultural land and provision of services to be covered.

10. **Agriculture**

    (a) Unsustainable patterns of modern industrialised agriculture.

    Monocultures, disappearance of traditional crop varieties, pollution risk due to use of pesticides and inorganic fertilizers; problems of irrigation – surface and ground water.

    (b) Environmental damage due to large farm units.

    Self-explanatory.

    (c) Food mountains in developed countries.

    Surplus and waste.

    (d) The Green Revolution.

    Discussion on whether Green Revolution is a success or a failure.

INTERNAL ASSESSMENT

Any **one** project/assignment from the prescribed syllabus.

Suggested Assignments

1. Make a survey of any one threat to the local environment with suggestions as to how the impact of the threat could be gradually reduced.

2. Make a functional model of an apparatus/equipment that could be used to alleviate the impact of any pollutant and, make a survey to study the effectiveness of this apparatus/equipment. (The report of the study is to form a part of the Project Work.)

CONTENTS

1. Understanding Our Environment — 13-26
2. Living Things in Ecosystems — 27-42
3. How Ecosystems work — 43-82
4. Water — 83-101
5. Air — 102-120
6. Atmosphere and Climate — 121-135
7. Soil and hand — 136-151
8. People — 152-165
9. Urbanisation — 166-179
10. Agriculture — 180-195

1 UNDERSTANDING OUR ENVIRONMENT

Environment is the surroundings or conditions in which a person, animal or plant lives or operates. It is the natural world, and/or a geographical area where organisms survive. Environment is derived from a French term *'environ'* which means surrounding. A term which closely relates to the environment is 'nature'. Nature is the natural component of the universe which includes living and non-living things. The word nature finds its origin in ancient Greek and Latin vocabulary. In Latin, the word *natura* means 'essential qualities'. While in Greek, *natura* means intrinsic characteristics of plants, animals and other components of the universe. Both the definitions hint at a fact that nature has all the components to initiate and facilitate the birth, growth, reproduction and death of all living organisms. Nature is a full-fledged system which keeps the life cycle of living organisms rolling on. The life cycles of living beings are very intricate. This is because the life cycle of one organism is linked to the life cycle of another organism. It is a complex network. All the biotic and abiotic factors have their life cycle in which they are created, sustained and then destroyed. Destruction of a life cycle initiates another life cycle. Environmental studies is an integrated, quantitative, and interdisciplinary approach to study the environmental systems. Therefore, it is an interdisciplinary field that includes physics, ecology, chemistry, botany, zoology, mineralogy, oceanography, geology, and atmospheric science to carry on the study of the environment and to formulate solution of environmental problems. Environmental Science is unique amongst the sciences through the application of all science, tools to the natural world facilitates our understanding of the environment.

> **Fascinating Fact**
>
> Many areas are using beet juice and salt mixture on their roads to keep them from freezing over. The beet juice prevents roads from icing over in temperatures up to -25°C, making it more effective than using a salt brine. A beet juice mixture is also less toxic to the environment.

There is a paramount need to create a consciousness about the environment. Human beings from all sections of the society and all ages must be responsible towards maintaining our environment. Therefore, to inculcate the environmental consciousness right from childhood, environmental studies has been introduced in schools and colleges academics. This aspect will be integrated in the entire educational process. The study of Environmental Science will enable us to—

 (i) Understand the connection between natural and human made environment.
 (ii) Understanding our dependence on the various components of environment (biotic, abiotic and human made).
 (iii) Develop a multidisciplinary perspective to understand the environmental issues or problems and analyse the impacts of our daily activities on its integrity.
 (iv) Develop favourable attitudes and habits to protect and preserve our environment.

1.0. MAIN ENVIRONMENTAL PROBLEMS

We are making advance development in the field of science and technology. Such progress have always aimed at upgrading our lifestyle or providing us a better living. The journey of progressing towards a better living has been accomplished by exploitation of resources. Human activities have been deteriorating the environment since centuries. Resource depletion, pollution, global warming, ozone layer depletion and loss of biodiversity are the major alarming environmental issues.

(i) Resource depletion occurs when the renewable and non-renewable natural resources become scarce due to high demand. The resources are being consumed much faster than they can be replenished. The resources can be broadly classified as renewable resources and non-renewable resources. Non-renewable resources like fossil fuels takes a long time to replenish. Therefore, such resources should be used judiciously. Use of renewable resources like hydropower, solar energy, wind energy, etc. should be encouraged as they do not get exhausted.

> **Fascinating Fact**
>
> Norway has very strict rules on advertising cars as "green" saying, "cars can do nothing good for the environment except less damage than others".

Let us have a look at depletion patterns of few important resources—

(a) Water—Even though our planet is 70% water, only a small percentage of that is a fresh water. The rest is salt water and not useful at all. The 2.5% of fresh water exists mostly as ice or permanent snow cover. Only a small percentage of water is available for use. Water resources are facing serious threats by human activities. These activities include pollution, urban growth, deforestation, and climate change. The three major sources of water pollution are municipal, industrial and agricultural. The hydrological cycle is the cycle

Understanding Our Environment

where water evaporates from the sea and is precipitated on land in the form of rain, hail and snow. The water is then stored in the ground as groundwater (which is ultimately discharged into waterways) or if it cannot be absorbed, it returns to the sea through run-off. Much of the pollution discharged deliberately or accidentally onto the land or directly into waterways will ultimately reach the sea where it will affect marine ecosystems.

(b) Soil—Soil is one of the most important natural resources on Earth. It is required both directly and indirectly for food production, manufacturing of industrial raw materials, and for generation of energy sources. Soil is essential for the function of ecosystems providing nutrients, oxygen, water and heat. Soil resources are being degraded by poor agricultural practices and chemical contamination. One of the most significant challenges facing current and future generations is the preservation of this irreplaceable natural resource from pollution and physical destruction. Soil contamination is the human-induced deposition of harmful substances which are not a product of natural accumulation or soil formation. Many human activities, ranging from mining activities, industrial and agricultural production to road transport, result in pollution that can accumulate in the soil or result in biological and chemical reactions in the soil. Soil erosion is the removal of soil by wind or water. This natural process is intensified by human activities, such as deforestation for agricultural purposes, changes in hydrological conditions, overgrazing and other inappropriate agricultural activities. Erosion can lead to soil degradation and eventually complete destruction.

(c) Forest—Over the years, the area under forest cover has decreased steadily, as forests have been cleared for agriculture, industry, housing and other development activities like the construction of roads, railways and hydroelectric plants. Communities living in and around forests remove fuelwood from forests. As long as the population was low, forests could meet the demand and still remain healthy, but the increasing population has severely depleted the forests. One of the most extracted and important resources of forest is timber. It is an important renewable natural resource in many societies around the world. If production is approached in a responsible way it can be both sustainable and economical. Timber is mostly used to create lumber for use in construction. They can also be used to make paper products, fibre board, hard board, plywood and particle board.

(d) Fossil Fuel—Fossil fuels are by far the largest source of energy in modern economies – coal and gas for electricity generation; and petrol, diesel and kerosene-type fuels for land, sea and air transport. Approximately two-thirds of the world's electricity is generated by coal-fired power plants. Coal is a fossil fuel created through a process known as coalification. Plants that formed millions of years ago in swamp forests died and formed layers of peat that were buried through geological processes, and then altered through heat and pressure in low oxygen environments. Natural gas is a fossil fuel created by the decomposition of organic material, usually from ancient marine organisms, in an anaerobic environment. There are two categories of natural gas deposits—conventional and unconventional. Conventional deposits are associated with oil reserves and unconventional deposits include coal bed methane, shale gas and tight-gas sandstone. Like natural gas, oil is created through the decomposition of organic matter in an anaerobic environment over millions of years. Natural gas supplies about 22% of the nation's energy needs and is used as an energy source for heating, cooking, and generation of electricity. Oil supplies 40% of the nation's energy needs and is used for the production of gasoline, diesel fuel, jet fuel, propane, and asphalt. Formation of fossil fuel is an extreme slow process. The extraction of fuel is happening at a much faster rate than the nature can replenishs them.

(e) Minerals—The term 'mineral' refers to a variety of materials found on the earth. It includes metals such as iron, copper, and gold; industrial minerals, like lime and gypsum; construction materials such as sand and stone; and fuels, such as coal and uranium. Mining by definition is an extractive industry, often with huge environmental and social impacts the mine has been closed. The products that comes out from the mines which can be used as a raw material for cellphones, tools and appliances, vehicles, and even roads. As the industrialised nations of the world continue such activities, the rapid depletion of energy and mineral resources is observed.

> **Fascinating Fact**
> About 87% of the electricity created in the world, comes from coal burning. Coal burning, followed by crude oil, and natural gas, is the biggest source of carbon dioxide emission in the world.

The general causes of resource depletion are :

1. Overpopulation—With increasing population, demands of the country increases which further results in the depletion of resources.

2. Overconsumption and waste—As the standards of living of people improve, they tend to consume more and waste even more.

3. Technological and industrial development—Technology advances and so the need of resources increases.

4. Pollution and contamination of resources—Water pollution and soil pollution are increasing at an alarming rate today due to the negligent attitude of people towards the environment.

> **Fascinating Fact**
> Pollution is one of the main environmental problems being discussed today. In every school or college, it's being taught upon, and the government is trying to combat this in every possible way. Fewer people know that it's the increasing pollution, which is leading the next generation to a weaker immune system and making them vulnerable to having various diseases.

Understanding Our Environment

Pollution has a direct effect on contamination of resources available in nature.

(ii) Pollution is the introduction of contaminants into the natural environment that cause adverse changes. Human activities like industrialisation, combustion of fuel, improper waste disposal introduce pollutants in the air, water and soil. Many products that we used in our day-to-day life contains chemicals that act as a potential pollutant. Some deodorants, air conditioners and other coolants emit out CFCs which degrade the ozone layer. The overuse of products that emit CFCs has already depleted the ozone layer. As a consequence, harmful UV radiation from the sun enters the biosphere.

> **Fascinating Fact**
>
> The amount of plastic making its way into the Earth's oceans is staggering.

1.1. TYPES AND CAUSES OF POLLUTION

1. Air Pollution

It is the most prevalent and dangerous form of pollution and is considered to go hand-in-hand with urbanization. These are directly affecting our existence. Smoke releases sulphur dioxide into the air making it toxic. It is caused mainly due to chimneys, factory stacks, vehicles and burning of wood. Release of sulphur dioxide and other greenhouse gases into air causes global warming and has the capacity to cause acid rain. Global warming or emission of these gases has increased temperatures, erratic rains, and droughts worldwide. This has heavily increased the cases of asthma, bronchitis and the more dangerous lung cancer, mainly in the metro cities. Carbon dioxide, carbon monoxide, particulate matter, dust are all air pollutants.

2. Water Pollution

Every living being depends directly on water. Other than direct dependencies, more than 60% of the species live in some form of water. Thus, water pollution is another major type of pollution that needs to be curbed. Major water pollutants are industrial effluents, sewage, domestic waste and spillage from ships and tankers. In addition, insecticides and pesticides run-off from fields and farms also pollute water. Water pollution is also a major cause of diseases caused to the non-aquatic species. Water pollution not only harms the aquatic beings but it also contaminates the entire food chain by severely affecting humans dependent on these. Water-borne diseases like cholera, diarrhoea have also increased in all places.

3. Soil Pollution

Soil pollution also known as land pollution, occurs due to incorporation of unwanted chemicals in the soil due to human activities. Use of insecticides and pesticides absorbs the nitrogen compounds from the soil, making it unfit for plants to derive nutrition from the soil. Release of industrial waste, mining and deforestation also exploits the soil.

4. Noise Pollution

It is caused when a noise which is of higher intensity than 85 db reaches our bare ears. Traffic, industries, faulty lifestyles are the major factors that causes noise pollution. Continuous exposure of high intensity sound may lead to psychological problems like stress, hearing impairment and hypertension.

5. Radioactive Pollution

This is considered as one of the most dangerous types of pollution because of its permanent effects. Radiation leakage from nuclear plant, or nuclear bombs are responsible for radioactive pollution. It can cause health problems like skin cancer, blood cancer, infertility, birth defects and blindness. It has the ability to permanently change the texture of soil, air and water. It can even cause mutation in species which can propagate for ages.

6. Light Pollution

Whenever illumination available is more than what is required in an area, light pollution is seen. It is more noticeable in big cities, on advertising boards and billboards, mainly during large scale events. It mainly affects the astronomical observations by making the stars very difficult to observe and study.

> **Fascinating Fact**
>
> Artificial lights can disrupt the migratory schedules of birds causing them to leave too early or too late in the season, missing ideal conditions for nesting.

(iii) Loss of biodiversity is the extinction of species (micro-organisms, plant or animal). The possible reasons for extinction of species is over-exploitation of resources, reduction of species habitat, selective cultivation, etc. Extinction occurs when species are diminished because of environmental forces (habitat fragmentation, global change, overexploitation of species for human use) or because of evolutionary changes in their members (genetic inbreeding, poor reproduction, decline in population numbers).

The major causes of extinction are :

1. Climatic Heating and Cooling—Climate Change is caused by a number of things. The effect that climate has on extinction is huge. The biodiversity of the Earth cannot keep up with the rapid changes in temperature and climate. The species are not used to severe weather conditions and long seasons, or a changing chemical make-up of their surroundings. As more species die, it is only

Understanding Our Environment

making it more difficult for the survivors to find food. The present day warmer climatic conditions that we are used to is perfect for diseases and epidemics to thrive.

2. Changes in Sea Levels or Currents—The changes in sea levels and currents is the impact of the melting freshwater. The denser, saltier water sinks and forms the currents that marine life depends on. The spreading and rising of ocean floor also affects the sea level. A small rise in the ocean floor can displace a lot of water onto land, that is already occupied. The gases from the volcanic activity can also be absorbed by the water, thus changing the chemical composition and making it unsuitable for some life.

3. Acid Rain—Acid rain forms when sulphur dioxide and/or nitrogen oxides are put out into the atmosphere. The chemicals get absorbed by water droplets in the clouds, and eventually fall to the earth as acid precipitation. Acid rain increases the acidity of the soil which affects plant life. It can also disturb rivers and lakes to a possibly lethal level.

4. Loss of Habitat—Most animals require a certain area of territory in which they can hunt and forage, breed and raise their young, and (when necessary) expand their population. As human civilization expands relentlessly into the wild, these natural habitats diminish. Land use practices like deforestation, urban and suburban development, agricultural cultivation, and water management projects that encroach upon and destroy natural habitat.

5. Overexploitation—Human beings depend on nature for their basic needs like food, clothing, shelter. But with technological advancements, we have explored many other uses of nature. Therefore, our need has turned into greed. Activities like hunting, fishing, etc. has led to extinction of various species and the result of over-exploitation of natural resources. In an ecosystem, each organism has an important role to play. Extinction or non-participation of one species considerably affects the ecological balance. The number of plants and animals appearing in the list of endangered species is increasing. An endangered species is a species which has been categorized as very likely to become extinct. For example – Siberian Tiger. Passenger pigeon is already extinct as a result of overhunting.

1.2. ENVIRONMENTAL PROBLEM : A GLOBAL PERSPECTIVE

Human beings developed machinery, industries, vehicles, constructions, etc. in order to lead a comfortable and an easy life. However, unsustained use of these inventions gave birth to environmental issues like pollution, global warming; ozone hole, resource exhaustion and loss of biodiversity. Eventually, the degrading environment is affecting the quality of our life. Therefore, it is essential to think that have we really progressed? As we discussed earlier, human development is often gauzed in terms of economic development or progress in technology. The nations are classified as developed, developing and under-developed based on economic and technological status. Environmental ethics are concerned with who owns resources and how they are distributed. The developed nations have exploited a huge amount of natural resources in the process of achieving the current economic and technological status. This is at the cost of poor people who are resource-dependent and live in developing nations. The economically advanced countries have exploited their resources to such an extent that they have exhausted nearly everywhere. Developed countries buy resources from resource-rich but economically deprived nations at a low cost. This depletes the natural resources of developing countries too. Changing this unfair economic practice is critical. Such a form of development has hampered environment and nature. If we overuse natural resources, our future generation will find it difficult to survive.

> **Fascinating Fact**
>
> If CFC-gases had not been banned, a large part of earth would be virtually uninhabitable by 2065. UV-radiation in Washington, D.C. or Southern Germany would be upto 650%, enough to cause sunburn in just five minutes.

> **Intext Questions**
>
> 1. How was the word 'nature' originated?
> 2. List out the major environmental problems.
> 3. What is CFC?

> **Fascinating Fact**
>
> A recent study from the World Economic Forum notes that 9 million tons of plastic enter oceans every year, which amounts to the equivalent of one garbage truck dumped into the ocean every minute.

1.3. ROOT CAUSE OF ENVIRONMENTAL PROBLEMS

The root cause of the environmental deterioration can be linked to the ever-growing population. The resource exploitation is being made to satisfy the needs and demands of this population. Population is defined as the number of living things that live together in the same place. The world population was estimated to have reached 7.5 billion in April 2017. Asia is the most populated continent, with its 4.3 billion residents making up 60% of the world population. Population growth is the rate at which a population expands. In the near future scarcity of food, fuel, clean and hygienic soil, water and air will immensely increase. The over-exploitation of resources is greatly hampering the buffering action and ability of nature to maintain the ecological balance. This concept can be better understood in terms of population crisis and consumption crisis.

Population crisis—The population crisis involves the exponential increase in the human population on earth. Developing countries are threatened by the population crisis as they are overpopulated. Asia is the most populated continent, with its 4.3 billion residents making up 60% of the world population. The world population is growing at approximately 2.4 % per year and are projected to reach

Understanding Our Environment

at least 2 billion by 2050. This is a scenario when there are too many organisms of a certain species is present in a certain habitat. This means that the number of organisms living there is larger than the carrying capacity of the habitat. In the near future, scarcity of food, fuel, clean and hygienic soil, water and air will immensely increase.

Consumption crisis—The consumption crisis involves the consumption of natural resources, pollution and extinctions caused by an exponential increase in the human population. The nature provides everything we consume, through mining, extraction, farming, and forestry. But there is a limit on the planet's resources. As we keep consuming more and more, the planet is overstressed by this over-exploitation of soil, water, minerals, forests, fish, etc. As a result, species, habitats, and even entire ecosystems will collapse.

1.4. SUSTAINABLE DEVELOPMENT

In 1987, the **World Commission on Environment and Development** introduced the term **Sustainable development** in its report *'our common future'*.

Sustainable development is the development that meets the needs of the present without compromising the ability of future generations to meet their own needs. The agenda of sustainable development is holistic and universal. The concept of sustainability links the concern for the carrying capacity of natural systems with the social, political, and economic challenges faced by humanity. For sustainable development to be achieved,

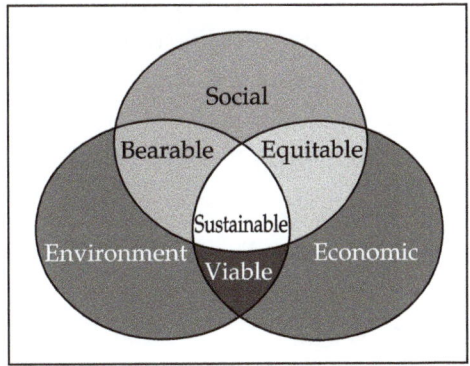

it is crucial to harmonise the three core elements: economic growth, social inclusion and environmental protection. These elements are interconnected and are all crucial for the well–being of individuals and societies. In September 2015, the United Nations General Assembly formally adopted a set of 17 Sustainable Development Goals (SDGs) that aim at transforming world by 2030. These goals focus at countering issues like :

(i) **People :** Ensuring healthy life, knowledge and inclusion of women and children.

(ii) **Planet :** Protecting our nature and ecosystem.

(iii) **Partnership :** Catalysing global solidarity.

(iv) **Justice :** Promoting safe and peaceful societies.

(v) **Prosperity :** Growing strong, inclusive and transforming economy.

(vi) **Equality :** Eradicating poverty and fight inequality.

Fascinating Fact

Even plants depend on the natural cycle of day and night. Artificial light at night can throw off a plant's response to the change of seasons. Prolonged exposure to artificial light prevents many trees from adjusting to seasonal variations.

Eco-village—One of the remarkable examples of sustainable development is an eco-village. An eco-village is a traditional or intentional community with the goal of becoming socially, culturally, economically and ecologically more sustainable. The population size of an eco-village is small which ranges from 50 to 200. The concept of eco-village is not very popular till date. Auroville is an eco-village situated in the plateau of South India. Auroville is home to over 2,000 people from 43 different countries and is one of the few places on Earth where biodiversity is actually increasing. The community is also a world leader in compressed-earth building techniques, rainwater harvesting, plant-based sewage treatment, solar and wind energy, and effective micro-organisms. Health of the residents is a very important aspect of sustainable and progressive development of any area or society. A balanced life is necessary in order to maintain a good health. A balanced life means being in control of all aspects of our life, such as :

1. Physical
2. Mental
3. Spiritual
4. Family
5. Financial
6. Work and Career
7. Social

Understanding Our Environment

Awareness of issues like personnel hygiene, public hygiene, drug abuse, narcotic addiction, alcohol consumption, child marriage, etc. are conducted because these issues affect the health of the whole community. Recent technologies of healthcare are introduced and implemented in the eco-villages. Eco-villages are also equipped with sustainable agriculture. The goal of sustainable agriculture is to meet society's food and textile needs in the present without compromising the ability of future generations to meet their own needs. Practitioners of sustainable agriculture seek to integrate three main objectives into their work: a healthy environment, economic profitability, and social and economic equity. Growers may use methods to promote soil health, minimise water use, and lower pollution levels on the farm. Consumers and retailers concerned with sustainability can look for "value-based" foods that are grown using methods promoting farm workers' well-being, that are environmentally friendly, or that strengthen the local economy.

Unfortunately, the practical application of sustainable development is unclear in many urban areas in developing countries. However, with current and emerging global challenges such as climate change, rapid urbanisation, environmental degradation, increasing poverty, food insecurity and financial crisis, a practical understanding of sustainable development is necessary and urgent especially in developing countries. Sustainability should be taken into consideration in all the fields like agriculture, industrialisation, urbanisation, infrastructure development, developing science and technology etc. The planning stage, execution stage and the monitoring stage should consider sustainable ways of carrying on the process. The unsustainable plans of development may yield short-term economic benefits, but it does not guarantee healthy and safe future for coming generations. This implies that we need to better understand the future limits to growth and use this understanding to reconfigure growth in a way that is increasingly sustainable. The sustainable way of progressing is the only way which ensures holistic development. Policies of government should inculcate clauses to promote sustainable societies. A sustainable society is one that can continue indefinitely. Its level of consumption should reflect environmental and resource balance. It should assure its citizens equality, freedom and a healthy standard of living. A sustainable society focuses on the current and future well-being of its citizens and the environment. Growth forever and obsession with the size of the commercial economy have displaced our responsible national goals. We must create a strategy for achieving a stable economy. We must develop measurement standards that clearly define personal, social and environmental health.

> **Fascinating Fact**
>
> Artificial lights can disrupt the migratory schedules of birds causing them to leave too early or too late in the season, missing ideal conditions for nesting. Birds that navigate by moonlight and starlight can wander off course.

Intext Questions

1. Define sustainable development.
2. Name the most populated continent.
3. What is consumption crisis ?

SUMMARY

- Environment is the surroundings or conditions in which a person, animal or plant lives or operates.
- Nature is the natural component of the universe which includes living and non-living.
- Environmental studies is an integrated, quantitative, and interdisciplinary approach to the study of environmental systems.
- The general causes of resource depletion are Over-population, Over-consumption and waste, Technological and industrial development and Pollution and contamination of resources.
- Resource depletion, pollution, loss of biodiversity are some of our environmental problems.
- The overuse of products that emit CFCs have created ozone holes.
- Population crisis involves the exponential increase in the human population on earth. Consumption crisis involves the consumption of natural resources, pollution and extinctions caused by an exponential increase in the human population.
- Sustainable development is the development that meets the needs of the present without compromising the ability of future generations to meet their own needs.
- In September 2015, the United Nations General Assembly formally adopted a set of 17 Sustainable Development Goals (SDGs) that aims at transforming world by 2030.
- An eco-village is a traditional or intentional community with the goal of becoming more socially, culturally, economically, and ecologically sustainable.
- A sustainable society is one that can continue indefinitely. Its level of consumption should reflect environmental and resource balance.
- People of all sections of the society and all the ages must be responsible towards maintaining our environment.

EXERCISE

A. Define each of these terms :
 1. Nature
 2. Eco-village

Understanding Our Environment

3. Overpopulation
4. Environment
5. Biodiversity
6. Environmental studies
7. Hydrological cycle
8. Mining
9. Endangered species

B. **Answer the following questions in brief :**
1. Why is ozone important to us ?
2. Differentiate between renewable and non-renewable sources of energy.
3. What are the possible reasons for loss of biodiversity ?
4. Why is EVS an interdisciplinary subject ?
5. 70% of the Earth is made up of water yet there is a shortage of water for human use. Why ?
6. Suggest a way of using timber without wasting it.
7. Write one point of difference between population crisis and consumption crisis.

C. **Answer these questions in detail :**
1. What are benefits of inculcating the concepts of environment in the academics at an early age ?
2. Explain the major environmental issues.
3. On what basis are the nations classified as developed, developing and under-developed ?
4. Explain the depletion patterns of each of these resources – soil, water, minerals, forest and fossil fuels.
5. How are fossil fuels formed ?
6. Explain the causes of resource depletion.
7. Write the effects of each of these types of pollution on the human health – Air pollution, water pollution, noise pollution and radioactive pollution.
8. Which are the major cause of extinction of species ?
9. Which are the main areas of focus of Sustainable Development Goals ?
10. Overpopulation crisis is said to be the root cause of environmental problems. Why ?
11. Eco-villages are a remarkable example of sustainable development. Explain this statement with an example.

WORKSHEET

A. Multiple Choice Questions :
1. The full form of CFC is _____.
2. The energy obtained from the water is called _____.

B. State any two ways of handling the following issues :
1. Environment and nature are closely related terms.
2. There is a paramount need to create a consciousness of the environment.

C. Read the following excerpts and answer the questions that follow. (open-ended questions) :
1. The world's **population** is growing by 1.10 percent per year, or approximately an additional 83 million people annually. The global **population** is expected to reach 8.6 billion in 2030.
   (a) How does population explosion lead to consumption crisis ?
   (b) Why do you think developing countries are more prone to bear the consequences of population explosion ?
2. Sustainable development is a coordinated, participatory and iterative process of thoughts and actions to achieve economic, environmental and social objectives in a balanced and integrative manner.
   (a) Name the three core elements of development.
   (b) How do you think sustainable development will be effective in overcoming the environmental issues ?

D. Activities :

Make a group of 5 members. Each group will take up any two Sustainable Development Goals as their topic. Put down your ideas on how these two goals can be accomplished in your city. Each group will make a presentation on their ideas. Make use of charts and Power Point slides to make your presentation effective.

2. LIVING THINGS IN ECOSYSTEMS

The Earth is the only planet having life on it. It is home to a large variety of life forms ranging from microscopic organisms to larger plants and organisms. The most important factors that make life on the earth possible are :

(i) It is at right distance from the sun.
(ii) Presence of water.
(iii) Presence of atmosphere.
(iv) Presence of solid crust.

It has been seen that life on earth is sustained by peculiar environmental conditions found here. The physical environment of the earth is made up of three important realms, which are the atmosphere, lithosphere and the hydrosphere. The combination and interaction of these three realms makes the sustenance of life possible. These three realms meet in a narrow zone called biosphere. The biosphere has all the physical requirements of life *i.e.* minerals, air, water and other climatic conditions like humidity and correct temperature. Our planet thus nurtures the life and sustenance of many different types of organisms. The organisms living in biosphere have acquired various habitats like forest, grassland, desert, wetland, coastland, etc. Biosphere is further divided into smaller units called ecosystem. An ecosystem is a region with a specific and recognizable landscape form.

2.0. WHAT IS AN ECOSYSTEM ?

An ecosystem is a community made up of living organisms and non-living components. The living organisms constitute the biotic components while the non-living organisms are the abiotic components. The non-living components of the eco-system are the water, inorganic and organic substances, climatic conditions and other geographical factors. It is not possible for a living component to sustain without these abiotic components. These components form the habitat of living organisms. Therefore, the living organisms are inseparable from the abiotic factors. The living component of the ecosystem ranges from extremely small bacteria which live in the air, water and on land to the huge terrestrial plants and animals.

1. Biotic factors—In an ecosystem, biotic factors include all the living parts of the ecosystem.

a. Plants : Most ecosystems depend on plants to perform photosynthesis, making food from water and carbon dioxide in the ecosystem. In ponds, lakes and the ocean, many of the plants are grasses, algae or tiny phytoplankton floating on or near the surface. Also in this category are the chemosynthetic bacteria that lives in deep ocean vents, which form the base of that food chain.

b. Animals : First-order consumers like mice, rabbits and seed-eating birds as well as zooplankton, snails, mussels, sea urchins, ducks and black sharks eat the plants and algae. Predators like coyotes, bobcats, bears, killer whales and tiger sharks eat first-order consumers. Omnivores like bears and rotifers (nearly microscopic aquatic animals) eat both plants and animals.

c. Fungi : Fungi like mushrooms and slime moulds feed off the bodies of living hosts or break down the remains of once-living organisms. Fungi serve an important role in the ecosystem as decomposers.

d. Micro-organisms : Protists generally are one-celled microscopic organisms, and they are sometimes overlooked in the ecosystem. Plant-like protists use photosynthesis, so they are producers. Animal-like protists such as paramecia and amoebas eat bacteria and smaller protists, so they form a part of the food chain. Fungus-like protists often serve as decomposers in the ecosystem. In deep-sea vents, chemosynthetic bacteria play the role of producers in the food chain. Bacteria act as decomposers, breaking down dead organisms to release nutrients. Bacteria also serve as food for other organisms.

> **Fascinating Fact**
>
> *Pseudomonas natriegens*, an ocean-dwelling bacterium, can go from birth to reproduction in 10 minutes flat. In five hours, a single cell could theoretically give rise to more than 1 billion offsprings.

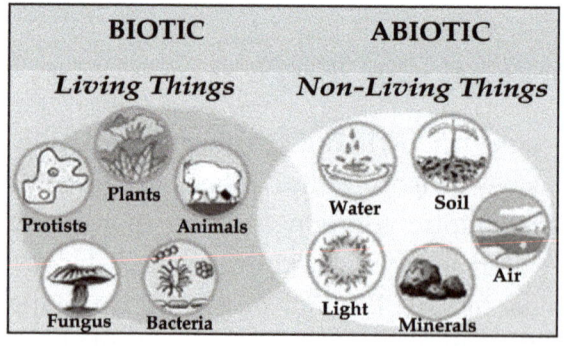

2. Abiotic factors—The abiotic factors in an ecosystem include all the non-living elements of the ecosystem. Examples of specific abiotic factors and how they may affect the biotic portions of the ecosystem include :

a. Air : In a terrestrial environment, air surrounds the biotic factors; in an aquatic environment, the biotic factors are surrounded by water. Changes in the chemical composition of the air, like air pollution from cars or factories, impacts everyone who breathes the air.

b. Soil : Most plants need soil for nutrients and to hold themselves in place with their roots. Soil is a reservoir of macronutrients and micronutrients

Living Things in Ecosystems

which are required for the growth of plants. Soil is also a habitat for many micro-organisms.

c. Water : Water is essential for life on Earth. The fact that water is essential to the chemical reactions within living organisms, is one of the key components for photosynthesis and is the placeholder in cells. Water also serves as a living environment for aquatic creatures. As such, changes in quantity and quality of water impact living systems. Water also has mass, creating pressure on aquatic environments. Clouds can even be the controlling factor in some ecosystems, such as the cloud forests of the tropics where plants draw their moisture from the air.

d. Light : Lack of light in the deeper ocean prevents photosynthesis, meaning that the majority of life in the ocean lives near the surface. Differences in daylight hours impact temperatures at the equator and the poles. The day-night rhythm of light impacts life patterns, including reproduction, for many plants and animals.

e. Temperature : Most organisms require a relatively stable temperature range. Mammals even have internal mechanisms to control their body temperature. Temperature changes, especially extreme and sudden changes, that go beyond an organism's tolerance, will harm or kill the organism.

> **? Intext Questions**
> 1. How does lack of light affect life under the ocean ?
> 2. Which are the two main categories of nutrients found in the soil ?
> 3. Why are decomposers important in our ecosystem ?

Interaction of Abiotic and Biotic Factors—A major difference between biotic and abiotic factors is that a change in any of the abiotic factors impacts

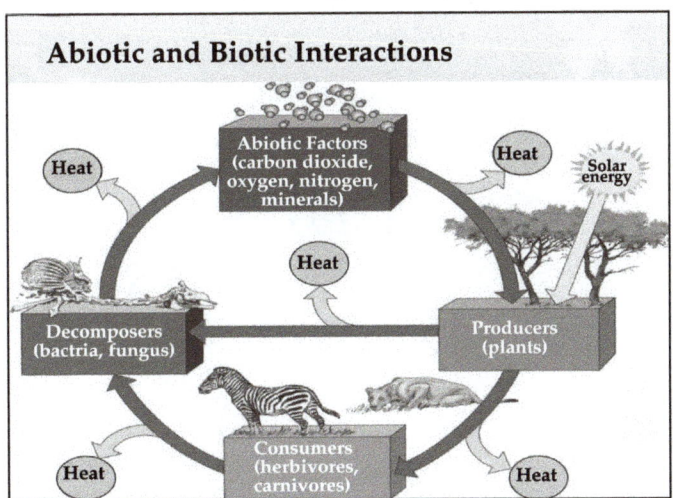

the biotic factors, but changes in the biotic factors do not necessarily result in changes to the abiotic factors. For example, increasing or decreasing salinity in a body of water may kill all the inhabitants in and around the water (except may be bacteria). The loss of the biota of the body of water does not necessarily change the salinity of the water, however all living organisms depend upon abiotic factors for their essentials like food, shelter and site of breeding. Plants use the abiotic factors of non-living components for carbon dioxide, water and energy from the sun. Plants also depend on soil for their mineral nutrients and support. These plants get preyed upon by some herbivorous organism or a parasite. Hence, plant being a biotic component interacts with the abiotic components. The abiotic components and biotic components influence each other. For example : the type of soil and the climatic conditions determine the type of flora and fauna found in that region. Thus, these biotic and abiotic components are linked to each other through nutrient cycles and energy flows. Water, air, energy, nitrogen, and soil minerals are essential abiotic components of an ecosystem. The energy is obtained from the sun. Energy enters in the ecosystem through the plants by the process of photosynthesis. Photosynthesis also takes in carbon, water and also mineral salts. Animals that feed on these plants play a major role in movement of matter and energy through the system. Most of the primary production in the terrestrial ecosystem is broken down by the decomposers. In a trophic system, the organisms that produces food through photosynthesis are the primary producers. The organisms that consumes the primary producers are the herbivorous animals, they are known as primary consumers or secondary producers. Secondary consumers are carnivorous animals that feeds on the primary consumers. The sequence of transfer of energy from plants to herbivores and to carnivores forms a food chain. In an ecosystem, there is continuous exchange of energy and carbon with the environment; mineral nutrients are cycled between plants, animals,

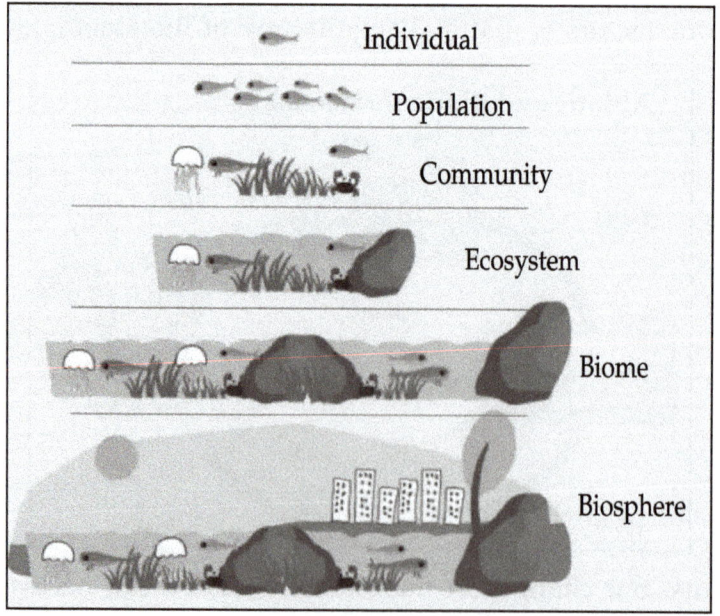

Living Things in Ecosystems

microbes and soil. Most of the nitrogen enters the system through biological nitrogen fixation. Nitrogen fixing bacteria are present freely in the soil or in symbiosis with plants. When these plant tissues are consumed, the nitrogen in the tissues is available to the animals and microbes. Deposition from the micro-organisms releases nitrogen from dead organic matter into the soil. Hence, abiotic and biotic components interact and work together in an environment that is best for all living organisms.

Earth is a planet for innumerable species. Human beings are just one of the 1.8 million species of plants and animals that exist on the earth. The life on earth can be organised into several different levels of function and complexity. These functional levels are : organisms, species, populations and communities.

3. Organism—An organism refers to any individual living thing that can react to stimuli, reproduce, and grow. Human beings, plants, animals and microbes are individually organisms. Organisms need other biotic and abiotic factors to survive and carry out their life processes. The organism performs all the life processes independently. However, parts of organism cannot exist independently of one another. An organism is fully adapted to its environment. It has a definite life span including definite series of stages like birth, hatching, growth, maturity, senescence, ageing and death.

4. Species—Species is *a group of interbreeding organisms that do not ordinarily breed with members of other groups*. It is a group of individuals that are genetically related and can breed to produce fertile young ones. Individuals are not members of the same species if their members cannot produce offspring that can also have children. If a species interbreeds freely with other species, it would no longer be a distinctive kind of organism. However, nowadays due to progress in science and technology, breeding between two species are being carried out. But such processes are artificially enforced by human beings, they do not occur naturally.

5. Population—A population is a group of organisms belonging to the same species that live in the same area and interact with one another. In ecology, a population is a group of individuals of the same species, inhabiting the same area, and functioning as a unit of biotic community. For example, all individuals of the common grass, *Cynodon,* in a given area constitute its population. Similarly, the individuals of elephants or tigers in an area constitute their population.

6. Community—A community is all of the populations of different species that live in the same area and interact with one another. A community is composed of all of the biotic factors of an area. Biotic community organisation results from interdependence and interactions amongst population of different species in a habitat. This is an assemblage of populations of plants, animals, bacteria and fungi that live in an area and interact with each other. A biotic community is a higher ecological category next to population. There are three types of biotic community, they are : animals, plants and decomposers (*i.e.,* bacteria and fungi). A biotic community has a distinct species composition and structure.

7. Ecosystems—The ecosystems are parts of nature where living organisms interact amongst themselves and with their physical environment. An ecosystem is composed of a biotic community, integrated with its physical environment through the exchange of energy and recycling of the nutrients. Ecosystems can be recognised as self-regulating and self-sustaining units of landscape, *e.g.*, a pond or a forest.

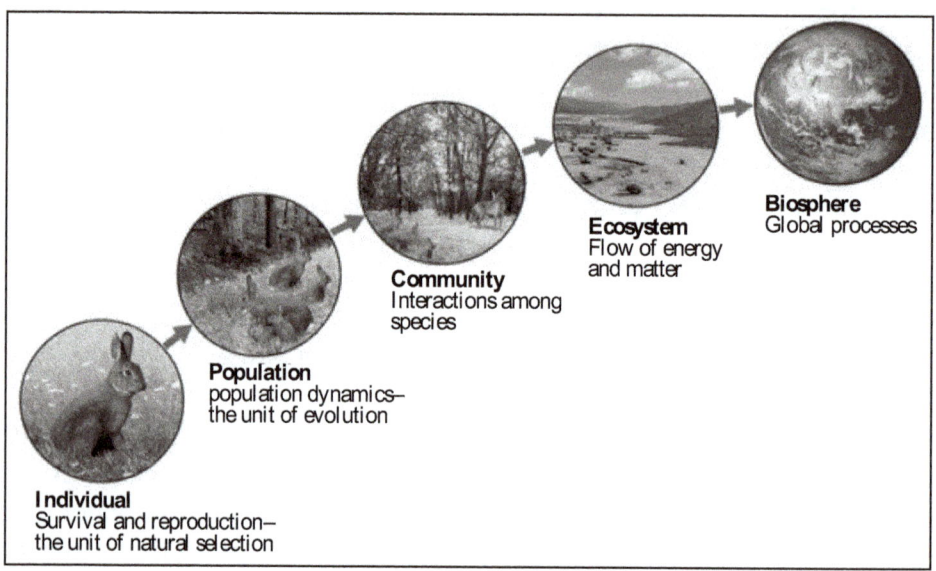

8. Landscape—A landscape is a unit of land with a natural boundary having a mosaic of patches, which generally represents different ecosystems.

9. Biome - This is a large regional unit characterised by a major vegetation type and associated fauna found in a specific climate zone. The biome includes all associated developing and modified communities occurring within the same climatic region, *e.g.*, forest biomes, grassland and savanna biomes, desert biome, etc. On a global scale, all the earth's terrestrial biomes and aquatic systems constitute the biosphere.

10. Biosphere - The entire inhabited part of the earth and its atmosphere including the living components is called the biosphere.

The global environment consists of three main sub-divisions :

(i) The hydrosphere which includes all the water components,

(ii) The lithosphere comprises the solid components of the earth's crust, and

(iii) The atmosphere formed of the gaseous envelope of the earth. The biosphere consists of the lower atmosphere, the land and the oceans, rivers and lakes, where living beings are found.

Living Things in Ecosystems

2.1. HABITAT AND ECOLOGICAL NICHE

In nature, species interact all of the time. Sometimes, their interactions can benefit both species, other times those interactions can cause harm. Nutrition or habitat are the main purposes of interaction between the species. The ecological niche describes how an organism or population responds to the distribution of resources and competitors and how it in turn alters those same factors. An ecological niche is impacted by ability to survive under changing conditions and also by competition. However, the term habitat should not be confused with the term niche. Each organism plays a particular role in its ecosystem. A niche is the role of species plays in the ecosystem. A niche will include the organism's role in the flow of energy through the ecosystem. This involves how the organism gets its energy, which usually has to do with what an organism eats, and how the organism passes that energy through the ecosystem, which has to do with what in turn eats the organism. An organism's niche also includes how the organism interacts with other organisms, and its role in recycling nutrients. Once a niche is left vacant, other organisms can fill that position. For example, when the Tarpan, a small wild horse found mainly in Southern Russia, became extinct in the early 1900s, its niche was filled by a small horse breed, the Konik. The habitat is the physical area where a species lives. Many factors are used to describe a habitat. The average amount of sunlight received each day, the range of annual temperatures, and average yearly rainfall can all describe a habitat. These and other abiotic factors will affect the kind of traits an organism must have in order to survive there. The temperature, the amount of rainfall, the type of soil and other abiotic factors all have a significant role in determining the plants that invade an area. The plants then determine the animals that come to eat the plants, and so on. A habitat should not be confused with an ecosystem: the habitat is the actual place of the ecosystem, whereas the ecosystem includes both the biotic and abiotic factors in the habitat.

The basic differences between both the terms are tabulated below :

Habitat	Niche
Organism's habitat is the place or surroundings where a species live.	Ecological niche describes how species live.
It is composed of biotic and abiotic parts of the ecosystem.	It is composed of all of the physical, chemical, and biological factors that a species needs to survive, stay healthy, and reproduce.
Habitat describes the effects of environment on the species.	The niche describes organisms' reaction to their environment.

> **? Intext Questions**
>
> 1. Which process marks the introduction of energy in the ecosystem ?
> 2. Name the functional levels of ecosystem.

2.2. INTERACTION OF SPECIES

Organisms living within an ecological community and species interaction forms the basis of many ecosystem properties and processes. The main modes of interaction between the species are explained below :

a. Predation—This is a relationship where one species depends entirely on other for its food and nutrition. The species which feeds on another one is called the predator whereas the one that is fed upon is called as the prey. Predator is usually stronger than prey. However, the prey organisms have developed many characteristics like camouflaging, mimicry and protective colouring to protect themselves from the predator.

b. Competition—It is a relationship when two or more species attempt to consume the same limited resources at the same time, which may be food, water, light, or any prey. Competition occurs when individuals or populations attempt to use the same limited resources. It can occur within the same species or with other species. Competition can be of two types— Indirect competition occurs when species do not even come in contact with one another, possibly feeding on the same plant in the day and the night. Direct competition occurs when species invade each other's niches. The more dominant species will prevail and have better access to the resource. This relationship can be further categorised as inter-specific competition and intra-specific competition.

1. Inter-specific competition may take place by interference or by exploitation. Interference is more direct; the two species actively fight or interfere with each other. Black walnut trees, for example, secrete compounds that inhibit the growth of other plants. Exploitation, by contrast, is a more indirect form where different species compete not by directly attacking or interfering with each other, but by exploiting the resource and thus leaving less available for their competitors.

Living Things in Ecosystems

2. Intra-specific competition is highly density-dependent, meaning that more the densely populated ecosystem, the more competition will occur. Intra-specific competition also features interference, where organisms directly fight for the resource, and exploitative competition, where they compete indirectly. Among sexually reproducing species, competition for mates is often an especially dramatic form of intra-specific competition. Male peacocks and elk both exhibit striking features, which they evolved as a result of sexual selection.

c. Parasitism—A parasite is an organism that lives on another organism and feeds on it. The parasite gets all of its nourishment and appropriate habitat from its host. The host is generally harmed by the parasite. Examples of parasites include ticks, fleas, tapeworms, leeches,

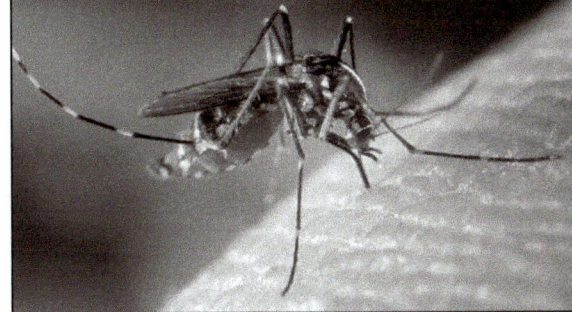

and mistletoe. These parasites reside in the human body. Parasites are classified into two categories –

1. Ectoparasite—Live on the outer body surface of the host. **For example**

- Athlete's foot fungus, fleas, mites, lice, and ticks.
- Some of these parasites also transmit disease organisms.

2. Endoparasite—Live inside their hosts, within cells or tissues, or in the alimentary canal. For example :

- *Mycobacterium tuberculosis*, the bacterium that causes tuberculosis.

Advantages and disadvantages of living in a host for parasites are tabulated below :

Advantages and Disadvantages of Living in or on a Host

	Ecoparasitism	Endoparasitism
Advantages	Ease of dispersal	Ease of feeding
	Safe from host's immune system.	Protected from external environment.

		Safer from natrunal enemies
Disadvantages	Vulnerability to natural enemies	Vulnerability to host's immune system
	Exposure to external environment	
	Feeding more difficult	Dispersal more difficult

> **Fascinating Fact**
>
> Tapeworms do not have a gut of their own. Instead, they use their specialised outer surface to absorb nutrients and excrete waste.

d. Mutualism—Mutualism is a close relationship between two species in which both are benefitted. During mutualism, each species depends upon the other for survival. For example - Humans have bacteria in the stomach that help to break down food that we eat. We benefit from them, and they survive on the food we eat.

e. Neutralism—Neutralism describes the relationship between two species which do interact but do not affect each other. It describe interactions where the fitness of one species has absolutely no effect whatsoever on that of other.

f. Commensalism—A relationship between species when one organism benefits and the other one is neither helped nor harmed. An example of this occurs between sharks and a type of fish called a Remora. Remoras attach themselves to Sharks and feed on scraps from the Shark's meals. They also use the Sharks as transportation. Similarly, birds build nest in trees. The trees are not hurt and they provide a habitat for birds.

g. Amensalism—Amensalism between two species involves one impeding or restricting the success of the other without being affected positively or negatively by the presence of the other. It is a type of symbiosis. Usually this occurs when one organism exudes

Living Things in Ecosystems

a chemical compound as part of its normal metabolism that is detrimental to another organism. The bread mould *Penicillium* is a common example of this; *Penicillium* secrete penicillin, a chemical that kills bacteria.

h. Synergism—It is a similar relationship like that of mutualism. Synergism is broadly defined as the combined effects of two or more organisms to produce a greater result than each would achieve individually. One of the best examples of synergism is sea anemone and a clownfish. The clownfish are always seen swimming within or between the tentacles of sea anemone. This protective shield is not a physical shield. The predators  of the clownfish stay away from the clownfish because the sea anemone will sting them if they come closer. Similarly, for the sea anemone, clownfish scare away the butterfly fish which eat sea anemones.

Law of Limiting Factor

In 1928, *Carl Sprengel* put forth a theory which stated that 'growth is not dictated by the resources, but the scarcest resource influences growth. This concept was further popularised by *Justus von Liebig*. Therefore, this law is also known as 'Liebig's law of minimum'. Liebig's law of minimum was improvised and defined in terms of the law of limiting factor. The law of limiting factor states that every living organism has limits to the environmental conditions it can endure. Environmental factors must be within appropriate levels for life to survive and sustain. These factors are primarily responsible for determining the growth and/or reproduction of an organism or population. It may be a physical factor such as temperature or light, a chemical factor such as particular nutrient, or a biological factor such as a competing species. The limiting factor may differ at different times and places. The Law of limiting factors can be summarised as too much or too little of any abiotic factor that can limit or prevent growth of a population of a species in an ecosystem.

Types of Limiting Factor

a. Density Dependent Factors—Density dependent factors are those factors whose effect on a population is determined by the total size of the population. Predation and disease, as well as resource availability, are all examples of density dependent factors. As an example, disease is likely to spread quicker through a larger, denser population, impacting the number of individuals within the population more than it would in a smaller, more widely dispersed population.

b. Density Independent Factors—A density independent limiting factor is one which limits the size of a population, but whose effect is not dependent on the size of the population (the number of individuals). Examples of density independent factors include environmentally stressful events such as earthquakes, tsunamis, and volcanic eruptions, as well as sudden climatic changes such as drought or flood, and destructive occurrences, such as the input of extreme environmental pollutants. Density independent factors will usually kill all members of a population, regardless of the population size.

c. Physical and Biological Limiting Factors—Limiting factors can also be split into further categories. Physical factors or abiotic factors include temperature, water availability, oxygen, salinity, light, food and nutrients; biological factors or biotic factors, involve interactions between organisms such as predation, competition, parasitism and herbivory.

> **? Intext Questions**
>
> 1. Write the statement of the theory put forth by Carl Sprengel.
> 2. During mutualism, each species depends upon the other for survival. Explain this statement with an example.

2.3. EVOLUTION

Evolution is the process of change in all forms of life over generations. The theory of evolution is based on the idea that all species are related and gradually change over time. Our planet has undergone many changes gradually over the years. Such changes have affected the habitat and food chain of many species. In conditions, evolution is necessary to adapt with changing conditions. The species which cannot evolve or modify to the changing conditions, may not be fit to survive or may even extinct. Thus, the modified characteristics may give the individual an advantage over other individuals which they can then pass on to their offspring. Charles Darwin's theory of evolution states that evolution happens by natural selection. Individuals with characteristics best suited to their environment are more likely to survive, finding food, avoiding predators and resisting disease. These individuals are more likely to reproduce and pass their genes on to their children. Individuals that are poorly adapted to their environment are less likely to survive and reproduce. Therefore, their genes are less likely to be passed on to the next generation. This type of evolution is by natural selection.

Co-evolution—When two species or groups of species have evolved alongside each other where one adapts to changes in the other. Such a type of evolution is called co-evolution. For example, when planktons modify their composition and structure, the fish which feeds on those planktons also evolves. It can lead to very specialised relationships between species, such as those between pollinator and plant and between parasite and host. It may also foster

Living Things in Ecosystems

the evolution of new species in cases where individual populations of interacting species separate themselves from their greater meta populations for long periods of time. Co-evolution is likely to happen when different species have close ecological interactions with one another. These ecological relationships include :

1. Predator—prey and parasite—host
2. Competitive species
3. Mutualistic species

Extinction—The mass extinctions reduce diversity by killing off specific lineages, and with them, any descendent species they might have given rise to. But mass extinction can also play a creative role in evolution, stimulating the growth of other branches. The sudden disappearance of plants and animals that occupy a specific habitat creates new opportunities for surviving species. Over many generations of natural selection, these ancestries and their descendent ancestries may evolve with special characteristics and adaptations to suit the new resources. In this way, mass extinction can level the evolutionary playing field for a brief time, allowing lineages that were formerly minor players to diversify and become more prevalent. By removing so many species from their ecosystems in a short period of time, mass extinctions reduce competition for resources and leave behind many vacant niches, which surviving lineages can evolve into.

We can thus say that ecosystems act as resource producers and processors. Our planet has been given with different types of ecosystems in the different geographical areas. The species have modified over generations to gain the suitable adaptations and are still undergoing evolution.

SUMMARY

- The earth is the only planet having life on it. It is home to a large variety of life forms ranging from microscopic organisms to larger plants and organisms.
- The physical environment of the earth is made up of three important realms, which are the atmosphere, lithosphere and the hydrosphere. The combination and interaction of these three realms makes the sustenance of life possible.
- Biosphere has all the physical requirements of life *i.e.* minerals, air, water and other climatic conditions like humidity and correct temperature.
- An ecosystem is a region with a specific and recognizable landscape form. An ecosystem is a community made up of living organisms and non-living components.
- In an ecosystem, biotic factors include all the living parts of the ecosystem. The abiotic factors in an ecosystem include all the non-living elements of the ecosystem.
- An organism refers to any individual living thing that can react to stimuli, reproduce, grow.

- Species is *a* group of interbreeding organisms that do not ordinarily breed with members of other groups.
- A population is a group of organisms belonging to the same species that live in the same area and interact with one another.
- A community is all of the populations of different species that live in the same area and interact with one another.
- A landscape is a unit of land with a natural boundary having a mosaic of patches, which generally represent different ecosystems.
- Biome is a large regional unit characterised by a major vegetation type and associated fauna found in a specific climate zone.
- The entire inhabited part of the earth and its atmosphere including the living components is called the biosphere.
- A niche is the role a species plays in the ecosystem. A niche will include the organism's role in the flow of energy through the ecosystem.
- The habitat is the physical area where a species lives.
- Predation is a relationship where one species depends entirely on other for its food and nutrition.
- Competition is a relationship when two or more species attempt to consume the same limited resources at the same time, which may be food, water, light, or any prey.
- A parasite is an organism that lives on another organism and feeds on it.
- Mutualism is a close relationship between two species in which both are benefit.
- Commensalism is a relationship between species when one organism benefits and the other one is neither helped or harmed.
- Synergism is defined as the combined effects of two or more organisms to produce a greater result than each would achieve individually.
- The law of limiting factor states that every living organism has limits to the environmental conditions it can endure.
- Evolution is the process of change in all forms of life over generations.

EXERCISE

A. Define each of these terms :

1. Organism 2. Species 3. Population 4. Community 5. Landscape 6. Biome 7. Niche 8. Habitat 9. Predation 10. Competition 11. Parasitism 12. Mutualism 13. Neutralism 14. Commensalism 15. Amensalism 16. Synergism 17. Evolution 18. Co-evolution 19. Extinction.

B. Answer in brief :

1. Differentiate between habitat and niche.

Living Things in Ecosystems

2. Which are the most important factors that make life on earth possible ?
3. State the law of limiting factors.
4. State the Darwin theory of evolution.

C. Answer the following in detail :
1. Explain the biotic factors of ecosystem.
2. Explain the abiotic factors of ecosystem.
3. How does a biotic and abiotic factor affect each other ?
4. What is competition ? Explain its types.
5. Explain the advantages and disadvantages of endo-parasitism.
6. Describe the types of limiting factor.

WORKSHEET

A. Fill in the blanks :

1. A tapeworm and a cat have _____ type of relationship.
   a. Mutualism   b. Predation   c. Synergism   d. Parasitism
2. The _____ is the thin region, or area, of the Earth that supports all life.
   a. Biosphere   b. Atmosphere   c. Hydrosphere   d. Lithosphere
3. Ecosystem is smallest unit of _____.
   a. Ionosphere   b. Lithosphere   c. Biosphere   d. Mesosphere
4. The set of ecosystems is called a _____.
   a. Biome   b. Climate   c. Subsystem   d. Structure

B. Justify each of these statements :

1. Ecosystem is a self-sustaining and self-regulating unit of landscape.
2. Mutualism is known as an obligatory relationship.
3. Some species survive while other go extinct.
4. Humans evolved from apes, yet apes do exist.

C. Read the following excerpts and answer the questions that follow. (open-ended questions) :

1. An aftificial ecosystem is not self-sustaining , and the ecosystem would perish without human assistance.
   (a) What is the difference between artificial and natural ecosystem ?
   (b) How does artificial ecosystem impacts the natural ecosystem ?
   (c) Why does artificial ecosystem perish with human intervention ?
2. Each species fits into an ecological community in its own special way and has its own tolerable ranges for many environmental factors.
   (a) How species with overlapping niches compete for resources ?
   (b) What makes a niche an ecological functional role rather than just ecological space ?

D. Activity :

1. Research and find out at least two examples for mutualism, predation, competition, synergism and parasitism (Examples should not include the ones given in this chapter)

3. HOW ECOSYSTEMS WORK

The term **environment** means our surrounding. The living beings are surrounded by non-living components such as air, water, soil, rocks, etc. These non-living factors are essential for the survival and sustenance of living organisms. Thus, the non-living factors become an important part of the environment of the living beings. The quality and quantity of non-living factors also affect the living beings. Ecology is the study of components of environment. Ecosystem is essentially a technical term for 'nature'. The term **ecology** was coined by *Ernst Haeckel*. Ecosystem is a self-regulating and self-sustaining structural and functional unit of the biosphere. This system depends upon the sun for its energy. As we know, Earth is the only planet having life on it with a large variety of organisms ranging from microscopic plants and animals to largest trees and animals. Ecosystems can be of any size and quantity based on the quantity of biotic and abiotic factors present. The sizes of ecosystems vary. They can be as large as the earth's biosphere itself or the Sahara Desert, or as small as a fishpond.

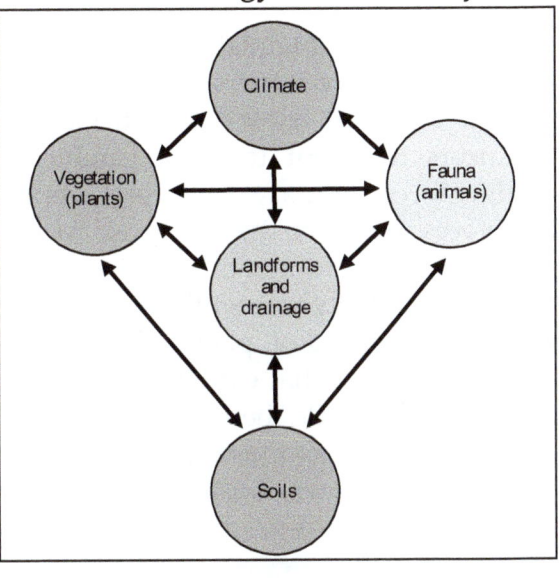

The given model shows the living and non-living components of an ecosystem. Each component is closely related and affects, or is affected by, each of the other components. The arrows in the diagram represent the inter-relationships that occurs between each part of an ecosystem. It is these specific interactions which cause each ecosystem to develop its own unique characteristics.

In an ecosystem, there is an exchange of materials and energy. Such an energy exchange can also occur with the adjoining ecosystems. Therefore, the adjoining ecosystems are all interconnected and interrelated. Biosphere is the collation of the vast network of all interconnected ecosystems. Biosphere is that part of land, air and water on the earth which supports life. Mainly there are two types of ecosystems. Namely terrestrial ecosystem and aquatic ecosystem.

1. Terrestrial ecosystem: This is the ecosystem which exists on land. It can be further divided into the following types :
- Forest ecosystem
- Grassland ecosystem
- Desert ecosystem

2. Aquatic ecosystem: This is the ecosystem which exists in water. It can be further divided into :
- Fresh water ecosystem (Pond or lake or river ecosystem)
- Marine ecosystem (Ocean ecosystem)

3.0. ENERGY FLOW IN ECOSYSTEM

Tropic level

Ecosystems maintain themselves by cycling energy and nutrients. The producers and consumers in an ecosystem can be arranged into several feeding groups, and each known is as trophic level (feeding level). In any ecosystem, producers represent the first trophic level, herbivores represent the second trophic level, primary carnivores represent the third trophic level and top carnivores represent the last level. At the first trophic level, primary producers (plants, algae, and some bacteria) use solar energy to produce organic plant material through photosynthesis. The animals at the second trophic level, which are herbivores feed on plants. The carnivores, which form the third trophic level are the predators that eat herbivores. However, some organisms feed on plants as wells as animals, hence these are called omnivores. The next trophic level comprises the decomposers, which include bacteria, fungi, moulds, worms, and insects, break down wastes and dead organisms and return nutrients to the soil. The decomposers process large amounts of organic material and return nutrients to the ecosystem in inorganic form, which are then taken up again by primary producers. It is estimated that on average about 10 % of net energy production at one trophic level is passed on to the next level. Processes like respiration, growth, reproduction and defecation consume the remaining portion of the energy. This is called 10% law which was put-forth by *Raymond Lindeman* in 1942.

> **? Intext Questions**
> 1. List out the types of terrestrial and aquatic ecosystem.
> 2. Why is tropic level also called as feeding level ?
> 3. Who put forth the 10% law ?
> 4. How is the 90% of the net energy lost ?

How Ecosystems Work

3.1. WHO EATS WHOM

Food Chain

When the light energy falls on the green surfaces of plants, a part of it transformed into chemical energy which is stored in various organic products in the plants. In the ecosystem, green plants alone are able to trap in solar energy and convert it into chemical energy. The chemical energy is locked up in the various organic compounds, such as carbohydrates, fats and proteins, present in the green plants. When the herbivores consume plants as food and convert chemical energy accumulated in plant products into muscular energy, degradation of energy will occur through its conversion into heat. The herbivores are consumed by carnivores of the first order (secondary consumers) then further degradation will occur. Similarly, when primary carnivores are consumed by top carnivores, again energy will be degraded. One form of life supports the other form. Thus, food from one trophic level reaches to the other trophic level and in this way a chain is established. This is known as food chain. A food chain may be defined as the transfer of energy and nutrients through a succession of organisms through repeated process of eating and being eaten. In food chain initial link is a green plant or producer which produces chemical energy available to consumers. Thus, a food chain is formed which can be written as follows :

Grass ⟶ Grasshopper ⟶ Frog ⟶ Hawk

Many food chains exist in an ecosystem. For example, in the food chain,

Grass ⟶ Rat ⟶ Snake ⟶ Eagle

Sometimes rats are not eaten by snakes, but eagles may hunt them. In such cases the length of the food chain is shortened.

Virtually all other living organisms depend upon green plants for their energy, the efficiency of plants in any given area in capturing solar energy sets the upper limit to long-term energy flow and biological activity in the community. Food chains are of three types:

1. Grazing food chain
2. Parasitic food chain
3. Saprophytic or detritus food chain

1. Grazing food chain

The grazing food chain starts from green plants and from autotrophs it goes to herbivores (primary consumers) to primary carnivores (secondary consumers) and then to secondary carnivores (tertiary consumers) and so on. The gross energy of a green plant in an ecosystem may ultimately be oxidised in respiration, it may be eaten by herbivorous animals and after the death and decay of producers it may be utilised by decomposers and converters and finally released into the environment. In herbivores, the assimilated food can be stored as carbohydrates, proteins and fats, and transformed into much more complex organic molecules.

The energy for these transformations is supplied through respiration. As in autotrophs, the energy in herbivores also meets three routes respiration, decay of organic matter by microbes and consumption by the carnivores. Likewise, when the secondary carnivores or tertiary consumers eat primary carnivores, the total energy assimilated by primary carnivores or gross tertiary production follows the same course and its disposition into respiration, decay and further consumption by other carnivores is entirely similar to that of herbivores.

2. Parasitic food chain

Parasites obtain nutrition from larger and smaller organisms without outright killing them. Producers, consumers, or both could fall prey to parasites. The energy transfer in this case is not significant as the prey is not killed. Therefore, the complete energy is not transferred or obtained. Only a partial amount of matter from the prey is consumed by the parasites.

3. Detritus food chain

The dead organic remains including metabolic wastes derived from grazing food chain are generally termed Detritus. The energy contained in detritus is not lost in ecosystem as a whole, rather it serves as a source of energy for a group of organisms called detritivores that are separated from the grazing food chain. In some ecosystems, more energy flows through the detritus food chain than through grazing food chain. In detritus food chain, the energy flow remains as a continuous passage rather than as a stepwise flow between discrete entities. The organisms in the detritus food chain are many and include algae, fungi, bacteria, slime moulds, actinomycetes, protozoa, etc. Detritus organisms ingest pieces of partially decomposed organic matter, digest them partially and after extracting some of the chemical energy in the food to run their metabolism, excrete the remainder in the form of simpler organic molecules.

3.2. FOOD WEB

Many food chains exist in an ecosystem, but these food chains are not independent. In ecosystem, one organism does not depend wholly on another. The resources are shared specially at the beginning of the chain. Thus, the food chains interrelate. This type of interrelationship links the individuals of the whole community. In this way, food chains become interlinked. A complex of interrelated food chains makes up a food web. Food web maintains the stability of the ecosystem. Most ecosystems are highly complex and consists of an extremely wide variety of species. Food web maintains the stability of the ecosystem. The greater the number of alternative pathways the more stable is the community of living things.

How Ecosystems Work

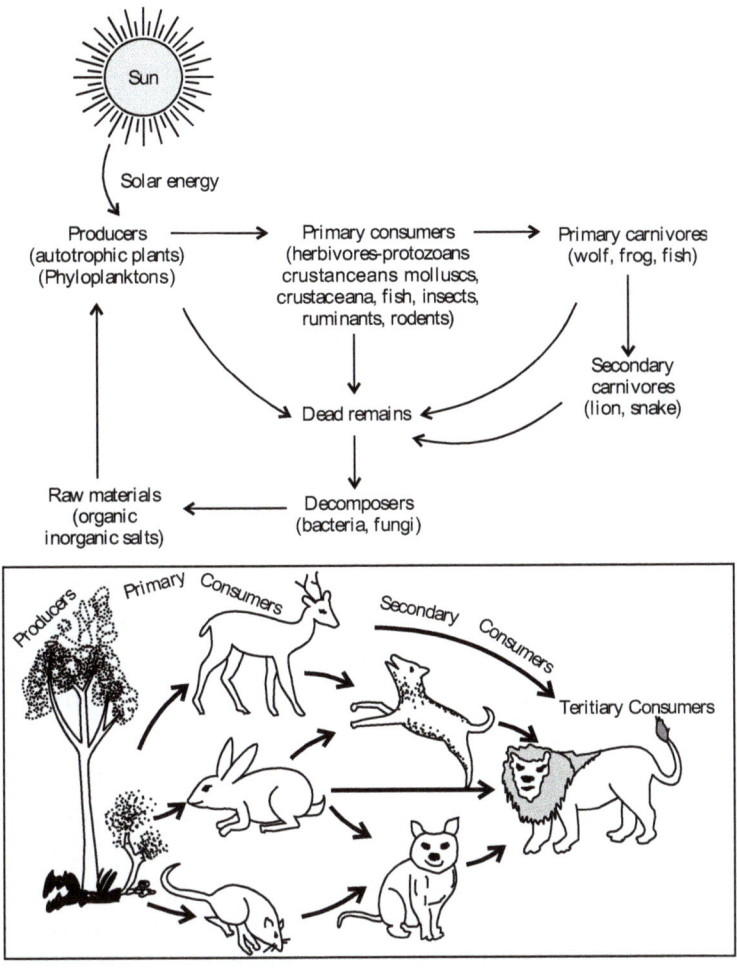

The differences between food chain and food web are tabulated below–

Food chain	Food web
A linear pathway showing the flow of energy.	A gathering of networks showing the flow of energy.
An organism of higher trophic level feeds on one specific organism of lower trophic level.	An organism of higher trophic level may feed on more members of lower trophic level.
Food chain has no effect on the adaptability and competitiveness of organisms.	Food web improves the adaptability and competitiveness of an organism.
The instability increases due to the increasing number of separate and confined food chains.	Stability increases due to the existence of the complex food chains.
If one group of an organism is extinct, the whole chain will be disturbed or disconnected.	The food web does not get disturbed by the disturbance of one group of organisms.

Food chain can be of types such as grazing, parasitic and saprophytic.	There are no different types of food web.
Food chain consists of 4-5 trophic levels of different species.	Food web contains numerous trophic levels of different populations of species.

Food Pyramid

The trophic structure of an ecosystem can be indicated by means of ecological pyramid. At each step in the food chain a considerable fraction of the potential energy is lost as heat. As a result, organisms in each trophic level pass on lesser energy to the next trophic level that they actually receive. This limits the number of steps in any food chain to 4 or 5. Longer the food chain lesser the energy is available for final members. Because of this tapering off of available energy in the food chain, a pyramid is formed that is known as ecological pyramid. The higher the steps in the ecological pyramid, the lower will be the number of individuals and the larger their size. In a food pyramid, the base trophic level is occupied by producer elements plants, algae, diatoms and other hydrophytes which are most abundant. At the second trophic level come the herbivores or zooplanktons which are lesser in number than producers. The third trophic level is occupied by carnivores which are still smaller in number than the herbivores and the top is occupied by a few top carnivores. Thus, in the ecological pyramid there is a relative reduction in number of organisms and an increase in the size of body from base to apex of the pyramid. The relationship between the amount of energy accumulated and the amount of energy utilised within one trophic level of food chain has an important bearing on how much energy from one trophic level passes on to the next trophic level in the food chain. The ratio of output of energy to input of energy is referred to as ecological efficiency.

Ecological efficiency can be measured by the following parameters :

(i) Ingestion : The amount of ingested food or energy taken by trophic level.

(ii) Assimilation : The amount of food absorbed and fixed into energy rich organic substances which are stored or combined with other mole cules to build complex molecules such as proteins, fats etc.

(iii) Respiration : The amount of energy lost in metabolism.

Fascinating Fact

The Antarctic Food Web is relatively simple compared to ecosystems in other parts of the world. There are fewer different species, but greater numbers of individuals of each.

How Ecosystems Work

> **? Intext Questions**
>
> 1. Write any one example of food chain.
> 2. Name the three types of food chains.
> 3. Why are decomposers crucial to the effective functioning of ecosystem ?
> 4. A food chain can have a maximum of 4-5 steps. Why?

3.3. THE CYCLING OF MATERIALS

A nutrient cycle refers to the movement and exchange of organic and inorganic matter back into the production of living matter. The process is regulated by the food web pathways previously presented, which decompose organic matter into inorganic nutrients. Nutrient cycle occurs within the ecosystems. In an ecosystem, the energy flows and the matter is recycled. This process happens through cycling of materials. These are water cycle, the carbon cycle, the nitrogen cycle and the energy cycle.

1. The Water Cycle

The rainwater runs along the ground and flows into the river or falls into the sea. The water that falls on the ground is absorbed by the soil which gets collected as the ground water. The plants take up ground water and use it during photosynthesis. However, some portion of absorbed water is lost by the plants during the process of transpiration. During day time, evaporation occurs where, the surface water from the water bodies are converted into water vapour. The water vapours rise up and forms clouds. The winds blow up the clouds and the clouds get heavier. As the clouds rises up it condense and form water droplets. When the clouds are heavy enough, they burst which fall on land as rain. Water cycle is the continuous transfer of water from air, sea, land and water in a repeated cycle. This continuous flow of water is sufficient to provide good living conditions on the planet. Some part of water which is present in the form of glaciers, snow and ice also contribute to the water cycle. The steps of water cycle are as follows :

Evaporation—Most water evaporates from the oceans, where water is found in highest abundance. However some evaporation also occurs from lakes, rivers, streams following rain.

Transpiration—It is the water loss from the surface area (particularly the stomata) of plants. It is estimated that, transpiration accounts for a massive 50% of land-based evaporation, and 10% of total evaporation.

Condensation—The process by which water vapour is converted back into liquid is called condensation. Water in the atmosphere condenses to form clouds around small particles, like bits of dust or smoke in the air.

Precipitation—Water returns to the earth through precipitation in the form of rain, sleet, snow or ice (hail). When rain occurs due to precipitation, most of it runs off into lakes and rivers while a significant portion of it sinks into the ground.

Infiltration—The process through which water sinks into the ground is known as infiltration and is determined by the soil or rock type through which water moves. During the process of sinking into the Earth's surface, water is filtered and purified. Depending on the soil type and the depth to which the water has sunk, the ground water becomes increasingly purified: the deeper the water, the cleaner it becomes.

Melting and Freezing—Some water freezes and is solidified as ice, in the form of glaciers and ice sheets. Similarly, water sometimes melts and is returned to oceans and seas.

However, human intervention in the water cycle occurs in two ways :

1. Withdrawals—We take water out of the system for various purposes like irrigation, domestic use, industrial use, etc. With increasing population, civilization and industrialization, the water consumption has significantly increased.

2. Discharges—We add substances to the water which could be potent or non-potent pollutant. As precipitation falls on the ground and moves into rivers and creeks, it picks up a whole range of pollutants. Pollutants may include farm pesticides, herbicides and fertilizers, gas, oil, pet waste, human waste from sewage treatment plants. Acid rain is one of the consequences of disturbed water cycle.

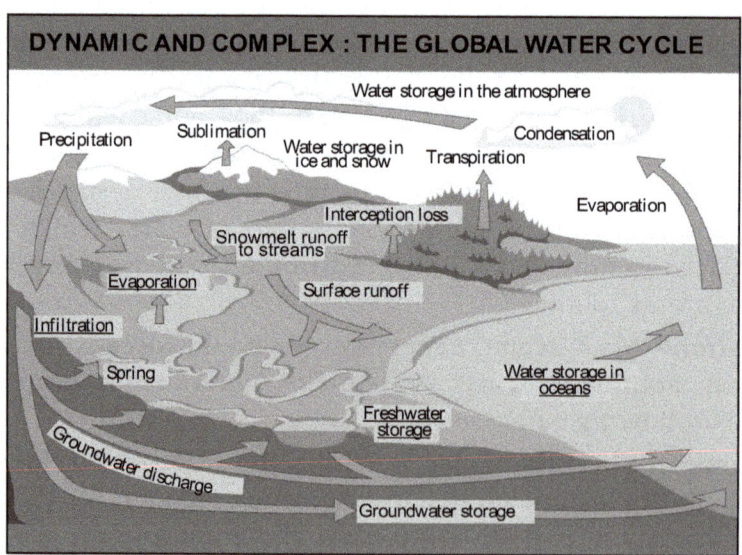

Fascinating Fact

Water is constantly being recycled so the water you drink today could be the same water dinosaurs drank millions of years ago.

How Ecosystems Work

2. The Carbon Cycle

Carbon is the fundamental element found in almost all the biotic and abiotic components. During photosynthesis, plants take up atmospheric carbon dioxide, combine it with water and convert it into glucose. Thus, the circulation of carbon atoms in the biosphere is a result of photosynthetic conversion of carbon dioxide into organic compounds by plants. In this process, plants release oxygen into the atmosphere on which animals depend for their respiration. In this manner, plants maintain the carbon and oxygen levels. Both plants and animals release carbon dioxide during respiration. During excretion, some amount of carbon is returned back. When plants and animals die, the carbon is returned to the soil. These processes complete the carbon cycle.

Carbon moves from one reservoir to another by these processes :

1. Combustion—Burning of wood and fossil fuels by factory and automobile emissions transfers carbon to the atmosphere as carbon dioxide.

2. Photosynthesis—Carbon dioxide is taken up by plants during photosynthesis and is converted into energy rich organic molecules, such as glucose, which contains carbon.

3. Metabolism—Autotrophs convert carbon into organic molecules like fats, carbohydrates and proteins, which animals can eat.

4. Cellular respiration—Animals eat plants for food, taking up the organic carbon (carbohydrates). Plants and animals break down these organic molecules during the process of cellular respiration and release energy, water and carbon dioxide. Carbon dioxide is returned to the atmosphere during gaseous exchange.

5. Precipitation—Carbon dioxide in the atmosphere can also precipitate as carbonated in ocean sediments.

6. Decay—Carbon dioxide gas is also released into the atmosphere during the decay of all organisms.

However, the emission from industries and vehicles are introducing more carbon dioxide and carbon monoxide into the atmosphere. With the increasing rate of deforestation, the carbon cycle and balance is disturbed. Since the Industrial Revolution, approximately 150 years ago, human activities such as the burning of fossil fuels and deforestation have begun to have an effect on the carbon cycle and the rise of carbon dioxide in the atmosphere. Human activities affect the carbon cycle through emissions of carbon dioxide (sources) and removal of carbon dioxide (sinks). The carbon cycle can be affected when carbon dioxide is either released into the atmosphere or removed from the atmosphere.

A. Burning of fossil fuels—When oil or coal is burned, carbon is released into the atmosphere at a faster rate than it is removed. As a result, the concentration of carbon dioxide in the atmosphere increases. Natural gas, oil and coal are fossil fuels that are commonly burned to generate electricity in power plants, for transportation, in homes and in other industrial complexes.

The primary industrial activities that emit carbon dioxide and affect the carbon cycle are petroleum refining, paper, food and mineral production, mining and the production of chemicals.

B. Carbon sequestration—When plants remove carbon dioxide from the air and store it, the process is called carbon sequestration. Agricultural and forestry methods can affect the amount of carbon dioxide being removed from the atmosphere and stored by the plants. These sinks of carbon dioxide can be farms, grasslands or forests. Human activity in managing farmland or forests affects the amount of carbon dioxide removed from the atmosphere by plants and trees. These sinks of carbon dioxide affect the carbon cycle by decreasing the amount of carbon dioxide in the air.

C. Deforestation—Deforestation is the permanent removal of trees from forests. Permanent removal of the trees means new trees will not be replanted. This large-scale removal of trees from forests by people results in increased levels of carbon dioxide in the atmosphere because trees are no longer absorbing carbon dioxide for photosynthesis. As a result, the carbon cycle is affected. Agriculture is one of the primary causes of deforestation. Farmers remove trees on a large-scale basis to increase acreage for crops and livestock.

D. Geologic Sequestration—Human activity can affect the carbon cycle by capturing carbon dioxide and storing it underground rather than permitting it to be released into the atmosphere. This process is called geologic sequestration.

> **Fascinating Fact**
>
> Like Earth, Mars has two permanent polar ice caps. The ones on Mars are mainly water ice, but also contain a lot of frozen carbon dioxide. 25-30% of Mars' carbon dioxide atmosphere is frozen at its poles.

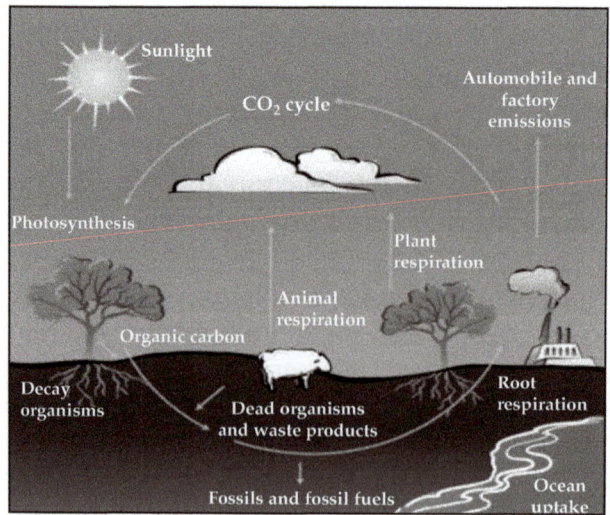

How Ecosystems Work

3. The Nitrogen Cycle

The excreta of the herbivores, omnivores and carnivores contain complex nitrogenous compounds. The excreta are decomposed by bacteria, worms and insects. These organisms break down the faecal matter into simple nitrogen compounds and release it into the soil. These compounds are absorbed by the plants for growth. The decomposition of dead remains of plants and animals also return the nitrogenous compounds to the soil in the similar way. In addition, nitrogen fixing bacteria convert atmospheric nitrogen into nitrates and nitrites. These bacteria are found in the soil. They further release nitrates and nitrites in to the soil. The plants absorb these compounds and use it for protein synthesis. Nitrogen enters the food chain through plants and decomposers and nitrogen fixing bacteria play a crucial role in converting nitrogen compounds into the usable form for plants.

The nitrogen cycle involves the following steps :

Lightning—Nitrogen can be changed to nitrates directly by lightning. The rapid growth of algae after thunderstorms is because of this process, which increases the amount of nitrates that fall onto the earth in rain water, acting as fertilizer.

Absorption—Ammonia and nitrates are absorbed by plants through their roots.

Ingestion—Humans and animals get their nitrogen supplies by eating plants or plant-eating animals.

Decomposition—During decomposition, bacteria and fungi break down proteins and amino acids from plants and animals.

Ammonification—The breakdown products of amino acids are further converted into ammonia by the decomposing bacteria. This process is called Ammonification.

Nitrification—It is the process of conversion of the ammonia to nitrates which is done by nitrifying bacteria.

Denitrification—In this process, bacteria convert ammonia and nitrate into nitrogen and nitrous oxide. Nitrogen is returned to the atmosphere to start the cycle over again.

However, human interventions are greatly impacting the nitrogen cycle. One of the ways in which this happens is by the mass production and use of nitrogen-based fertilizers. Plants take in nitrogen to produce proteins and for cellular processes also. Fertilizer contains nitrogen and is widely used on farms to increase and improve the growth of crops. However, fertilizer often ends up in runoff, which occurs when heavy rainwater collects on the soil and runs into bodies of water. This greatly increases the amount of nitrogen that ends up areas of water as well as in soil, which can be harmful to ecosystems.

Another way humans affect the nitrogen cycle is by the burning of fossil fuels, known as combustion. Fossil fuels contain nitrogen that, when burned, is released into the atmosphere in the form of nitrous oxides. Nitrous oxides are the chief components of acid rain, a type of pollution that is harmful to forests and bodies of water.

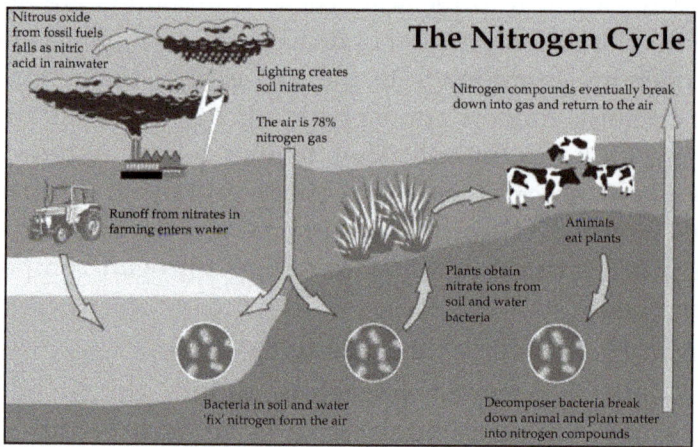

These cycles are a part of global life processes. These biogeochemical cycles have specific features in each of the ecosystems. The geographical features of an area also affect these cycles. If these cycles are disturbed beyond a limit, our environment will be destroyed and our survival will become difficult.

Intext Questions

1. Which are the nitrogenous products formed during nitrification and de-nitrification ?
2. Which chemicals result in the formation of acid rain ?
3. How does deforestation affect the carbon cycle ?
4. How does solid forms of water participate in the water cycle ?

Interdependence of natural cycle

Plants and animals depends on each other to survive. This is called interdependence. Survival of plants and animals is impossible without abiotic components like water, soil, sunlight, rocks, etc. of the ecosystem. All of the biogeochemical cycles are mainly involved and proper maintenance of ecosystem with proper energy flow across primary producers and consumers at tertiary stage. As seen above, bio-geochemical cycles proceed in steps. However, these cycles are inter-dependent on each other. Water is the most important link to all of these cycles. Water is capable of dissolving and transporting most of the compounds and intermediates formed during the carbon, nitrogen and other nutrient cycles. Plants are also another important linking factor. For example : algal bloom is the result of disturbed nitrogen cycle. Algal bloom results in

How Ecosystems Work

reduced carbon dioxide in that area. The reason for algal bloom is introduction of nitrogenous fertilizers in the lakes. Over accumulation of chemical fertilizers leads to disturbed water cycle and acid rain. Thus, it is not correct to say that human activities affect only a certain portion of environment. Though a major and direct impact is seen in one place, there could be side-effects on the other places too.

(E) Ecological succession

Ecological succession is the process through which ecosystems tends to change over a period of time. Succession implies to seasonal change or man-made changes. These changes alter the community of plants and animals. For example : if a forest is cleared, it initially becomes a colony of certain species of plants and animals, which gradually changes through an orderly process of community development. Succession is therefore a series of progressive changes in the composition of an ecological community over time. Succession could be categorised as primary succession and secondary succession. There are two main types of succession—certain—primary and secondary.

Primary succession is the series of community changes which occur on an entirely new habitat which has never been colonized before. For example, formation of new islands, on new volcanic rock, and on land formed from glacial retreats. When the rock cools, seeds blown by the wind may lodge in crevices. There they can germinate and take root. Often these first colonizing plants are weedy species, such as fast-growing grasses. After these plants germinate and grow, they die and decompose, and their remains create pockets of soil from which other plants as well as fungi can grow. Over time, as vegetation covers more and more of the island, seeds from other plants arrive. As the plant community develops, harder, taller-growing species begin to shade out the first colonizers and eventually dominate. More plants and animals arrive, and the ecosystem changes with each new arrival. Over several decades, as populations of different species become established, the ecosystem's structure becomes more stable.

Secondary succession is the series of community changes which take place on a previously colonized, but disturbed or damaged habitat. For example, areas which have been cleared of existing vegetation or destructive events such as fires. The stages of secondary succession are similar to those of primary succession. As we know insects and weeds from the surrounding ecosystems first recolonize the disturbed area, and these species are replaced by hardier plants and animals as time goes on. If this landscape remains undisturbed for a long enough time, the evolving biological community can once again attain a stable ecological structure. Although calamities like wildfires and other disturbances can certainly ruin a landscape, the soil often retains some amount of seeds that can sprout shortly after the effects of the disturbance pass, so ecosystems within the landscape can recover through secondary succession. Sometimes, however, catastrophic disturbances, such as massive volcanic eruptions or advancing glaciers, effectively eliminate all of the biological activity in a landscape. In these cases, any seeds that survive the disturbance are covered with large amounts of ash, rock, or ice, which isolates them from the landscape's future development. Consequently, the landscape can return to life only though primary succession.

Communities change gradually from one stage to another. One stage merges gradually into the next stage. 'Climax' is the final stage. Succession will not go any further than the climax community. The final stage does not mean that there will be no further change. When large organisms in the climax community, such as trees, die and fall down, then new openings are created in which secondary succession will occur.

The features of ecological succession are as follows :

a. Succession takes place because through the processes of living, growth and reproduction, organisms interact with and affect the environment within an area, gradually changing it.
b. Succession is not partial. It involves a transformation of the whole community.
c. The actual species involved in a succession in a particular area are controlled by factors such as the geology and history of the area, the climate, microclimate, weather, soil type and other environmental factors.
d. Succession occurs on many different timescales, ranging from a few days to hundreds of years.

The nature has its own mechanisms to ensure the creation, continuity and destruction of ecosystem at appropriate period of time. But the human activities are interfering and affecting nature's mechanisms.

SUMMARY

- Ecology is the study of components of environment. Ecosystem is essentially a technical term for 'nature'. The term ecology was coined by Ernst Haeckel.
- Ecosystem is a self-regulating and self-sustaining structural and functional unit of the biosphere. Sun is the primary source of energy for this system.
- Terrestrial and aquatic are the two main types of ecosystem.
- The producers and consumers in an ecosystem can be arranged into several feeding groups, each known as trophic level (feeding level).
- It is estimated that on an average about 10 % of net energy production at one trophic level is passed on to the next level.
- Food from one trophic level reaches to the other trophic level and in this way a chain is established. This is known as food chain.
- A complex of interrelated food chains make up a food web.

How Ecosystems Work

- Human activities affect the carbon cycle through emissions of carbon dioxide (sources) and removal of carbon dioxide (sinks).
- Nitrogen enters the food chain through plants and decomposers and nitrogen fixing bacteria play a crucial role in converting nitrogen compounds into the usable form for plants.
- Plants and animals depend on each other to survive. This is called interdependence. Survival of plants and animals is impossible without abiotic components like water, soil, sunlight, rocks, etc. of the ecosystem.
- Ecological succession is the process through which ecosystems tend to change over a period of time.
- Communities change gradually from one stage to another. One stage merges gradually into the next stage. 'Climax' is the final stage.

EXERCISE

A. Define each of these terms :

1. Ecology, 2. Ecosystem, 3. Tropic level, 4. Food chain, 5. Food web, 6. Food pyramid, 7. Transpiration, 8. Carbon sequestration, 9. Geological sequestration, 10. Ecological succession, 11. Bio-geochemical cycle.

B. Answer each of these questions in brief :

1. State the 10% law.
2. How does water naturally get purified during the process of infiltration ?
3. How has industrial revolution affected the carbon cycle ?
4. Write the difference between Nitrification and Denitrification ?
5. How does lightning affect the nitrogen content in the soil ?
6. Which factors affect the succession of the actual species in a particular area ?
7. How do detritus obtain nutrition ?

C. Answer the following in detail :

1. Differentiate between food chain and food web.
2. Enlist the features of ecological succession.
3. Explain the human activities that affect the carbon cycle.
4. How does human intervention affect the water cycle ?
5. Explain the parameters used to measure the ecological efficiency.
6. Which are the main types of food chain? Explain each type with an appropriate example.
7. Explain the steps involved in water cycle in a proper sequence.

WORKSHEET

A. Fill in the blanks :
1. The term ecology was coined by ____.
2. During transpiration, the water is lost through the ___ in plants.
3. ____ is a series of progressive changes in the composition of an ecological community over time.
4. Algal bloom is the result of disturbed ____ cycle.

B. Write one food chain each of these types :
1. Grazing food chain
2. Parasitic food chain
3. Detritus food chain
4. Ocean food chain

C. Justify these statements :
1. Food chain is independent of the adaptability and competitiveness of organisms.
2. The final stage in the ecological succession does not mean that there will be no further change.
3. Agricultural activities have resulted in carbon sequestration.
4. Algal bloom disturbs the aquatic food chain.
5. In detritus food chain the energy flow remains as a continuous passage rather than as a stepwise flow between discrete entities.
6. Glaciers and polar ice-caps contains the pure form of water.

D. Read the following excerpts and answer the questions that follow. (open-ended questions)
1. Environment Protection Agency (EPA) of United States of America has implemented rules and regulations to limit the underground injection of carbon dioxide. Underground injection is done for purposes such as enhanced oil recovery and enhanced gas recovery (EGR). What could be the main reason for implementation of these rules and regulations ?
2. The energy transfer in certain types of food chain is not significant. Identify such a food chain and justify the statement.
3. Some birds and animals seasonally migrate. How do these birds and animals affect the food chain and food web of that particular area?

E. Activity :
1. List out all possible human interventions that affect the food chain and food web. Conduct a group discussion on how we can control such activities.

4 KINDS OF ECOSYSTEMS

The Earth is the only planet which is a home for a large variety of species of plants, animals and microorganisms. Biosphere is the part of our planet which has conditions appropriate to support life. Biosphere is a part of hydrosphere, atmosphere and lithosphere. There are a variety of ecosystems. Landforms are the natural physical features of the earth's surface, for example—valleys, plateaus, mountains, plains, hills or glaciers. Landforms possess many different physical characteristics and are spread throughout the planet. Together, landforms constitute a specific terrain and their physical arrangement in the landscape forms what is termed as topography. The physical features of landforms include slope, elevation, rock exposure, stratification and rock type. These can be formed by a variety of natural forces, including erosion from water and wind, plate movement, folding and faulting, and volcanic activity.

4.0 FORESTS

Terrestrial ecosystems in their natural state are found in different types of forests, grasslands, deserts, semi-arid areas and coastal regions. Forests are formed by a community of plants, which is predominantly covered by trees, shrubs, climbers and ground cover. Forests are essential for life on earth. 300 million people worldwide live in forests and 1.6 billion depend on them for their livelihoods. Forests also provide habitat for a vast array of plants and animals, many of which are still undiscovered. They protect our watersheds. Forests are so much more than a collection of trees. Forests are home to 80% of the world's terrestrial biodiversity. These ecosystems are complex webs of organisms that include plants, animals, fungi and bacteria. Forests take many forms, depending on their latitude, local soil, rainfall and prevailing temperatures. The abiotic components of forests are soil, mountain, hill, river valley, etc. while plants, animals and microorganisms form the biotic components. The abiotic factors like climate, temperature and soil determine the types of forests. Coniferous, deciduous, evergreen, rainforest, mangrove delta are some types of forests.

1. Tropical Rainforests—Tropical rainforests are rainforests that occur in the areas of tropical rainforest climate in which there is no dry season. The tropical rainforest is hot, moist biome found near Earth's equator. The world's largest tropical rainforests are in South America, Africa, and Southeast Asia.

The combination of constant warmth and abundant moisture makes the tropical rainforest a suitable environment for many plants and animals. Tropical rainforests contain the greatest biodiversity in the world. However various human activities are causing threat to the tropical rainforest. The human activities include oil extraction, deforestation, mining, war, selective agriculture, cattle grazing, industrialisation, pollution, hunting and poaching and construction.

Climate—Tropical rainforests are defined by the fact that they are hot and wet, typical of tropical climates. Found near the equator where it is warm, these regions have rainfall year-round, with little to no dry season. The hot and humid conditions create an ideal environment for the growth of bacteria and other microorganisms. They cover about 6% of the Earth's surface and are found all over the world but mostly in South America in Brazil. Even though they cover small percentage of land on Earth, they are home to the largest number of plants and animal species in such a concentrated area.

Location—Tropical rainforests are found in the world's hottest and wettest areas, namely those closest to the equator. The world's largest tropical rainforests are in Amazon basin in South America, lowland regions in Africa, and the islands of Southeast Asia. While they are found in abundance in Sumatra and New Guinea, small areas are also found in Central America and parts of Australia.

Some of the world's best-known rainforests are :
- The Amazon rainforest in Brazil
- El Yunque, a rainforest in Puerto Rico that attracts millions of tourists
- The Congo basin in Africa

Flora and Fauna—The combination of lots of moisture and consistent year-round warm weather makes tropical rainforests particularly lush areas of plant life. It is estimated that tropical rainforests are home to a staggering 15 million different species of plants and animals, making them some of the world's most

Kinds of Ecosystems

diverse locations. A wide range of animals ranging from microbes to big animals are seen here.

2. Temperate Fainforest—Temperate rainforests are coniferous or broad leaf forests that occur in the temperate zone and receive heavy rainfall. Temperate rainforests experience vast amounts of rainfall, but feature a cooler average temperature compared to tropical rainforests. Temperate rainforests are characterised by mild climates or temperatures. Essentially, these areas do not experience extremely cold or extremely hot temperatures. Temperate rainforests have two different seasons. Winter is quite long and wet, and the summer is short, dry and foggy.

Climate—Temperate rainforests are characterised by mild climates or temperatures. Essentially, these areas do not experience extremely cold or extremely hot temperatures. Temperate rainforests have two different seasons. One season (winter) is quite long and wet, and the other (summer) is short, dry and foggy. Throughout the long-wet season, the temperature hardly falls below freezing point, which is 0°C or 32°F. Throughout the short, dry and foggy season, the temperature hardly exceeds 27°C or 80°F. Also in summer, when it's relatively dry, the weather is considerably cool as the fog supplies sufficient moisture to enable the rainforest to thrive. Ideally, the fog contributes 18-30 cm (7-12") of precipitation every summer. These biomes are very mild due to their closeness to the ocean on one side and mountain ranges on the other. During winter months, the ocean water emits heat, leaving the coastal areas warmer and absorbs heat during summer months, leaving the coastal areas cooler.

Location—Temperate rainforests are located along some coasts in temperate zones. The biggest temperate rainforests are located on the Pacific coast of North America. They extend from Oregon to Alaska for about 1,200 miles. Smaller temperate rainforests also exist. They can be located on the southeast coast of Chile, South America. A few other coastal strips exist that have temperate rainforests such as small parts in the U.K., New Zealand, Japan, South Australia and Norway.

Flora and Fauna—The undergrowth in temperate rainforests is lush, consisting mainly of mosses, lichens, and ferns. In the course of growth during spring, when the tree leaves have not wholly formed, there is a lot of light penetrating to the forest floor. This aspect allows plant species to thrive on the ground, which explains why plant species that exist on the ground surface grow, flower and produce fruits before late summer. There is a huge diversity of life in temperate rainforest biomes. Frogs, turtles, insects, birds, spiders and salamanders are just some of the animal species found here. Bird species like cardinals, broad-winged hawks, pleated woodpeckers and snowy owls exist in this biome. Some of the mammals present in this biome include raccoons, porcupines, red foxes, white-tailed deer, and opossums.

> **Intext Questions**
> 1. Name some physical features of landforms.
> 2. Write the names of any three rainforests.
> 3. Which forest is close to the equator ?

3. Temperate Deciduous Forest—Temperate deciduous forests are located in the mid-latitude areas which is between the polar regions and the tropics. The deciduous forest regions are exposed to warm and cold air masses, hence this

area has four seasons. The temperature varies widely from season to season with cold winters and hot, wet summers. During the fall, trees changes its colour and then lose their leaves. This is in preparation for the winter season. As it gets so cold, the trees adapt themselves to the winter by going into a period of dormancy or sleep. They also have thick bark to protect them from the cold weather. Trees grow and flowers bloom during the spring and summer growing seasons.

Climate—An average temperature of -30°C to 30°C is experienced in these forests. Summers are hot and winters are cold. Average rainfall per year is approximately 750 to 1,500 mm. Temperate deciduous forests are most notable because they go through four seasons. Leaves change its colour in autumn, fall

Kinds of Ecosystems

off in the winter, and grow back in the spring; this adaptation allows plants to survive cold winters.

Location—Temperate deciduous forests are located in the mid-latitude areas which means that they are found between the polar regions and the tropics. Temperate deciduous forests are seen in Eastern United States, Canada, Europe, China and Japan region.

Flora and Fauna– Popular vegetation of temperate deciduous forests are broad leaf trees (oaks, maples, and beeches), shrubs, perennial herbs, and mosses. Birds like broad-winged hawks, cardinals, snowy owls, and pileated woodpeckers are found in this biome. Mammals include white-tailed deer, raccoons, opossums, porcupines and red foxes.

4. Taiga—Taiga also known as boreal forest or snow forest, is a biome characterised by coniferous forests consisting mostly of pines, spruces, and larches. Taiga is the Russian word for forest and is the largest biome in the world. Taiga, also known as coniferous or boreal forest, is the largest terrestrial

biome on earth. Long, cold winters, and short, mild, wet summers are typical of this region. In the winter, chilly winds from the arctic cause bitterly cold weather in the Taiga. The length of day also varies with the seasons. Winter days are short, while summer days are long because of the tilt of the earth on its axis. Precipitation is relatively high in the Taiga and falls as snow during the winter and rain during the summer.

Climate—The most part of Taiga biome climate is dominated by Arctic air. Uniquely cold winds carry along extremely cold air from the Arctic Circle to this biome. During clear nights, when cloud cover is unavailable, the temperatures even plummet further. Due to the Earth's tilt, the taiga biome faces away from the sun during winter. Therefore, the radiation barely reaches the ground to heat it up. Winters come with exceedingly cold conditions and lasts for six months. Summer experiences rainy, hot and short season in this biome. In the

Taiga biome, fall is the shortest season. Spring is characterised by scintillating flowers, melting ponds, and animals coming out of hibernation.

Location—The Taiga biome is situated in the north part of the northern hemisphere and occurs in the continents of America, Asia, and Europe. It spans across Alaska, Canada, Scandinavia and spreads through the northern hemisphere.

Flora and Fauna—Since the climate of Taiga biome is extremely cold, there are only a few varieties of plants. Coniferous tree with cones are the most dominant tree species in this biome. There are four dominant kinds of conifers here—evergreen, spruce, pine, tamarack and fir. Under specific conditions, broadleaved trees like aspen and birch have developed ability to endure the harsh conditions in this biome. The cold temperatures limit the number of animal species that can survive in the tiger biome throughout the year. Typical examples of large animals that live in the Taiga biome include bears, deer, and mice. Typical examples of smaller animals that live in this biome include moles, squirrels, chipmunks, bobcats, and ermine. The Taiga biome harbours numerous species of birds and insects like woodpeckers, bald eagles, warblers, and chickadee.

Threats to the Forest—Forests have long been threatened by a variety of destructive agents. Destructive agents could be natural or man-made. Natural threats such as fire, insects and diseases are integral to forest dynamics. Man-made disruption of forests includes deforestation, pollution, global warming, etc. The main reasons of deforestation are agricultural expansion, livestock ranching, timber extraction, infrastructure expansion and extraction of other forest resources.

4.1. GRASSLANDS, DESERTS AND TUNDRA

1. Tropical Savanna—It is a biome characterised by tall grasses and occasional trees. Tropical savannas or grasslands are associated with the tropical wet and dry climate type. In tropical savanna climate, the dry season can become severe, and often conditions of drought prevail during the course of the year. Tropical savanna climate often features tree-studded grasslands, rather than thick jungle.

Climate—The climate of this biome varies with the pre-existing season. There are two distinct seasons consisting of a wet and a dry season. The wet season comes

Kinds of Ecosystems

during the summer period while the dry season comes during the winter. The climate during the dry season is disastrous to animal and plant life since most plants wither and dry up leading to no food for the animals. Most of the rain in the Savanna biome is from the wet season. With the warmth of the Savanna, there is more rainfall. Also, there is the sprouting of healthy plants owing to the presence of adequate water. Rivers flow and ponds of water fill with water.

Location—It is located between the two tropics, Tropic of Cancer to the north and the Tropic of Capricorn to the south. The area between the tropics is what is known as the tropical grasslands. The biome covers over half of Africa, most of South America and portions of Asia such as India.

Flora and Fauna—There are a variety of plant species in this biome, both tree and grass species. Trees such as acacia, baobab, pine and palm as well as grass namely rhodes grass, red oat grass, lemon grass and star grass grow in the biome. This biome supports one of the world's most renowned species of animals such as zebras, gazelles, wildebeests, warthogs, and elephants which are herbivores. Carnivores in the biome include lions, cheetahs, hyenas and leopards.

2. Temperate Grasslands—Temperate grasslands are located north of the Tropic of Cancer. Temperate grasslands have hot summers and cold winters. They typically have between 10 to 35 inches of precipitation a year, much of it occurring in the late spring and early summer. Snow often serves as a reservoir of moisture for the beginning of the growing season. Seasonal drought and occasional fires help to maintain these grasslands.

Climate—Temperate grassland biome climate varies depending on the season. Summers are usually hot, and temperatures can go up to 90 degrees Fahrenheit. Winters are usually cold, and temperatures can fall to below zero degrees Fahrenheit in specific areas. This biome experiences long, hot summers depending on the latitude of the temperate grassland.

Location—A vast majority of these biomes are found in Africa, South America, North America, Hungary, and Russia. North of the Tropic of Cancer is where most grasslands occur. In the larger North America, temperate grassland biomes flourish in the western regions of the nation, where they are commonly referred to as plains. In South America, temperate grassland biomes are commonly referred to as Pampas.

Flora and Fauna—The dominant vegetation in temperate grassland biome is grass like blue-eyed grass, purple needle grass, buffalo grass and rye grass. Examples of animal species existing in temperate grassland biome include antelopes, pronghorn, bison, coyotes, badgers, including small animals and birds such as quails, grouses, blackbirds, owls, hawks, grasshoppers, snakes, spiders, and leafhoppers.

3. Prairies—Prairies are the temperate grasslands of North America. The word 'Prairie' originated from the Latin word 'priata' which means meadow. It is a region of flat, gently sloping or hilly land. Tall trees, up to two meters high, dominate the landscape. The Prairies are located in the heart of the continent.

Climate—The climate is of continental type with extreme temperatures. The summers are warm, with temperatures of around 20°C and winters are very cold with temperatures of around – 20°C.

Location— Prairies are located in North America.

Flora and Fauna - Prairies are practically treeless. Based on availability of water, the plants found in the area is differ.

- Trees such as willows, alders, and poplars grow in areas where you get water.
- Where rainfall is above 50 cm, farming is practiced as the soil is fertile. The main crop here is maize. The other crops that are grown in this area include potatoes, soybean, alfalfa, and cotton.

The American Buffalo or the bison is the main animal in the Prairies. Other animals found in this region are rabbits, prairie dogs, coyotes, and gophers.

4. Steppes—A steppe is a dry, grassy plain. Steppes occur in temperate climates, which lie between the tropics and polar regions.

Climate—Temperate regions have distinct seasonal temperature changes, with cold winters and warm summers. Steppes are semi-arid, meaning they receive 25 to 50 centimetres (10-20 inches) of rain each year.

Location—It is mostly found in the USA, Mongolia, Siberia, Tibet and China.

Flora and Fauna—The main ones are different types of grasses. The grasses are separated into 3 different groups, depending on how much rain

Kinds of Ecosystems

they get. A lot of the animals that live in Steppea are grazing animals, such as rabbits, mice, antelopes, horses, etc. Smaller animals have little defence from predators.

5. Pampas—These are flat and fertile plains. The average temperature in the Pampas is 18° C.

The pampas have a high sun or dry season in the summer, which in the Southern Hemisphere is in December. The wind blows most of the time. The climate in the pampas is humid and warm.

Climate—The average temperature in the Pampas is 18° C. The pampas have a 'high sun' or dry season in the summer, which in the Southern Hemisphere is in December. The wind blows most of the time. The climate in the pampas is humid and warm.

Location—These forests range from the Atlantic Ocean to the Andes Mountains. It is found primarily in Argentina and extends into Uruguay.

Flora and Fauna—The plants in the pampas include cattails, water lilies and reeds. Some animals include seed eating birds such as the Double Collard Seedeater, the great Pampas Finch, the grassland Yellow Finch, and the Long-Tailed Reed Finch.

Threats to Grasslands

a. There are high possibilities of transformation of marginal grasslands into deserts as rainfall patterns change.
b. Development of urban areas is increasingly cutting into grassland habitats.
c. When native grasses and their soil-retaining roots are eradicated, fallow ploughed lands lose topsoil to dust and erosion.
d. Ecological disturbance, such as fire or destruction of vegetation by overgrazing, can lead to replacement of native grass species by weedy introduced non-native species.

Intext Questions

1. Which is the main animal in prairies ?
2. In which areas are steppes found ?
3. What is the taiga region also known as ?
4. Which forests are semi-arid in nature ?

6. Desert—A desert witnesses little rainfall, resulting in less vegetation than in more humid areas of the globe. Deserts are areas of land that are arid, or dry, and get less than 10 inches of rain per year. Deserts can be hot or cold. Plants and animals in the desert ecosystem have adaptations that allow them to survive the lack of rainfall and extreme temperatures. Hot deserts are warm year-round and very hot in the summer. During the day, temperatures often reach over 100 degrees Fahrenheit. In the evening, the temperature drop sometimes below the freezing. Much of the time rain does not fall, but when it does, it is only for a short amount of time. The ground is usually rocky or sandy. Most of the hot deserts in the world are located just north and south of the equator, where it is the hottest. The largest hot desert is the Sahara Desert in Northern Africa. The Sahara covers over 3 million square miles and has some areas that receive no rainfall for years. Cold deserts are cool year-around with very cold temperatures in the winter. Temperatures in cold deserts are often below freezing. Heavy snows happen during the winter, with most of the rainfall happening during the spring months. The ground can be solid ice in colder temperatures and rocky or spongy soil in milder temperatures. The cold deserts of the world are mostly located on the coasts near oceans and closer to the north and south poles. The largest cold desert, and the largest desert in the world, is the continent of Antarctica.

Climate—Due to the availability of little moisture in the air to capture and hold on to the heat emanating from the high temperatures during the day, desert nights are typically cold. A combination of extreme temperature fluctuations and incredibly low levels of water makes the desert biome a very harsh land mass to live in.

Location—Most deserts occur far away from the coasts, in locations where moisture emanating from the oceans and seas hardly reaches. However, some

Kinds of Ecosystems

deserts are situated on the west coast of some continents like the Atacama in Chile and Namibia in Africa, culminating in coastal fog deserts whose aridity is caused by cold ocean currents. The desert biomes of the world are located in six biogeographic domains including—The Australian deserts, Afrotropic deserts, the Indo-Malay region, the Neotropic deserts, the Nearctic deserts and Palearctic domain.

Flora and Fauna—The most common plants that thrive in desert biomes include Cacti, small shrubs, succulents, and grasses. Animals in the desert biome include Bobcats, Coyotes, Javelina, Desert tortoise, Cactus wren, Desert kangaroo Rat, Sonoran desert toad, Thorny devil, Desert bighorn ship, Armadillo lizard and Sonoran pronghorn antelope.

Threats to desert

a. Human activities such as firewood gathering and the grazing by animals are also converting semi-arid regions into deserts.
b. Global warming is increasing the incidence of drought, which dries up water holes.
c. Higher temperatures may produce an increasing number of wildfires that alter desert landscapes by eliminating slow-growing trees and shrubs and replacing them with fast-growing grasses.
d. Grazing animals can destroy many desert plants and animals.

7. **Tundra**—Tundras are among the Earth's coldest, harshest biomes. Tundra ecosystems are treeless regions found in the Arctic and on the tops of mountains, where the climate is cold and windy and rainfall is scant. The summer is brief, with temperatures above freezing point and lasting for only a few weeks at most. However, this "warm" summer coincides with periods of almost 24-hour daylight, so the plant growth can be enormous.

Location—There are two main types of tundra biomes in the world, one at the Arctic Circle in the northern hemisphere, and the other that is found on the top of the highest mountains in the world.

The Arctic Tundra: Located in the northern hemisphere, the arctic tundra is, quite literally, the world's north pole. It spans almost 20% of the earth's surface, and is located at latitudes 55° to 70° N. It is extremely cold, and is one of the world's least populous areas.

a. Alpine tundra is found on mountain tops that are too cold for trees to grow, particularly in the highest elevations.
b. The Antarctic region is actually significantly colder than the arctic, so it is not technically considered tundra. Overall the yearly average temperature can be as low as -70°F (-56°C) so it is characterised by entirely different ecosystems.

Climate—The arctic tundra, which is located in the northern hemisphere surrounding the north pole, is characterised by extremely cold and dry conditions, similar to a frozen desert. In summer months, the sun can shine almost around the clock, which is why so many plants and animals need this time for survival. Alpine tundra experiences freezing temperatures and dry air. Though they are located in higher elevations, because of these heights, alpine tundra is often subjected to larger concentrations of sunlight at a time, because the air and atmosphere is thinner, thereby allowing the rays to penetrate strongly.

Flora and Fauna—Common plants found in the tundra biome are Reindeer moss, Crowberry, Heath, Liverwort, Tussock grass, Willow, Lichen, Dwarf trees and small birches. The main types of animals that are found in the tundra are those that eat plants and those that eat animals, fish, insects, and birds.

Herbivores—Voles, Lemmings, Squirrels, Arctic hare, Snowshoe rabbits, Caribou/reindeer, Musk oxen, Mountain goats

Carnivores—Wolves, Wolverines, Arctic foxes, Polar bears

Fish—Salmon, Cod, Trout, Flatfish

Birds—Falcons, Ravens, Loons, Sandpipers, Terns, Gulls, Snow buntings, Harlequin duck

Threats to Tundra Forests

a. Greenhouse gas emissions cause the Earth's temperature to rise. As tundra warms, permafrost melts and releases methane and carbon dioxide lying beneath the permafrost.
b. As temperatures rise in the tundra, the amount of summer moisture may decline, resulting in problems such as wildfires and drought. Climate change causes an indirect food supply problem in the tundra. As it gets warmer, shrubs in the tundra replace lichens and other vegetation.
c. Oil spills can be a problem in tundra regions because it's harder to clean spills around ice floes than it is to clean spills in open waters.
d. Tourists can also disturb some native species invading animal nesting grounds.
e. Mining for minerals in the tundra harms the environment. When people dig holes and disturb the soil; it could take years for vegetation to return.

Kinds of Ecosystems

4.2. FRESHWATER ECOSYSTEM

Freshwater ecosystems are a subset of Earth's aquatic ecosystems. They include lakes and ponds, rivers, streams, springs, and wetlands. It supports a range of plant and animal ecosystems whose composition is shaped by the availability of food, oxygen (O), temperature and sunlight. Freshwater environments are less extensive than the sea, but they are important centres of biodiversity. This is especially so in dry environments, like deserts, where isolated ponds and streams provide a habitat for plants and animals. The 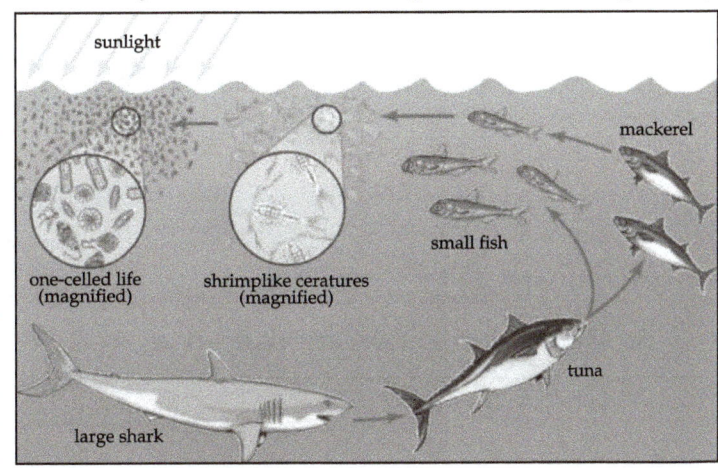 diversity of a freshwater ecosystem depends upon temperature, availability of light, nutrients, oxygen, and salinity. Many human activities threaten the health of freshwater ecosystems. For instance, acid rain created from sulphur (S) and nitrogen oxide (NO) emissions turns many lakes and streams acidic, leaving them unable to support various fish species. The building of dams to create hydro-electric power plants blocks the routes of migratory fish such as salmon. Deforestation adds silt to a stream or river and slows it down, which may increase flooding.

1. Lake Ecosystem—Lake ecosystems are a prime example of stationery or stagnant ecosystems. Lake systems are diverse, ranging from a small, temporary rainwater pool to a few inches deep. It consists of all abiotic factors like light, temperature, minerals, air, soil, etc. The biotic components include phytoplanktons, aquatic animals, algae and micro-organisms.

2. Pond Ecosystem—Ponds are freshwater ecosystem. They are still water body with no wave action. As the size of the pond is relatively small, a constant temperature is always maintained. Algae forms the basis of food chain in the ponds. Food web and food chain is composed of aquatic plants, insect, fish, amphibians and reptiles.

3. Marshes—Marshes are defined as wetlands frequently or continually inundated with water, characterised by emergent soft vegetation adapted to saturated soil conditions. There are different kinds of marshes, ranging from the prairie potholes to the everglades, coastal to inland, freshwater to saltwater. All these receive most of their water from surface water, and many marshes are also fed by groundwater.

4. Swamps—A swamp is defined as a wetland dominated by trees or dense shrub thickets, although in popular parlance it is commonly applied to many other sodden ecosystems, including marshes, bogs, fens and mires. They are found in the subarctic region to the heart of the tropics, native to a significant range of climate zones. They may be permanent or seasonal in nature, and when left undisturbed, foster a wild, primal atmosphere.

5. Rivers—Following are the characteristics of river ecosystem—
 a. Flowing water that is mostly unidirectional
 b. A state of continuous physical change

Kinds of Ecosystems

c. Many different (and changing) microhabitats

d. Variability in the flow rates of water

Bacteria are present in large numbers in river waters. They play a significant role in energy recycling. Bacteria decompose organic material into inorganic compounds that can be used by plants and by other microbes. Rivers are also a home to many kinds of phytoplanktons and aquatic plants.

Threats to Rivers

Construction of large dams—This disrupts the natural flooding cycles, reduces flows, drains wetlands, cuts off rivers from their floodplains, and inundates riparian habitats, resulting in the destruction of species, intensification of floods and a threat to livelihoods in the long term.

Deforestation and loss of natural habitats including wetlands—This reduces natural flood control and destroys the habitats used by fish, waterbirds and many other species for breeding, feeding and migrating.

Excessive water abstraction—River water is extracted for agricultural irrigation, domestic consumption and urban or industrial use. Over-exploitation of river water has resulted in disturbed ecosystem, dried-up river beds and death of river flora and fauna.

Pollution—Pollution is caused by runoff from agricultural chemicals, poorly-managed and sometimes out of date industrial processes, and lack of adequate treatment for sewage and other urban wastes. The results may include water that is unfit to drink, massive fish kills, and complete loss of underwater plants. Through rivers, the pollutants enter the food chain.

6. **Wetlands**—Wetlands comprise areas that are transition between terrestrial (land) areas and aquatic (water) areas. The wetlands ecosystem represents a richly diverse web of plants and animals interacting together. A wetland can take in many forms. Some types of wetlands include marshes,

fens, bogs, riparian wetlands, swamps and estuaries. Wetlands that exist away from oceans obtain their water from ground water and precipitation; wetlands in coastal environments receive precipitation and ground water. In wetlands, the water table sits at or is close to the surface of the land, and shallow water often covers the area. Some other characteristics of wetlands may include land supporting aquatic vegetation, a substrate of saturated soil and substrates not comprised of soil but inundated with water during the growing season. The water in wetlands ecosystems can be freshwater, saltwater, brackish water or flowing water.

Threats to Wetlands

a. A major threat is the draining of wetlands for commercial development, including tourism facilities, or agricultural land.
b. Alien invasive species have severe impacts on local aquatic flora and fauna, and can upset the natural balance of an ecosystem.
c. Pollution in wetlands is a growing concern, affecting drinking water sources and biological diversity.
d. Increase in temperature is causing polar ice to melt and sea levels to rise. This in turn is leading to shallow wetlands being swamped and some species of mangrove trees being submerged and drowned.

4.3. MARINE ECOSYSTEM

Marine ecosystems are aquatic ecosystems whose waters possess a high salt content. Out of all of the types of ecosystems on the planet, marine ecosystems are the most prevalent. The marine ecosystem includes—marshes, tidal zones, estuaries, the mangrove forest, lagoons, sea grass beds, the sea floor, and the coral reefs. The threats that have impacted the marine ecosystems are pollution, global warming and overfishing. Due to global warming, polar ice caps melts and cause flood in the oceans. The oil spills and the pollution caused from marine vehicles are contaminating the water. Thus, the marine life is getting affected. Over-fishing and unbalanced fishing is a reason for extinction of various marine species of fish.

1. Estuary—An estuary is a partially enclosed, coastal water body where freshwater from rivers and streams mixes with salt water from the ocean. Estuaries, and their surrounding lands, are places of transition from land to sea. Although influenced by the tides, they are protected from the full force of ocean waves, winds and storms by landforms such as barrier islands or peninsulas. Many different habitat types are found in and around estuaries, including shallow open waters, freshwater and saltwater marshes, swamps, sandy beaches, mud and sand flats, rocky shores, oyster reefs, mangrove forests, river deltas, tidal pools and sea grass beds.

Kinds of Ecosystems

Following are the threats to estuary—

1. Increased nutrients and algal blooms.
2. Loss of habitat and biodiversity.
3. Contaminants and pollutants.
4. Accelerated rates of sedimentation.
5. Disturbance of acid sulphate soils.
6. Changes to freshwater and tidal flows
7. Invasive species
8. Climate change.

2. Coral Reefs—Corals are members of the Phylum Cnidaria, a diverse group that includes jellyfish, hydroids, and sea anemones. Corals are colonial organisms made up of individual polyps. Coral reefs are one of the most biologically diverse ecosystems on earth. This means that fluctuations in the abundance of one species can drastically alter both the diversity and abundances of others.

While natural causes such as hurricanes and other large storm events can be the stimulus for such alterations, it is more commonly anthropological forces that effect these types of shifts in the ecosystem.

Following are the threats to the coral ecosystem—

a. **Climate change—**Corals cannot survive if the water temperature is too high. Global warming has already led to increased levels of coral bleaching, and this is predicted to increase in frequency and severity in the coming decades.

b. **Overfishing—**This affects the ecological balance of coral reef communities, warping the food chain and causing effects far beyond the directly overfished population.

c. **Careless tourism—**Careless boating, diving, snorkeling and fishing happens around the world, with people touching reefs, stirring up sediment, collecting coral and dropping anchors on reefs. Some tourist resorts and infrastructure have been built directly on top of reefs, and some resorts empty their sewage or other wastes directly into water surrounding coral reefs.

d. **Pollution**—Urban and industrial waste, sewage, agrochemicals, and oil pollution are poisoning reefs. These toxins are dumped directly into the ocean or carried by river systems from sources upstream. Some pollutants, such as sewage and runoff from farming, increase the level of nitrogen in seawater, causing an overgrowth of algae, which hampers the growth of reefs by cutting off their sunlight.

e. **Sedimentation**—Erosion caused by construction (both along coasts and inland), mining, logging, and farming is leading to increased sediment in rivers. The destruction of mangrove forests, which normally trap large amounts of sediment, is exacerbating the problem.

f. **Coral mining**—Live coral is removed from reefs for use as bricks, road-fill, or cement for new buildings. Corals are also sold as souvenirs to tourists and to exporters who do not know or don't care about the longer term damage done, and harvested for the live rock trade.

Ocean Ecosystem

The ocean is divided up into three zones, or layers, based on how much sunlight they receive. The top layer is called the euphotic zone, which receives lots of sunlight. It starts at the ocean's surface and goes down to about 230 feet on average. The second layer is the disphotic zone, which receives some sunlight, but not enough for plants to survive. The third layer is the aphotic zone, which gets no light at all. The aphotic zone is extremely cold and few marine animals can survive here.

Marine plants grow in the euphotic zone of the ocean, as they need sunlight to create food through photosynthesis. Seaweeds, marine algae and sea grasses are the common sea plants. Kelp is one of the common marine algae. Phytoplankton is another important plant found in the ocean. This is the food for many ocean creatures, from the largest whales to the smallest fish. The ocean contains a large variety of animal life, including fish, mollusc, dolphins, seals, walruses, whales, crustaceans, bacteria, sea anemones and many others. Most marine animals live in the top two ocean zones, where they have access to plants and other ocean animals to eat. Very few species live in the deep ocean. Anglerfish is one such animal.

Threats to the ocean ecosystem—

a. Due to global warming the sea levels are rising. This could bring floods in the coastal areas.

b. Many pesticides and nutrients used in agriculture flow into the coastal waters, resulting in oxygen depletion that kills marine plants and shell fish.

c. Factories and industrial plants discharge sewage and other runoff into the oceans.

Kinds of Ecosystems

> - Oil spills from the marine vehicles pollute the oceans.
> - Ocean ecosystem suffers overfishing. Edible fish and other species of fish are harvested on a large scale for various commercial benefits.

Fascinating Fact

Half of all the oxygen we breathe is produced in the ocean.

Polar Ecosystems—Life in the planet's polar regions can be incredibly difficult. The cold winds whip across the landscape. Winter temperatures can reach deep into the negative degree Celsius, and the winter night can last for months. But these landscapes are home to a rich diversity of wildlife both on land and under the sea surface. Polar environments are in the Arctic and Antarctic regions. Arctic regions are in the Northern Hemisphere, while Antarctica is in the Southern Hemisphere. The climate of both polar regions consists of long cold winters and short cool summers. The difference between two regions are tabulated below—

Arctic region	Antarctic region
At sea—700 km to nearest land	Inland—1,300 km to nearest sea
Contains a wide range of landscapes; plains, mountains, some very large significant rivers and lakes, rolling hills, huge stretches of tundra and the edge of the taiga.	98% covered in icy mountains, glaciers or smooth ice-sheet.
Plant life in the Arctic is characterised largely by what grows on the tundra.	Plant life in the Antarctic on the other hand is much less plentiful.
The Arctic has many large land animals including reindeer, musk ox, lemmings, arctic hares, arctic terns, snowy owls, squirrels, arctic fox and polar bears.	The largest land animal in the Antarctic is an insect, a wingless midge, *Belgica antarctica*, there are however a great many animals that feed in the sea though come onto the land for part or most of their lives. These include huge numbers of adelie, chinstrap, gentoo, king, emperor, rockhopper and macaroni penguins.
There are many indigenous people who live around the Arctic.	Antarctica has never had any native people living there.

Threats to Polar Ecosystem

1. Global warming—Results in warming of the sea and loss of sea ice and land-based ice, this is greatest long-term threat to the region. Already some ice shelves have collapsed and ice slopes and glaciers have retreated.

2. Tourism—With the pollutants that accompany ships and aircraft, the possibility of oil spills and the effects of lot of people and infrastructure on wildlife and the wider environment.

3. Ozone depletion—CFC's and other ozone depletors are responsible for the ozone hole that has appeared over Antarctica for over 30 years.

4. Over fishing—Around the world including the Arctic Ocean and the Southern Ocean surrounding Antarctica humans are taking fish out of the water faster than fish can reproduce and be replaced.

5. Exploitation of resources—The Arctic holds some of the world's largest untapped oil and gas reserves, but getting those precious resources whether on land or offshore can have devastating environmental impacts. Infrastructure for these development projects can destroy habitat, fragment migration routes, and drain freshwater resources.

4.4. BIOECOGRAPHIC ZONES OF INDIA

The Indian mainland could be divided into ten bio-geographic regions. Biogeography is the study of the distribution of species (biology), organisms, and ecosystems in geographic space and through geological time. There are ten biogeographic zones in India.

1. Trans-Himalayan region—Consists of Ladakh in Jammu and Kashmir, Lahul-Spiti in Himachal Pradesh and small areas of Sikkim. It constitutes 5.6% of the total geographical area, includes the high altitude, cold and arid mountain areas. This zone has sparse alpine steppe vegetation that harbours several endemic species and is a favourable habitat for the biggest populations of wild sheep and goat in the world and other rare fauna that includes Snow Leopard and the migratory Blacknecked Crane (*Grus nigricollis*). The cold dry desert of this zone represents an extremely fragile ecosystem.

2. Himalayan region—This region consists of four subregions :

(a) Northwest Himalaya which extends from Kashmir to the River Sutlej in Himachal Pradesh.

(b) Western Himalaya which comprises Garhwal and Kumaon and includes eight hilly districts of Uttaranchal.

(c) Central Himalaya, most of the regions fall in Nepal.

(d) Eastern Himalaya which includes Kingdom of Bhutan and Indian states of Sikkim and Arunachal Pradesh.

It constitutes 6.4% of the total geographical area, includes some of the highest peaks in the world. The Himalayan zone makes India one of the richest areas in terms of habitat and species.

3. Northeast India—This region consist of states of Assam, Meghalaya, Manipur, Mizoram, Nagaland and Tripura. Northeast Region constitutes 5.2 %

Kinds of Ecosystems

of the total geographical area. This region represents the transition zone between the Indian, Indo-Malayan and Indo-Chinese bio-geographical regions as well as being a meeting point of the Himalayan mountains and peninsular India. The Northeast is thus the biogeographical 'gateway' for much of India's fauna and flora and also a biodiversity hotspot.

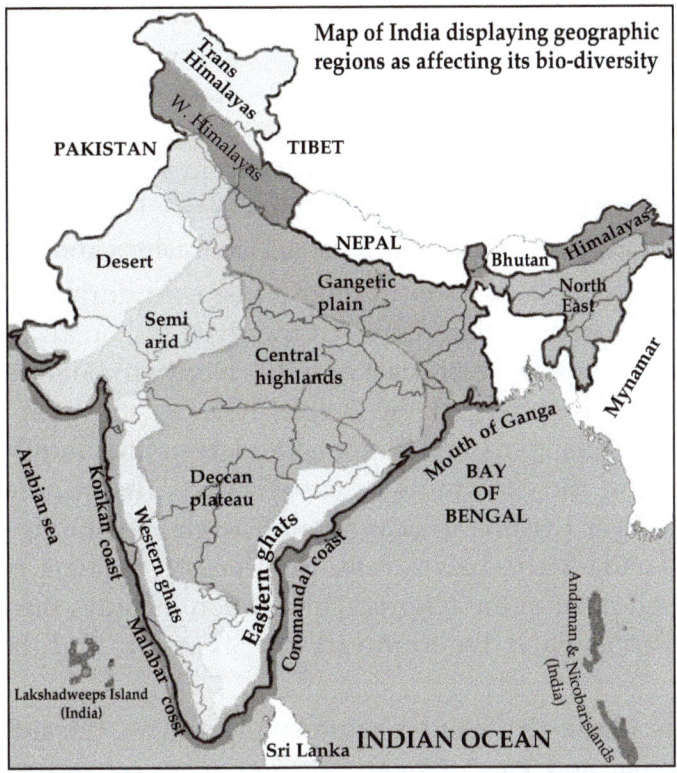

Map of India displaying geographic regions as affecting its bio-diversity

4. Indian Desert—Indian Desert covers nearly 12% of land, most of which is located in the state of Rajasthan. In the north it extends into Punjab through Ferozpur, Sangrur and Bhatinda districts and in the northeast it joins with desert areas of Haryana, in parts of Mahendragarh and Hissar Districts. In the west, are the Thar-Parkar, Cholistan and Thal deserts of Pakistan. In the South, it extends into Gujarat mainly in the Kutch, Mehsana and Banaskantha districts and to some extent in the Saurashtra region.

5. Semi-arid region—It consists of the Deccan plateau in Central India, Malwa plateau in Northwest India, and Saurashtra region in Gujarat. The Semi-arid region merges with the Desert on the western side and with the Gangetic plain in the north. The Semi-arid region occurs in eastern Rajasthan, Gujarat except Kutch, Western Madhya Pradesh, parts of Uttar Pradesh, Haryana, Punjab and Southern parts of Jammu and Kashmir.

6. Western Ghats—Western Ghats on the northwest coasts of India extends from the river Tapti in the north to Kanyakumari in the South. It consists of a chain of ancient mountains parallel to the west coast of the Indian peninsula and occupies only 5% of India's land area. It is one of the major tropical evergreen forest regions in India and represents one of the two biodiversity 'hot spots'. Western Ghats are home to viable populations of most of the vertebrate species found in peninsular India, besides an endemic faunal element of its own.

7. Deccan peninsula—Deccan peninsula has five divisions which are Deccan plateau North, Deccan plateau South, Eastern high lands, Chhota Nagpur and Central highlands. The Northern plateau is very dry. Eastern highland is a small province and it also consists of Eastern Ghats and moist hills and valleys of Chattisgarh-Dandakarunya area. Central highland includes both Vindhya and Satpura hill ranges. Southern Deccan plateau falls in states of Karnataka, Andhra Pradesh, Tamil Nadu and Kerala and possibly Orissa. The Central Indian forests include Eastern Madhya Pradesh, Northwest Maharashtra and Northwest Orissa.

8. Eastern Ghats—It spreads through Orissa, Andhra Pradesh and Tamil Nadu. They extend over a length between the river Mahanadi in the North and Vaigai in the South along the east coast of India. Northern boundary is Mahanadi basin and Southern boundary is the Nilgiri hills. In the west it merges with the tips of Basthar, Telangana and Karnataka plateau and Tamil Nadu uplands, while coastal area in the east limits its eastern part. The Middle Eastern Ghats extends from the river Krishna to near about Chennai, including the Nallamalai, Palakonda, Velikonda-Seshachalam hills. South-eastern Ghats run towards the Western Ghats and meet in the Nigiris. This section includes the Javadi hills, the Kollimalai, the Pacchamalai, the Kalrayan, the Shevaroys and the Biligirirangan Hills.

9. Gangetic plain—It includes regions adjacent to Terrai-Bhabar tracts in Uttar Pradesh, Bihar and West Bengal. Gangetic plain constitutes around 10.8% of the total geographical area. The Gangetic plain is topographically homogenous for hundreds of kilometers. The characterstic fauna of this region include Rhino (*Rhinoceros unicornis*), Elephant, Buffalo, Swamp Deer, Hog-Deer and Hispid Hare.

10. Coastal areas—It includes the coastal areas of different states. Coastal region constitutes 2.5 % of the total geographical area with sandy beaches, mangroves, mud flats, coral reefs and marine angiosperm pastures make them the wealth and health zones of India.

Each type of ecosystem has its peculiarity and characteristic features. These peculiarities determine not only the type of organisms that grow but also their adaptations.

SUMMARY

- Biosphere is the part of our planet which has conditions appropriate to support life. Biosphere is a part of hydrosphere, atmosphere and lithosphere.

Kinds of Ecosystems

- Landforms are natural features of landscape, natural physical features of the earth's surface, for example- valleys, plateaus, mountains, plains, hills or glaciers.
- Landforms are the natural features and shapes existent on the face of the earth.
- Forests are formed by a community of plants, which is predominantly covered by trees, shrubs, climbers and ground cover.
- Terrestrial ecosystem includes tropical savannas, temperate grasslands, prairies, steppes, pampas, deserts, tropical rainforest, temperate deciduous forest and taiga.
- Freshwater ecosystem includes lakes, ponds, wetlands, marshes, swamps and rivers.
- Marine ecosystem are estuaries, coral reefs and oceans.
- Arctic and Antarctic regions are the two regions of polar ecosystem.
- The Indian mainland could be divided into ten bio-geographic zones.

EXERCISE

A. Define each of these terms :

1. Landform, 2. Priata, 3. Biogeography, 4. Topography, 5. Estuary.

B. Answer each of these in brief :

1. Briefly explain the climatic conditions of -
   a. Tropical rainforest, b. Temperate rainforest, c. Taiga, d. Savanna, e. Prairies, f. Pampas, g. Polar areas, h. Desert
2. Where are these forests located ?
   a. Tropical rainforest, b. Temperate rainforest, c. Taiga, d. Savanna, e. Prairies, f. Pampas g. Polar areas h. Desert
3. Write any three characteristics of wetland.
4. Differentiate between Arctic ecosystem and Antarctic ecosystem.
5. Which are the four sub-regions of Himalayas ?
6. Why is Trans-Himalayan area a fragile ecosystem ?
7. Differentiate between temperate and temperate deciduous forest.
8. Which are the four types of conifers in taiga ?
9. Write the characteristics of river ecosystem.

C. Answer each of these in detail—

1. List out the threats to –
   a. Grasslands, b. Desert, c. Tundra, d. River, e. Wetlands, f. Estuary, g. Coral ecosystem, h. Polar areas.
2. Explain the types of freshwater ecosystem.
3. State the commercial uses of corals.

WORKSHEET

A. **Fill in the blanks :**
1. _____ is the biogeographical gateway for India's flora and fauna.
2. The Congo basin is situated in _____.
3. Coral belongs to the phylum _____.

B. **Justify the following statements :**
1. Deforestation causes flooding in freshwater.
2. Plants of temperate deciduous undergo period of sleep.
3. There is no dry season in tropical rainforest.
4. Oil spills affect the marine life.

C. **Read the following excerpts and answer the questions that follow. (open-ended questions) :**
1. Tropical rainforest contain the greatest biodiversity.
   (a) What are threats to tropical rainforest ?
   (b) Which factors facilitate greatest biodiversity in tropical rainforest ?
2. Steppes can support high densities of grazing animals.
   (a) Which factors favour grazing animals in steppes ?
   (c) Where is steppes located ?

D. **Activity :**
1. Make a chart of different types of ecosystem. Compare the type of flora and fauna grown in all these ecosystems.

5 WATER

Earth is made up of four layers that is hydrosphere, biosphere, lithosphere and atmosphere. A hydrosphere is the collective mass of water found on, under and over the surface of planet. Hydrosphere is much more extensive than the land. It is estimated that 71% of the earth's surface is occupied by seas and oceans. Out of all the water on Earth, saline water in oceans, seas and saline groundwater make up about 97% of it. Only 2.5–2.75% is fresh water, including 1.75–2% frozen in glaciers, ice and snow, 0.5–0.75% as fresh groundwater and soil moisture, and less than 0.01% of it as surface water in lakes, swamps and rivers. Over 68 percent of the fresh water on Earth is found in icecaps and glaciers, and just over 30 percent is found in ground water. Only about 0.3 percent of our fresh water is found in the surface water of lakes, rivers, and swamps. Of all the water on Earth, more than 99 percent of Earth's water is not usable. The portion of saline water on the earth is called as sea. Large seas areas are called oceans. Seas are separated from the oceans by a series of peninsulas.

5.0. WATER RESOURCES

Water resources are the sources of water that are potentially useful to the living beings. The resources of water in which the water is found on, is detailed below.

1. Polar ice caps—Polar ice caps are the dome-shaped sheets of ice found near the North and South Poles. They are formed because high-latitude polar regions receive less heat from the Sun than other areas on Earth. They remain frozen year-round, and they serve as sources for glaciers that feed ice into the polar seas in the form of icebergs. As a result, average temperatures at the poles can be very cold. Earth's north pole is covered by the floating ice

> **Fascinating Fact**
>
> The average thickness of the ice on Antarctica is over a mile.

pack and the Greenland ice sheet over the arctic ocean. While the Antarctica ice sheet lays a covering over the south pole. However, due to the climatic changes like global warming, the temperature in the polar region is rising. The satellite pictures of these regions show a considerable shrink of ice caps.

Snow—Snow is the form of ice that precipitates from the atmosphere. Polar regions are the major snowprone areas. Snow forms when tiny ice crystals in clouds stick together to become snowflakes. If enough crystals stick together, they will become heavy enough to fall to the ground. Snowflakes that descend through moist air that is slightly warmer than 0°C will melt around the edges and stick together to produce big flakes. Snowflakes that fall through cold, dry air produce powdery snow that does not stick together. Snow is formed when temperatures are low and there is moisture in the atmosphere in the form of tiny ice crystals.

However, due to various human activities, the atmospheric temperature at the poles has risen up. As temperatures rise, the polar ice caps start to melt and break apart causing the polar ice caps to shirnk 9% every 10 years. The changing environment at the poles affects native people, animals, and plants. Animals such as seals, polar bears, and whales may be forced to change their natural migration patterns. People who live in coastal villages may have to abandon their homes as sea levels rise. The effects of the melting polar ice caps may one  day be felt well beyond the poles. As the polar ice caps shrink, sea levels begin to rise, creating serious problems for coastal areas around the globe.

2. Surface water—Surface water is any water that collects on the surface of the earth. This includes oceans, seas, lakes, rivers, or wetlands. Man-made bodies of water are not considered surface water since they generally rest on artificial surfaces, not the ground itself. Surface water is lost through evaporation and regained through precipitation (rain) or recruited from ground-water sources. Surface water that is not saline can also be lost by seeping into the ground, where

Water

it becomes groundwater, used by plants, mankind for life support, industrial purposes or agricultural purposes, or can enter the sea where it becomes saline water. A few types of surface water are defined below –

a. River—A river is a natural flowing watercourse, usually freshwater, flowing towards an ocean, sea, lake or another river. From its source, a river flows downhill as a small stream. Precipitation and groundwater add to the river's flow. It is also fed by other streams, called tributaries. The end of a river is its mouth. Here, the river empties into another water body like a larger river, lake, or the ocean.

b. Lake—A lake is a large body of water (larger and deeper than a pond) within a body of land. Lakes do not flow, like rivers, but many have rivers flowing into and out of them. Since they are often fed by rivers, springs or precipitation (rain and/or snow), lakes are primarily freshwater. However, some of the more famous lakes, like the Dead Sea and the Great Salt Lake, are saline lakes and contain only saltwater.

c. Wetlands—Wetlands are ecosystems saturated with water, either seasonally or permanently. Wetlands occur where water meets land. A wetland is a place where the land is covered by water, either salt, fresh or somewhere in between. Marshes and ponds, the edge of a lake or ocean, the delta at the mouth of a river, low-lying areas that frequently flood, all of these are wetlands.

d. Oceans and seas—An ocean is a large area of salt water between continents. Oceans are much bigger than sea. Oceans are a large body of water constituting a principal part of the hydrosphere. While sea is a division of an ocean or a large body of salt water partially enclosed by land. Oceans do not have any substantial wildlife present in them since they are away from the land. Seas, on the other hand, have a variety of animal and plant life because of favourable conditions.

> **Fascinating Fact**
>
> Earth's longest chain of mountains, the Mid-Ocean Ridge, is almost entirely beneath the ocean, stretching across a distance of 65,000 kilometres.

> **Intext Questions**
>
> 1. What are peninsulas ?
> 2. In what ways is river water recharged ?
> 3. List out the forms of wetlands.
> 4. What is meant by tributary ?

(i) Rivers of controversy

As we know water is one of the major and inevitable resource for survival and sustenance of all living beings. In India, rivers are not considered as a mere resource, but are worshipped. Thus, our citizens are connected spiritually to majority of the rivers. Various mythological and historical incidents and stories are linked to the rivers of India. Ever since the beginning of civilisation, rivers have been a crucial aspect of dispute. Below is detailed account of few rivers that have been in controversy –

1. Kaveri river dispute

The Kaveri or Cauvery river water dispute is one of the most talked about and oldest river disputes in India, dating back all the way to the 19th century. It is a dispute between Tamil Nadu and Karnataka. Karnataka, which has always contended that it does not receive a fair share of the water and an agreement from 1924 favoured Madras Presidency, has demanded a renegotiated settlement. Tamil Nadu says that change in the current water sharing deal will affect millions of farmers in the state. A tribunal constituted in 1990 gave a verdict in 2007. The issue remains unresolved due to a review petition, and controversies.

2. Krishna river water dispute

Like Kaveri, Krishna river water dispute also has its roots in the colonial period. It is about a disagreement between Maharashtra, Karnataka and Andhra Pradesh, regarding sharing the water from the river which flows into the Bay of Bengal. The Government of India constituted the first Krishna Water Disputes Tribunal in 1969 to resolve the dispute and KWDT-II was constituted in 2004. The controversy was solved in 2010, with the formation of Telangana as a separate state.

3. Godavari water dispute

Another river which has caused a standoff between states is the Godavari river which flows through Andhra Pradesh, Madhya Pradesh, Chhattisgarh, Orissa and Karnataka. A tribunal for resolving the issue was constituted in 1969

Water

alongside the Krishna Water Disputes Tribunal, and its verdict was made binding on all states by the government of India in 1980.

4. Barak river dispute

The Barak is one of the two major rivers flowing through India's north east region, and originates from Manipur, before flowing through Mizoram and Assam, and going across the border into Bangladesh. It is the cause for a tussle between Manipur and Assam and is also at the centre of an international water dispute between India and Bangladesh.

(ii) Dam

Dam is a structure built across a stream, a river, or an estuary to retain water. Dams are built to provide water for human consumption, irrigating arid and semi-arid lands, or used in industrial processes. Dams are primarily used for generating hydropower. The construction of large dams completely change the relationship of water and land, destroying the existing ecosystem balance which, in many cases, has taken thousands of years to create. One of the first problems with dams is the erosion of land. Dams hold back the sediment load  normally found in a river flow, depriving the downstream of this. In order to make up for the sediments, the downstream water erodes its channels and banks. This lowering of the riverbed threatens vegetation and river wildlife. Changes in the microclimate, loss of vegetable cover, variation in water table, landslides, sedimentation of reservoirs, drying up of spring are some of the effects of dam.

Dams of India

After independence India has made lot of progress in dams and water reservoirs. Today India is one of the world's most prolific dam-builders. There are around 4300 large dams already constructed and many more in the pipeline. The major dams of India are –

1. Tehri Dam - Uttarakand

Tehri Dam is located on the Bhagirathi River, Uttarakhand. Tehri Dam is the highest dam in India, with a height of 261 meters and the eighth tallest dam in the world. The high rock and earth-fill embankment dam first phase was completed in 2006 and other two phases are under construction. The water reservoir is used for irrigation, municipal water supply and the generation of 1,000 MW of hydroelectricity.

2. Bhakra Nangal Dam – Himachal Pradesh

Bhakra Nangal Dam is a gravity dam across the Sutlej river in Himachal Pradesh. Bhakra Nangal is the largest dam in India, with a height of 225 meters and second largest dam in Asia. Its reservoir, known is as the "Gobind Sagar Lake".

A gravity dam is a dam constructed from concrete or stone masonry and designed to hold back water by primarily using the weight of the material alone to resist the horizontal pressure of water pushing against it.

3. Sardar Sarovar Dam – Gujrat

Sardar Sarovar Dam, also known as Narmada Dam, is the largest dam to be built, with a height of 163 meters, over the Narmada River in Gujarat. Drought prone areas of Kutch and Saurashtra are highly benefitted by this project. The gravity dam is the largest dam of Narmada Valley Project with power facilities up to 200 MW. The dam is meant to benefit the 4 major states of India—Gujarat, Madhya Pradesh, Maharashtra and Rajasthan.

4. Hirakud Dam - Odisha

Hirakud Dam is built across the Mahanadi River in tribal state Orissa. Hirakud Dam is one of the longest dams in the world about 26 km in length. There are two observation towers on the dam, one is "Gandhi Minar" and another one is "Nehru Minar". The Hirakud Reservoir is 55 km long and is used as multipurpose scheme intended for flood control, irrigation and power generation.

5. Nagarjuna Sagar Dam - Telangana

Nagarjuna Sagar Dam is the world's largest masonry dam with a height of 124 meters, built across Krishna River in Telangana. Nagarjuna Sagar Dam has the largest man-made lake in the world. The dam is 1.6 km long with 26 gates.

6. Cheruthoni Dam - Kerela

Cheruthoni Dam, the largest concrete gravity dam in Kerala, is located close to Idukki arch dam. It is the third highest dam in India with a 454 feet-high across River Cheruthoni.

7. Indira Sagar Dam – Madhya Pradesh

Indira Sagar Dam built on the Narmada river with a height of 92 m is concrete gravity dam, located in Khandwa district of Madhya Pradesh. Indira Sagar project was the key project on Narmada river providing excellent storage site of water. Indira Sagar Dam has the biggest reservoir in India.

Water

8. Krishnaraja Sagar Dam - Karanataka

Krishnaraja Sagar Dam is built across Kaveri River near Mysore in Karnataka. It is one of the principal and largest dams built on the river Kaveri in Karnataka in, South India. The Kaveri is one of the major rivers in India and there is a famous and beautiful Brindavan Gardens attached to the dam.

9. Mettur Dam – Tamil Nadu

Mettur Dam is built across Kaveri River at Salem district in Tamil Nadu with a height of 120 ft. It is one of the largest and one of the oldest dams built in India. Mettur Dam has biggest and the most power generating capacity dam in Tamil Nadu.

> **Fascinating Fact**
>
> In 1975, the Banqiao Dam in China was among many dams that were destroyed after the extreme rains of Typhoon Nina. It is estimated that between 90000 and 230000 lives were lost as a result of the Banqiao Dam breaking.

> **Intext Questions**
>
> 1. Why are rivers worshipped in India ?
> 2. List out the major dams of India.
> 3. Which states were involved in Barak water dispute ?

5.1. GROUNDWATER

Groundwater is the water found underground in the cracks and spaces in soil, sand and rock. It is stored in and moves slowly through geologic formations of soil, sand and rocks called aquifers. When rain falls to the ground, some of it flows along the land surface to streams, rivers or lakes, some moisturizes the ground. Part of this water is used by vegetation; some evaporates and returns to the atmosphere. Part of the water also seeps into the ground, flows through the unsaturated zone and reaches the water table. Groundwater can be found almost everywhere. The water table may lie deep or shallow depending on several factors such as the physical characteristics of the region, the meteorological conditions and the recharge and exploitation rates. Heavy

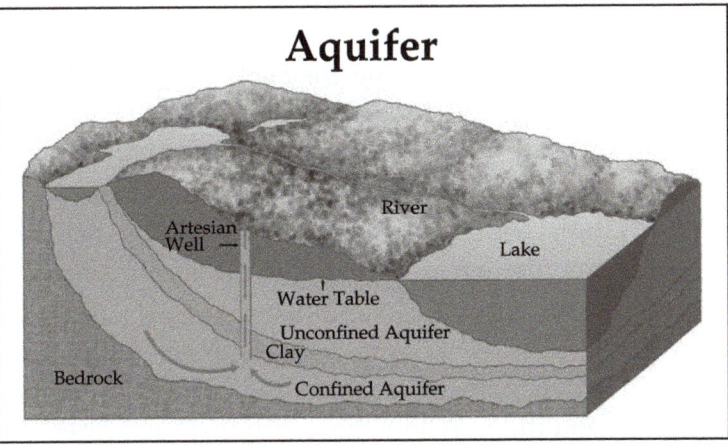

rains may increase recharge and cause the water table to rise. But on the other hand, an extended period of dry weather may cause the water table to fall. When groundwater reaches an aquifer it does not stand still. It normally will keep flowing but much slower than before reaching the aquifer.

Groundwater plays a very important role in keeping the water level and flow into rivers, lakes and wetlands. Specially during the drier months, when there is little direct recharge from rainfall, it provides the environment with groundwater flow through the bottom of these water bodies and becomes essential for the wild life and plants living in these environments. Groundwater also plays a very relevant role in sustaining navigation through inland waters in the drier seasons. By discharging groundwater into the rivers it helps in keeping the water levels higher.

However, as a result of human activities, groundwater gets contaminated. Causes of ground water pollution are –

a. When hazardous waste is disposed of or dumped incorrectly, the chances of its spilling and leaching into soil and water are much.

b. Landfills are another direct cause of pollution in groundwater. The longer a landfill remains full of waste, the more the toxins from that waste seep into the soil below and around the landfill. This leads to groundwater contamination almost immediately. When landfills are very large, the amount of groundwater polluted by them is significant.

c. Sometimes, when surface water in the area becomes polluted, it can lead to those pollutants evaporating into atmospheric air and water. In turn, polluted air can drift into areas where humans are more present, and polluted rain can fall as acid rain. This damages the environment and can also cause serious health risks for people in the area, too.

d. Diesel and gasoline are well-known indirect causes of groundwater pollution. In some instances, these fuels, when kept in underground storage, can leak significantly and seep into the ground around them, leading to groundwater contamination.

e. Some septic systems are installed incorrectly or become damaged over time without regular maintenance. This causes human waste to leach into the surrounding soil, which in turn causes a lot of pollution very fast.

f. Road salts, solvents, and chemicals used on roads, in lawns, and around the home are some of the leading manmade causes of groundwater pollution. When these products are used on land surfaces or homes, they are easily washed away by natural rainfall. Much like chemicals and other man-made solutions, pesticide is prone to washing into the soil after heavy rainfalls, especially when it is used frequently by farmers and other members of the agricultural industry. The chemicals

Water

involved in pesticides are very dangerous for both human and animal consumption, and when they reach groundwater, they can almost never be completely removed.

Effects of groundwater pollution are –

g. Nutrient pollution—Groundwater pollution can cause certain types of nutrients that are necessary in small amounts to become far too abundant to sustain normal life in a given ecosystem. Fish might start dying off quickly because they are no longer able to process the water in their water supplies, and other animals might become sick from too much of certain types of nutrients in the water they drink. Plants might not be able to absorb water as easily, and the entire ecosystem will suffer.

h. Toxic water in ecosystems—When groundwater that supplies lakes, rivers, streams, ponds, and swamps becomes contaminated, this slowly leads to more and more contamination of the surface water as well. When this happens, fish, birds, animals and plants that live in the area become sick and die off quickly. This is a huge factor in the destruction of the wetlands, which rely heavily on groundwater to recharge their lakes and ponds after drought periods. In turn, people who use this land for hunting, fishing, and even for their own sources of clean water are affected by this type of pollution.

i. Diseases like hepatitis, dysentery, cholera, poisoning could be some diseases associated with the ground water pollution.

Water is used by us for a wide range of activities in our lives. Apart from the domestic uses, water is required in large scales in industries, hydropower stations and agriculture. The water is fetched and channelised through pump sets, installing a network of pipelines or by building dams.

Undoubtedly, water is an important resource for survival and sustenance of living organisms. Various human activities and overexploitation has led to depletion of water. Appropriate measures should be taken by government as well as individuals to conserve water.

Some measures are given below –

(i) Desalination of sea water—This is one way of reusing the water. The salt and minerals from the sea/ocean water are removed using appropriate purification methods like distillation, reverse osmosis, electrodialysis and nanofiltration. The purified water serves all purposes like the fresh water. However, desalination of sea water requires more time and is expensive too. The productivity of desalination of sea water is not satisfactory. In addition, there might be a few environmental consequences like disturbed ecosystem, imbalance in the water table and hampered life of flora and fauna.

(ii) Water conservation—Water conservation is the practice of using water efficiently to reduce unnecessary water usage. Water is an essential asset for the nourishment of all life and is the fundamental demand for all activities appropriate for local use to agricultural and industrial. With the regular expanding weight of the human population, there has been a serious tension on water resources. On a daily basis we can adopt a few measures to conserve water. Some of the measures at domestic level are given below –

   a. Turn off the tap while brushing your teeth.
   b. Choose efficient fixtures for faucets.
   c. Install water-saving showerheads.
   d. Cover swimming pools to reduce evaporation.
   e. Install drip water or sprinkler in your gardens.
   f. Install low flow shower heads and low flow toilet flushes.
   g. Do not run the dishwasher or washing machine until it is fully loaded.
   h. Fix the leaking pipes and taps.

(iii) Water harvesting—Rainwater harvesting is a very popular method of conserving water especially in the urban areas. Rainwater harvesting means collecting rainwater on the roofs of building and storing it underground for later use. This method raises the declining water table, recharges groundwater and can help augment water supply. Water harvesting can be undertaken through a variety of ways

   a. Capturing runoff from rooftops
   b. Capturing runoff from local catchments
   c. Capturing seasonal flood waters from local streams
   d. Conserving water through watershed management

These techniques can serve the following purposes :

   a. Provide drinking water.
   b. Provide irrigation water.
   c. Increase groundwater recharge.
   d. Reduce stormwater discharges, urban floods and overloading of sewage treatment plants.
   e. Reduce seawater ingress in coastal areas.

Intext Questions

1. What is an aquifer ?
2. Draw a neat labelled diagram to depict an aquifer.
3. What are the sources of toxic substances in a water body ?

5.2. FRESHWATER POLLUTION

Any activity that occurs on the land can affect water quality because pollutants on land or in the air can wash into waterways when it rains. For example, rain that washes over your yard may pick up excess fertilizers and pesticides and carry them into your local water body. This may also happen on farmland. When rain washes over driveways, roofs, and streets, it can pick up oil, rubber and other residues. On hot days, paved surfaces heat up rain runoff that can then enter a waterway and raise water temperatures. Such pollutants can be categorised as point sources and non-point sources. Point source pollutants come from a single point. Factory discharge pipes are an example of point sources of pollution because they come from a single source. Point sources of pollution threaten the health of rivers and other water bodies. The major threat to today's water quality is pollution without an easily identifiable source, or non-point source pollution. Non-point-source pollution accounts for more than half of all surface water pollution. We all contribute to non-point source pollution. Using fertilizers and pesticides in our lawns, failing to clean up after our pets, and washing our cars cause non-point source pollution. Every time it rains or snows, natural and man-made pollutants on the land are washed into streams and wetlands. These pollutants include pesticides, fertilizers, metals, manure, road salt and motor oil that originate from farms, lawns, paved surfaces, landfills and home septic systems. In addition, air pollutants contaminate rainwater. Another significant contributor to non-point source pollution is soil erosion. Although erosion is a natural process, an unnatural acceleration of this process may be caused by construction sites, dirt roads, and other land disturbances.

Freshwater pollution is the contamination of inland water with substances that make it unfit for its natural or intended use. Pollutants are of two types – point sources and non-point sources. A point source is a single, identifiable source of pollution, such as a pipe or a drain. Industrial wastes are commonly discharged to rivers and the sea in this way. Non-point sources of pollution are often termed 'diffuse' pollution and refer to those inputs and impacts which occur over a wide area and are not easily attributed to a single source. They are often associated with particular land uses, as opposed to individual point source discharges. Pollution may be caused by faecal waste, chemicals, pesticides, petroleum, sediment, or even heated discharges. In addition, these pollutants are contaminating the groundwater too.

Waste water treatment plants—Waste water treatment plant is an efficient way to save water. Waste water from households is treated at a treatment plant to remove the physical, biological and chemical matter. Waste water needs to be treated before it can be reused or released into a water body. Waste water treatment removes impurities from waste water. Sewage comprises of waste water released from homes, industries, hospitals and offices and also the water collected during rains. Sewage treatment is the step wise procedure which involves removal of wastes from the water. Sewage treatment is also called as waste water treatment.

Waste water treatment involves physical, chemical and biological treatment of water. Waste water is allowed to pass through different steps in a sequence.

Physical and biological treatment of waste water is explained step wise below -

a. **Bar Screens**—Bar screens are the screens that prevent the flow of large objects in waste water. These screens help to remove large objects like rags, plastic bags, cans, napkins and sticks from sewage.

b. **Grit Dhamber**—Waste water from the bar screens is allowed to pass through grit chambers in a slow manner. The slow movement of water makes grit, sand and dust particles to settle down.

c. **Clarifier**—A clarifier is a tank with its central part inclined downwards so as to allow faeces to settle down. The waste settled at the bottom is termed as sludge.

d. Sludge is transferred to a separate tank where it is decomposed using bacteria. Finally, a skimmer is used to remove oils and grease. Clarified water is obtained after the separation of all physical contaminants from the sewage.

e. **Aerator**—The clarified water is passed into an aerator. An aerator pumps air into the water to settle the bacteria to the bottom of the tank as activated sludge. Bacteria under aerated conditions consume impurities left in the water. The water present in the top is 95% clean and is let out into a water source while the activated sludge is dried in a sand bed and is used as manure. Using bacteria in decomposing waste is the biological treatment.

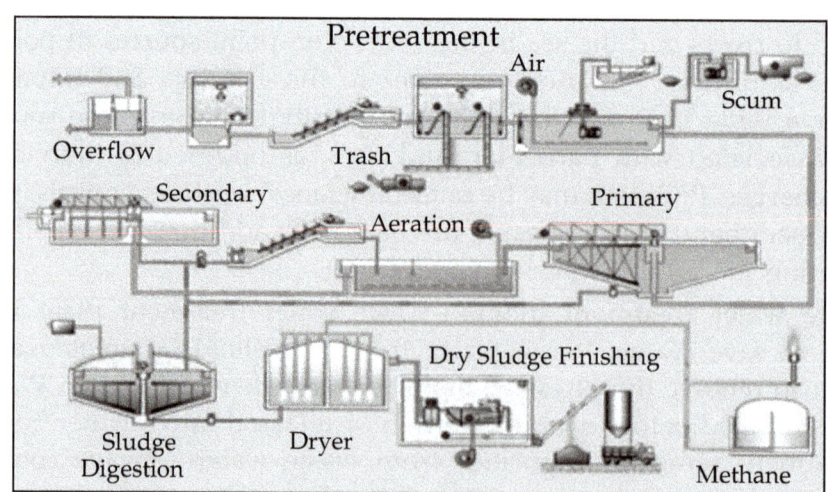

Water

Chemical treatment of waste water :

a. Chlorine tablets or chlorine gas is used to treat waste water chemically.
b. Water will be clean on the dissolution of a chlorine tablet. Hence, chlorine tablets are used to disinfect water in treatment plants.
c. Chlorine gas is introduced through many pipes into a tank with water stored after physical and biological treatment.
d. Ozone is also used in chemical purification of water.

Purification of water

a. Drinking water sources are subjected to contamination and require appropriate treatment to remove disease-causing agents. Purification of water follows these steps –
b. Coagulation and flocculation are often the first steps in water treatment. Chemicals with a positive charge are added to the water. The positive charge of these chemicals neutralises the negative charge of dirt and other dissolved particles in the water. When this occurs, the particles bind with the chemicals and form larger particles, called floc.
c. Floc settles to the bottom of the water supply, due to its weight. This settling process is called sedimentation.
d. Once the floc has settled to the bottom of the water supply, the clear water on top will pass through filters of varying compositions (sand, gravel, and charcoal) and pore sizes, in order to remove dissolved particles, such as dust, parasites, bacteria, viruses, and chemicals.

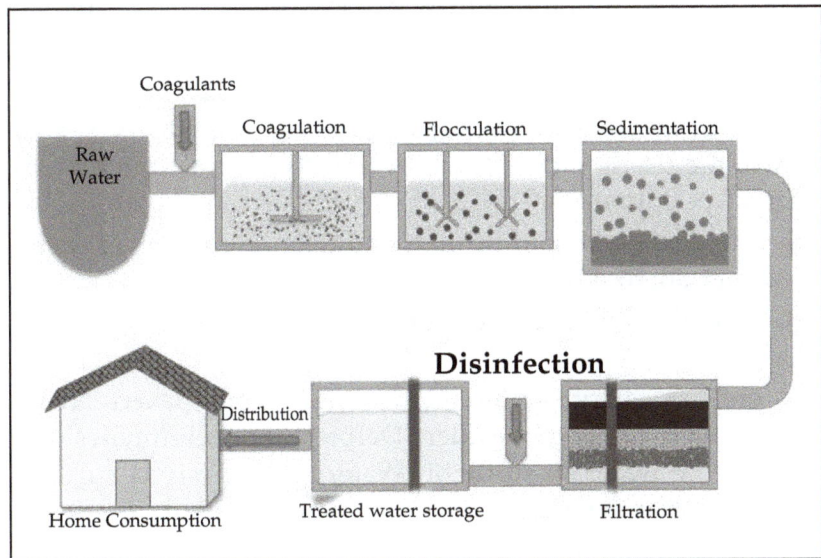

e. After the water has been filtered, a disinfectant (for example, chlorine, chloramine) may be added in order to kill any remaining parasites, bacteria, and viruses, and to protect the water from germs when it is piped to homes.

We know that water is crucial for sustenance and survival of life. Water is an important abiotic component of the ecosystem. Thus, conserving water is not only our responsibility but also our need.

Artificial eutrophication—The phenomenon of a sudden increase in the organic and inorganic nutrient supply in an aquatic environment is referred to as Eutrophication. These nutrients are basically nitrogen and phosphorous, and they favour overgrowth of algae and grazing bacteria, which then results in oxygen depletion. Organic pollutants from man's activities like effluents from the industries and homes can radically accelerate the aging process. Thus, this phenomenon is also called anthropogenic or man-made eutrophication.

Some effects of artificial eutrophication are –

a. Overgrowth of algae can interfere with the health and diversity of indigenous fish, plant, and animal populations. It can also limit the recreational use of lakes and estuaries.
b. Algal blooms can fully cover up the water surface and block sunlight, which causes the death of underwater plants and animals.
c. Fish and other marine animals may die due to depletion of dissolved oxygen. This may lead to a decrease in aquatic biodiversity.
d. Some algal cells present in the algal blooms may also produce certain harmful toxins. These toxins are harmful to fishes and birds may cause certain diseases in humans *e.g.*, diarrhoea, gastroenteritis, nausea etc.

Thermal pollution - Thermal pollution is the degradation of water quality by any process that changes ambient water temperature. Its causes and effects are listed below.

Causes of thermal pollution –

a. Some industries and power plants use natural waters as a coolant, and release the used warm waters back into natural water bodies, causing thermal pollution.
b. The rate of metabolism in many aquatic animals may increase due to a warmer surrounding.
c. Geothermal vents and hot springs introduce excess heat into bodies of water.
d. Soil erosion, deforestation, and runoff from paved areas are other artificial sources of hot water. Deforestation eliminates shade, which exposes the water to sunlight. Water on hot paved surfaces gets hot, then runs off into nearby bodies of water, raising the water temperature.

Effects of thermal pollution –

a. Warm water holds less oxygen than cool water. Thus, oxygen content is decreased.

Water

b. Fish and amphibians may move away from the warm water to a more-suitable location, disrupting the ecosystem for animals that remain and are dependent on them. This disturbs the food chain and food web of that area.

c. The sudden heating can kill off vulnerable organisms or drive them away. This is one of many serious issues for threatened and endangered animal species.

? Intext Questions

1. Define point source and non-point source of pollution with appropriate examples.
2. Draw a neat labelled diagram to show steps involved in water purification.
3. What is a floc ? Name its constituents.

5.3. OCEAN POLLUTION

The ocean remains one of the most expansive, mysterious and diverse places on Earth. Unfortunately, it is being threatened by pollution from people on land and from natural causes. Marine life is dying, and as a result the whole oceanic ecosystem is threatened simply by various sources of pollution. If we are to preserve ocean and its natural beauty, drastic measures have to be taken to combat this pollution and keep what we hold most dear. Before, it was assumed that because the ocean was so big, vast and deep, that the effects of dumping trash and litter into the sea would only have minimal consequences. But as we have seen, this has proven to not be the case. While all four oceans have suffered as a result of human consequence for over millennia by now, it has accelerated in the past few decades. Oil spills, toxic wastes, floating plastic and various other factors have all contributed to the pollution of the ocean.

Causes of ocean pollution –

There are various ways by which pollution enters the ocean. Some of them are :

1. Sewage

Pollution can enter the ocean directly. Sewage or polluting substances flow through sewage, rivers, or drainages directly into the ocean. This is often how minerals and substances from mining camps find their way into the ocean.

The release of other chemical nutrients into the ocean's ecosystem leads to reduction in oxygen levels, decay of plant life, moreover a severe decline in the quality of the sea water itself. As a result, all levels of oceanic life, plants and animals, are highly affected.

2. Toxic Chemicals from Industries

Industrial and agricultural wastes are another most common form of wastes that are directly discharged into the oceans, resulting in ocean pollution. The dumping of toxic liquids in the ocean directly affects the marine life as they are considered hazardous and secondly, they raise the temperature of the ocean, known as thermal pollution, as the temperature of these liquids is quite high. Animals and plants that cannot survive at higher temperatures eventually perish.

3. Land Runoff

Land runoff is another source of pollution in the ocean. This occurs when water infiltrates the soil to its maximum extent and the excess water from rain, flooding or melting flows over the land and into the ocean. Oftentimes, this water picks up man-made, harmful contaminants that pollute the ocean, including fertilizers, petroleum, pesticides and other forms of soil contaminants. Fertilizers and waste from land, animals and humans can be a huge detriment to the ocean by creating dead zones.

4. Large Scale Oil Spills

Ship pollution is a huge source of ocean pollution, the most devastating effect of which is oil spills. Crude oil lasts for years in the sea and is extremely toxic to marine life, often suffocating marine animals to death once it entraps them.

5. Ocean Mining

Ocean mining in the deep sea is yet another source of ocean pollution. Ocean mining sites drilling silver, gold, copper, cobalt and zinc create sulphide deposits up to three and a half thousand meters down into the ocean. While we have yet to gather scientific evidence to fully explain the harsh environmental impacts of deep sea mining, we do have a general idea that deep sea mining causes damage to the lowest levels of the ocean and increase the toxicity of the region. Further it leads to leaking, corrosion and oil spills that only drastically further hinder the ecosystem of the region.

Effects of Ocean Pollution

1. Effect of Toxic Wastes on Marine Animals—Oil spill is dangerous to marine life in several ways. The oil spilled in the ocean could get on to the gills and feathers of marine animals, which makes it difficult for them to move or fly properly or feed their children. The long-term effect on marine life can include cancer, failure in the reproductive system, behavioural changes, and even death.

2. Disruption to the Cycle of Coral Reefs—Oil spill floats on the surface of water and prevents sunlight from reaching to marine plants and affects the process of photosynthesis. Skin irritation, eye irritation, lung and liver problems can impact marine life over long period of time.

3. Depletes Oxygen Content in Water—Most of the debris in the ocean does not decompose and remain in the ocean for years. It uses oxygen as it degrades. As a result of this, oxygen levels go down. When oxygen levels go

Water

down, the chances of survival of marine animals like whales, turtles, sharks, dolphins, penguins for long time also decrease.

4. Failure in the Reproductive System of Sea Animals—Industrial and agricultural wastes include various poisonous chemicals that are considered hazardous for marine life. Chemicals from pesticides can accumulate in the fatty tissue of animals, leading to failure in their reproductive system.

5. Effect on Food Chain—Chemicals used in industries and agriculture get washed into the rivers and from there are carried into the oceans. These chemicals do not get dissolved and sink at the bottom of the ocean. Small animals ingest these chemicals and are later eaten by large animals, which then affects the whole food chain.

6. Affects human health—Animals from impacted food chain are then eaten by humans which affects their health as toxins from these contaminated animals gets deposited in the tissues of people and can lead to cancer, birth defects or long-term health problems.

SUMMARY

- A hydrosphere is the collective mass of water found on, under and over the surface of planet.
- It is estimated that 71% of the earth's surface is occupied by seas and oceans.
- Out of all the water on Earth, saline water in oceans, seas and saline groundwater make up about 97% of it.
- Snow is the form of ice that precipitates from the atmosphere. Polar Regions are the major snow prone areas.
- Surface water is any water that collects on the surface of the earth. This includes oceans, seas, lakes, rivers, or wetlands.
- Kaveri river dispute, Krishna river water dispute, Godavari water dispute and Barak river dispute are some of the major water disputes of our country.
- Dams are built to provide water for human consumption, irrigating arid and semi-arid lands, or used in industrial processes.
- Groundwater is the water found underground in the cracks and spaces in soil, sand and rock. It is stored in and moves slowly through geologic formations of soil, sand and rocks called aquifers.
- Groundwater plays a very important role in keeping the water level and flow into rivers, lakes and wetlands.
- Desalination of water is a way conserving water where the salt and minerals from the sea/ocean water are removed using appropriate purification methods like distillation. The purified water serves all purposes like the fresh water.
- Freshwater pollution is the contamination of inland water with substances that make it unfit for its natural or intended use.
- Sources of pollutants are of two types – point sources and non-point sources.

- A point source is a single, identifiable source of pollution, such as a pipe or a drain.
- Non-point sources of pollution are often termed 'diffuse' pollution and refer to those inputs and impacts which occur over a wide area and are not easily attributed to a single source.
- Waste water treatment plant is an efficient way to save water.
- The phenomenon of a sudden increase in the organic and inorganic nutrient supply in an aquatic environment is referred to as Eutrophication.

EXERCISE

A. Define each of these terms :
   1. Wetland 2. Lake 3. Water conservation 4. Rainwater harvesting 5. Freshwater pollution 6. Eutrophication 7. Thermal pollution 8. Ocean mining.

B. Answer each of these questions in brief :
   1. In what form is water distributed in our planet ?
   2. How is snow formed ?
   3. Differentiate between ocean and sea.
   4. In which state is Krishnarajasagar dam located ? State one tourist attraction situated here.
   5. What are the disadvantages of desalination of sea water ?
   6. What is the purpose of building a dam ?

C. Answer each of these questions in detail—
   1. Explain any 4 types of surface water.
   2. Explain the types of water found in the solid form.
   3. State the causes of –
      (a) Ocean pollution
      (b) Thermal pollution
      (c) Groundwater pollution
   4. State the effects of –
      (a) Ocean pollution
      (b) Thermal pollution
      (c) Groundwater pollution
   5. List out the measures of water conservation that can be taken at a domestic level.

Water

WORKSHEET

A. Fill in the blanks :
1. Greenland ice sheet is covered over the ____ ocean.
2. ____ and ____ are the saline lakes.
3. ____ is the highest dam in India.
4. ____ is the reservoir of Bhakra Nangal Dam.
5. The observation towers of Hirakund dam are ____ and ____.

B. Justify the following Statements :
1. Polar ice caps are formed near North and South poles.
2. Chlorine is added in water treatment plant.
3. Deforestation leads to thermal pollution.

C. Read the following excerpts and answer the questions that follow. (open-ended questions) :
1. Karnataka state faced a few major river disputes since 19th century with its neighbouring states.
   (a) Name these river disputes.
   (b) Which river dispute was solved ? What was the verdict ?
2. Sardar Sarovar Dam is built on the Narmada river. This project was initiated in 1961. Many local people raised their concerns and grievance towards this project.
   (a) What could be the possible negative consequences of building a dam ?

D. Activity :
1. Make a short report of any one river dispute (apart from the ones mentioned in this chapter) and present it in the class.

6 AIR

Pollution is caused when contaminants are induced into the natural environment which brings about adverse change. Pollution is thus defined as the effect of undesirable change in our surroundings that has harmful effects on plants, animals and human beings. Substances which cause pollution are called as pollutants. Human activities like urbanisation, industrialisation and other advancements in technologies has reaped us immense economic gain along with an easy and comfortable lifestyle. But, we have contaminated and polluted our air, water and land on which life exists to gain these benefits. The biodegradable pollutants such as sewage, kitchen waste decompose over time and do not cause much harm to the environment. The non-biodegradable wastes such as plastic, DDT, radioactive waste is hazardous. The

pollutants once added are difficult to eliminate. Many a times one type of pollution gives rise to another type of pollution. For example, in urban areas huge traffic is a reason for air pollution. But traffic congestion is also a reason for sound pollution. Important types of pollution are—Air, water, soil and noise. Pollution can be broadly categorised as point pollution and non-point pollution. Point pollution comes from localised, specific and identifiable

Air

sources. For Example—sewage pipes and industrial smokestacks. Non-point pollution comes from dispersed or uncontained sources like vehicle exhaust. Pollution can take the form of chemical substances or energy, such as noise, heat or light. Its unpleasant effects are damaging for the healthy survival and also the contamination in most cases is not completely reversible. Pollution is drastically rising in all the countries due to rise in human activity associated with modern technology and population growth. Even the daily normal livelihood requirements are high contributing factors to never ending pollution of all sorts. Thus, pollution control is the responsibility of every citizen around the globe.

6.0. MAJOR SOURCES OF AIR POLLUTION

Air pollution is the addition of harmful substances in air that degrades the air quality, causing severe damage to the environment and the health of living beings. Air quality is defined as the degree to which the air in a particular place is pollution-free. Air pollution is not a recent phenomenon, its origin can be traced back to the times when man first started using firewood for his daily chores. However, it became more noticeable by the beginning of 20th century with advancement of urbanisation, transportation and industrialisation. The unpleasant effects of air pollution are damaging for the healthy survival and also the contamination is seen in many cases which are not completely reversible. Air pollution is drastically rising in all the countries due to rise in human activity associated with modern technology and population growth. Even the daily normal livelihood requirements are high contributing factors to never ending pollution of all sorts. Thus, pollution control is the responsibility of every citizen around the globe.

Its major sources are–

1. Natural disaster—A natural disaster is a major adverse event resulting from natural processes of the Earth; examples are floods, hurricanes, tornadoes, volcanic eruptions, earthquakes, tsunamis. These have adversely affected the vital sectors of our development as agriculture, communication, irrigation, power projects and rural and urban settlements. Let us understand how these natural disasters turn into a cause of air pollution. An earthquake is the shaking of the earth's surface caused by rapid movement of the earth's crust or outer layer. The tremors caused during the earthquake damage can often break the gas pipes and electric lines that

cause fires. Such a combustion leads to air pollution. Cyclone is an area of low atmospheric pressure surrounded by a wind system blowing in anti-clockwise direction, formed in the northern hemisphere. In common terms, cyclone can be described as a giant circular storm system. During cyclone, the fine dust and mud particles are raised from the ground. This increases the amount of suspended particulate matter in the air. Similar effect can be seen in case of a tornado also. When volcanoes erupt or in case of forest fires, a mixture of gases and particles are emited into the air. The gases include oxides of sulphur, nitrogen and carbon. These oxides are potential air pollutants.

> **Intext Questions**
> 1. List some non-biodegradable pollutants that we generate in our daily life.
> 2. How does cyclone result in air pollution?

2. Domestic combustion—Household activities such as cooking and heating with traditional technologies, and lighting with kerosene, generate emissions of a range of health harmful pollutants. A significant population still cook using solid fuels (such as wood, crop wastes, charcoal, coal and dung) and kerosene in open fires and inefficient stoves. These cooking practices are inefficient, and use fuels and technologies that produce high levels of household air pollution with a range of health-damaging pollutants, including small soot particles that penetrate deep into the lungs. Saturated hydrocarbons will generally give a clean flame while unsaturated carbon compounds will give a yellow flame with lots of black smoke. This results in a sooty deposit on the vessel. However, limiting the supply of air results in incomplete combustion of even saturated hydrocarbons giving a sooty flame. The gas or kerosene stove used at home has inlets for air so that a sufficiently oxygen-rich mixture is burnt to give a clean blue flame. If you observe the bottoms of cooking vessels getting blackened, it means that the air holes are blocked and fuel is getting wasted. Fuels such as coal and petroleum have some amount of nitrogen and sulphur in them. Their combustion results in the formation of oxides of sulphur and nitrogen which are major pollutants in the environment. The types and amounts of pollutants produced depend upon the type of appliance, how well the appliance is installed, maintained, and vented, and the kind of fuel it uses.

Pollution caused due to domestic combustion can be controlled by –

(a) Appliance selection—Choose vented appliances that have been tested and certified to meet current safety and emission standards.

Air

(b) Proper installation—Improperly installed appliances can release dangerous pollutants, thus, they should be installed properly with the help of the experts or the concerned person.

(c) Ventilation—Adequate supply of air is needed to reduce the indoor level of pollutants. This supply of air is also important to carry pollutants upto the chimney, stove pipe or flue to the outside. The appliance should have vent connected to it. Nothing should block the vent and there should be no holes or cracks in the vent.

(d) Inspection and maintenances—Combustion appliances should be regularly inspected and maintained because appliances that are not working properly can release harmful and even fatal amounts of pollutants, especially carbon monoxide. If air holes of gas stove or gas ranges are blocked, then required amount of oxygen cannot participate in the combustion leading to incomplete combustion.

3. Air pollution on wheels (Vehicular pollution)—Auto vehicles are installed with an internal combustion engine which burns the fossil fuels. During this combustion reaction, harmful gases are released. When the fuel is burnt inside the engine of vehicles, pollutants like Carbon monoxide, Hydrocarbons, oxides of Nitrogen and Sulphur and Lead are released into air. Since the number of vehicles are increasing all over the world, amount of pollutants is also

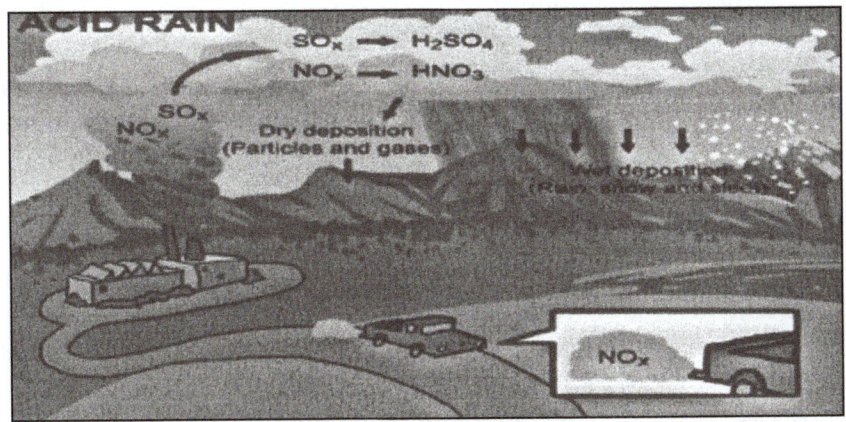

increasing considerably. Vehicular exhausts release a significant amount of particulates which leads to respiratory disorders. These pollutants contribute to acid rain and global warming as well. Vehicular pollution has grown at an alarming rate due to growing urbanisation in India. The air pollution from vehicles in urban areas, particularly in big cities, has become a serious problem. The pollution from vehicles has begun to tell through symptoms like cough, headache, nausea, irritation of eyes, various bronchial and visibility problems. The main pollutants emitted from the automobiles are hydrocarbons, lead or benzene, carbon monoxide, sulphur dioxide, nitrogen dioxide and particulate matter. The main cause of vehicular pollution is the rapidly growing number of vehicles. The other factors of vehicular pollution in the urban areas are two-stroke engines, poor fuel quality, old vehicles, inadequate maintenance, congested traffic, poor road condition and old automotive technologies and traffic management system. Using four-stroke engine and catalytic converters will reduce vehicular pollution to a significant extent. Travelling through public transports or car-pooling whenever possible can considerably help in reducing pollution. Engines of vehicles can be switched off when we are waiting at the traffic signal. Vehicles should be properly maintained.

4. Industrial air pollution—Industrial pollution is generally referred to the undesirable outcome when factories (or other industrial plants) emits harmful by-products and waste into the environment such as emissions to air or water bodies (water pollution), deposition on landfills etc., (land pollution) or emission of toxic chemicals into the atmosphere (air pollution). Smoke contains undesirable gases like carbon dioxide, sulphur dioxide and carbon monoxide, besides solid and liquid particulate matter, in the form of dust and spray mist, which cause air pollution. In most of the industries, coal or other fossil fuels are used to create heat energy. This releases a lot of carbon dioxide apart from other pollutants. With the increasing urbanisation and industrialisation, the demand for different industrial products increases. Thus, industries multiply their production rate, affecting the air quality.

> **Fascinating Fact**
>
> Air pollution is a leading cause of many common killers. It accounts for about one-third of deaths from stroke, chronic respiratory disease, and lung cancer as well as one quarter of deaths from heart attack. 92 per cent of the global population live in places with unhealthy air quality.

Causes of Industrial Pollution

1. Lack of Policies to Control Pollution—Lack of effective policies and poor enforcement drive allowed many industries to bypass laws made by pollution control board which resulted in mass scale pollution that affected lives of many people.

2. Unplanned Industrial Growth—In most industrial townships, unplanned growth took place wherein those companies flouted rules and norms and polluted the environment with both air and water pollution.

3. Use of Outdated Technologies—Most industries still rely on old technologies to produce products that generate large amount of waste. To avoid high cost and expenditure, many companies still make use of traditional technologies to produce high end products.

4. Presence of Large Number of Small Scale Industries—Many small scale industries and factories that don't have enough capital and rely on government grants to run their day-to-day businesses often escape environment regulations and release large amount of toxic gases in the atmosphere.

Air

5. Inefficient Waste Disposal—Water pollution and soil pollution are often caused directly due to inefficiency in disposal of waste. Long term exposure to polluted air and water causes chronic health problems, making the issue of industrial pollution into a severe one. It also lowers the air quality in surrounding areas which causes many respiratory disorders.

6. Leaching of Resources from Our Natural World—Industries require large amount of raw material to make them into finished products. This requires extraction of minerals from beneath the earth. The extracted minerals can cause soil pollution when spilled on the earth. Leaks from vessels can cause oil spills that may prove harmful for marine life.

6.1. MAJOR AIR POLLUTANTS

Air pollutants are emitted from a range of both man-made and natural sources. Air pollutants can be released directly into the atmosphere (primary emissions) or can form as a result of chemical interaction involving precursor substances. The air pollutant emissions cause air pollution, however, reductions in emissions do not always automatically result in similar cuts in concentrations. There are complex links between air pollutant emissions and air quality. These include emission heights, chemical transformations, reactions to sunlight, additional natural and hemispheric contributions and the impact of weather and topography. Significant cuts in emissions are essential for improving air quality.

(a) Carbon monoxide—It is a colourless, odourless gas that is produced by incomplete burning of carbon-based fuels including petrol, diesel, and wood. It is also produced from the combustion of natural and synthetic products such as cigarettes. The main source of carbon monoxide is vehicular emission. Carbon monoxide is absorbed into the bloodstream more readily than oxygen, so the relatively small quantities in inhaled air can have harmful effects. Prolonged exposure can cause tissue damage and individuals suffering from cardiovascular disease are particularly at risk.

(b) Oxides of nitrogen—Emissions from traffic, electricity generating stations and industry are the main source of nitrogen oxides. Nitrogen dioxide can affect the throat and lung. The main effects are emphysema and cellular damage. It impacts visually as it has a brown colour and gives rise to a brown haze. Oxides of nitrogen contribute to the formation of acid rain.

(c) Oxides of sulphur—They are produced from burning coal, mainly in thermal power plants. Some industrial processes, such as production of paper and smelting of metals, produce sulphur dioxide. The main source of sulphur dioxide is burning coal and oil and emissions by industries. It is an irritant gas which attacks the throat and lungs. Prolonged exposure can lead to increase in respiratory illnesses like chronic bronchitis. It contributes to the formation of acid rain which damages vegetation and buildings.

(d) Ozone—It occurs naturally in the upper layers of the atmosphere. This important gas shields the earth from the harmful ultraviolet rays of the sun. However, at the ground level, it is a pollutant with highly toxic effects. Vehicles and industries are the major source of ground-level ozone emissions. Ozone makes our eyes itch, burn, and water. It lowers our resistance to colds and pneumonia.

(e) Lead—It is present in petrol, diesel, lead batteries, paints, hair dye products, etc. The main source of lead in air is from petrol engine exhaust emissions. High concentrations can retard the mental development in children. Long-term exposure to low levels of lead can affect the nervous system. The introduction of unleaded petrol has dramatically reduced emissions.

(f) Hydrocarbons—Hydrocarbons in the form of gasoline, petroleum, coal, kerosene, charcoal, natural gas etc. have widespread uses in our day-to-day lives. They are also a main source of fuel for the industrial and manufacturing sector. Pollution is caused due to the incomplete combustion of these hydrocarbon fuels. Hydrocarbon vapours can cause health effects. Inhaling Formaldehyde can cause irritation. It is a major contributor to eye and respiratory irritation caused by photochemical smog. Ethylene causes injury to the leaves of sensitive plants. Effects are epinasty, chlorosis, curling, leaf abscission and growth retardation.

(g) Benzene—Benzene comes from petrol emissions and the evaporation of petrol at petrol stations. It is a carcinogen. Acute short-term inhalation may cause drowsiness, dizziness, headaches, as well as eye, skin, and respiratory tract irritations, and, at high levels, unconsciousness.

(h) Particulates—Particulate matter includes a wide range of pollutants—road dust, diesel soot, fly ash, wood smoke, nitrates in fertilisers, sulphate aerosols, lead, arsenic, etc. Dust consists of particles larger than about ten microns which are formed by the physical processes such as grinding or breaking up of rocks and soil. These dust particles remain suspended in the air for sometime and then settle at the ground quickly. The dust particles of size ranging from 10-100 micron which are suspended in the air are known as Suspended Particulate Matter (SPM).

Sources—The principal source of Particulate matter is the combustion of fossil fuels such as coal, gasoline, and wood. This is formed through chemical reactions, fuel combustion (e.g., burning coal, wood, diesel), industrial processes, farming (ploughing, field burning), and unpaved roads or during road constructions.

Health effects—Short-term exposures can worsen heart or lung diseases and cause respiratory problems. Long-term exposures can cause heart or lung disease and sometime premature deaths.

Air

Environmental effects—Particulate matter such as cement dust, magnesium-lime dust and carbon soot deposited on vegetation can inhibit the normal respiration and photosynthesis mechanisms within a leaf.

Toxic air pollutants are those pollutants that cause or may cause cancer or other serious health effects, such as reproductive effects or birth defects. Air toxins may also cause adverse environmental and ecological effects. Examples of toxic air pollutants include benzene, found in gasoline; perchloroethylene, emitted from some dry cleaning facilities; and methylene chloride, used as a solvent by a number of industries.

> **? Intext Questions**
> 1. List out types of pollution.
> 2. How does air pollution affect our health ?
> 3. What are consequences of air pollution on the plants ?

Classification of Air pollutants

Air Pollutants can be solid particles, liquid droplets, or gases. They can be natural or manmade. These pollutants have been classified into primary and secondary categories.

The primary pollutants are "directly" emitted from the processes such as fossil fuel consumption, volcanic eruption and factories. The major primary pollutants are oxides of sulphur, oxides of nitrogen, oxides of carbon, particulate matter, methane, ammonia, chlorofluorocarbons, toxic metals etc.

The secondary pollutants are not emitted directly. The secondary pollutants form when the primary pollutants react with themselves or other components of the atmosphere. Most important secondary level air pollutants are Ground Level Ozone, Smog and POPs (Persistent Organic Pollutants).

1. Classification of air pollutants based on composition

(i) Gaseous pollutants—These pollutants exist in gaseous state at normal temperature and pressure. The three main types of gaseous air pollutants are following :

(a) Sulphur dioxide (SO_2)

(b) Oxides of nitrogen ($NOx = NO + NO_2$)

(c) Ozone (O_3)

Sulphur dioxide and nitric oxide (NO) are the primary air pollutants, and ozone is a secondary pollutant (though there are negligible direct emissions of the gases itself).

Nitrogen dioxide (NO_2) is both a primary and secondary air pollutant. Other important gaseous pollutants are—ammonia, carbon monoxide, volatile organic compounds (VOCs) and persistent organic pollutants (POPs).

(ii) Particulate air pollutants—These are not gaseous substances. They are suspended droplets, solid particles or mixtures of the two.

2. Particulate matter—There are many sources of particulate matter (dust) including vehicle exhaust emissions, soil and road surfaces, construction works and industrial emissions. Particulate matter can be formed from reactions between different pollutant gases. Small particles can penetrate the lungs and cause damage.

(a) Grit –It consists of the small loose particles of stone or sand. The release of grit from domestic hearths and factory chimneys is a major source of pollution in industrial areas. These are released due to incomplete combustion of fuels. These pollutants cause lung irritation, asthma, bronchitis etc.

(b) Dust Particles—Dust particles forming in everyday events or construction or agricultural activities etc. is also a pollutant. They attach to other pollutants and become more harmful. In humans, they may cause allergies and other respiratory diseases.

(c) Smoke—Smoke primarily consists of particles and can include other gaseous air pollutants, including nitrogen oxides, carbon monoxide, and hydrocarbons that may be toxic. The invisible fine particles in smoke are of special concern because they can lodge deep into the lungs and cause serious health effects, such as aggravated asthma, nose and throat irritation, bronchitis and lung damage. Some particles may even get into the bloodstream and affect the heart.

(d) Lead oxide—The sources of lead oxide are industrial effluents (mostly lead oxide), solder (metallic), lead paint and lead containing soldering fluxes. Effects of over exposure of lead oxide on human health include reduced fertility, still-birth and risk of nervous system impairment.

(e) Chloroflorocarbons (CFC)—These are gases that are released mainly from air-conditioning systems and refrigeration. When released into the air, CFCs rise to the stratosphere, where they come in contact with few other gases, which leads to a reduction of the ozone layer that protects the earth from the harmful ultraviolet rays of the sun.

(f) PAH (Poly Aromatic Hydrocarbons)—This encompasses a wide range of compounds that consist of two or more aromatic rings made entirely of Carbon and Hydrogen. Airborne PAH, when inhaled, is believed to produce lung cancer. Benzo(a)pyrene (BaP) is the most common PAH in ambient air and is therefore used as a marker to set air quality and emission standards.

(g) Soot—Incomplete combustion of coal and charcoal always leaves behind a black powder-like substance. This is soot. It is extremely small in size and toxic in nature. It can travel through our windpipe and settle in our lungs. Soot can cause a variety of diseases from Asthma to Bronchitis. Also, soot contains SO_2 and NO_2 that form acid rain.

Air

(h) **Asbestos Dust**—Asbestos is a highly toxic substance. Any activity related to it like manufacturing asbestos sheets or asbestos insulation can release asbestos dust. This is very harmful and a major cause of atmospheric pollution. Prolonged exposure to asbestos may cause Asbestosis, Lung Cancer and Mesothelioma.

(i) **Aerosols (Smog)**—An aerosol is a suspension of fine solid particles or liquid droplets, in air or another gas. They are fine, air borne particles consisting at least in part of solid material. Aerosols can be natural or anthropogenic. The continental and oceanic source are the natural sources of aerosols.

(b) **Continental source**—Clean continental air often contains less than 3,000 particles per cubic centimetre (of which half are water-soluble), polluted continental air typically 50,000/cm^3 (of which two-thirds are soot, and the rest are mostly water-soluble). Urban air typically contains 160,000/cm^3, mostly soot, and only 20% is water-soluble. Desert air has about 2,300/cm^3 on average, almost all water-soluble. Clean marine air generally has about 1,500/cm^3, about all water-soluble.

(c) **Oceanic source**—The ocean is a major source of natural aerosols. Air-sea exchange of particulate matter contributes to the global cycles of carbon, nitrogen, and sulphur aerosols, such as dimethyl sulphide (DMS) produced by phytoplanktons. Ocean water and sea salt are transferred to the atmosphere through air bubbles at the sea surface. As this water evaporates, the salt is left suspended in the atmosphere.

(d) **Anthropogenic sources**—Dust and smoke are the anthropogenic sources of aerosols. They include sulphate, nitrate, and carbonaceous aerosols, and are mainly from fossil fuel combustion sources.

Aerosols play an important role in the global climate balance. Atmospheric aerosol particles play important role in radiation budget of the Earth as they scatter and absorb both shortwave solar radiation and longwave terrestrial radiation. They are also highly involved in the formation of clouds and precipitation since they operate as cloud condensation and ice nuclei. Aerosols can form the abundance and distribution of atmospheric trace gases by complex chemical reactions, and can affect significantly the cycles of nitrogen, sulphur, and atmospheric oxidants. Due to the increasing anthropogenic emission of aerosols since the industrial revolution, they can also affect the global climate change. However, the effects of aerosols on climate are not one-way, moreover excessively uncertain. The climate forcing by aerosols can be realised in two ways, basically—in direct and indirect radiative forcing.

(i) **Direct effect**—Aerosol particles reflected a part of shortwave solar radiation back into the space, cooling the Earth's atmosphere. This cooling effect of aerosols, especially by sulphate components may be compensated by the absorption of longwave terrestrial radiation primarily by elemental (black) carbon aerosols and dust particles.

(ii) **Indirect effect**—Aerosol particles can also affect the radiation balance by formation of cloud droplets. Cloud droplets are formed in the troposphere by condensation of water vapour onto aerosol particles (cloud condensation nuclei, or ice nuclei) when the relative humidity exceeds the saturation level.

(iii) They can reduce visibility.

(iv) Aerosols can cause breathing problems.

(v) Aerosols directly scatter sunlight and reflect it back out to space. They can also react with clouds in complex ways, causing the clouds to reflect more light back out to space. This prevents the sun's warmth from reaching the earth's surface.

Intext Questions

1. How does aerosol affect radiation balance in the atmosphere ?
2. List out the pollutants arising from combustion of fossil fuel.
3. Which are the common types of PAH ?

Bhopal Gas Tragedy

The Bhopal Gas Tragedy, 1984 was a catastrophe. In the early morning hours of December 3, 1984, a rolling wind carried a poisonous gray cloud from the Union Carbide Plant in Bhopal, Madhya Pradesh (India). Forty tons of toxic gas (Methyl-Iso-Cyanate, MIC) was accidentally released from Union Carbide's Bhopal plant, which leaked and spread throughout the city. The result was a nightmare that still has no end, residents awoke to clouds of suffocating gas and began running desperately through the dark streets, victims arrived at hospitals; breathless and blind. The lungs, brain, eyes, muscles as well as gastro-intestinal, neurological, reproductive and immune systems of those who survived were severely affected. When the sun rose the next morning, the magnitude of devastation was clear. Dead bodies of humans and animals blocked the street, leaves turned black and a smell of burning chilli peppers lingered in the air.

Air

An estimated 10,000 or more people died. About 500,000 more people suffered agonizing injuries with disastrous effects of the massive poisoning. None can say, if future generations will not be affected. Besides air, water and soil pollution, effects of this disaster on human health were devastating. People suffered from respiratory disorders, genetic changes which caused cancer. Exposure to methyl isocyanate led not only to miscarriage but it also damaged growing foetus and affected fertility in men and women. Even long time after the disaster, traces of many toxins were found in the breast milk of mothers and were in turn transmitted to the recipient babies.

Thermal Inversions (Los Angeles)—Temperature inversion layers also called thermal inversions or just inversion layers, are areas where the normal decrease in air temperature with increasing altitude is reversed and air above the ground is warmer than the air below it. Inversion layers can occur anywhere from close to ground level up to thousands of feet into the atmosphere. Inversions act to prevent mixing in the lower regions of the troposphere, so pollutants become trapped quite easily and contribute to the formation of smog. During an inversion episode, temperatures increase with increasing altitude. The warm inversion layer then acts as a cap and stops atmospheric mixing. This is why inversion layers are called stable air masses. Topography can also play a role in creating a temperature inversion since it can sometimes cause cold air to flow from mountain peaks down into valleys. This cold air then pushes under the warmer air rising from the valley, creating the inversion. In addition, inversions can also form in areas with significant snow cover because the snow at ground level is cold and its white colour reflects almost all heat coming in. Thus, the air above the snow is often warmer because it holds the reflected energy. Inversion layers are a significant factor in the formation of smog in Los Angeles because they create stable atmospheric conditions. Air pollution is a regional problem in Los Angeles, a metropolitan city located in Southern California. However, more specifically, air pollution is a problem that greatly affects its local inhabitants. Los Angeles is located in a chaparral, and its geography is a huge contributor to the problem of air pollution. Located between the Pacific Ocean and surrounding mountains, Los Angeles has the ideal geography for temperature inversions, which often magnifies pollution.

Photochemical Smog (Mexico city)—Photochemical smog is a type of smog produced when ultraviolet light from the sun reacts with nitrogen oxides in the atmosphere. It is visible as a brown haze, and is most prominent during the morning and afternoon, especially in densely populated, warm cities. Cities that experience this smog daily include Los Angeles, Sydney, Mexico City, Beijing, and many more. NO_2, ozone and PANs are called photochemical oxidants because they can react and oxidise certain compounds in the atmosphere or within a person's lungs that are not normally oxidised. Even small traces of these chemicals can affect the respiratory tract of humans and animals, and damage crops and trees. Mexico City is one of the largest cities in the world with a population close to twenty million people. The majority of the population is exposed daily to fumes produced by 3.6 million vehicles. This, of course, means that many roads throughout Mexico City are highly congested. The city is situated at 2,240 metres above sea level, and because there's less oxygen at this altitude, most of the air pollution is the result of incomplete combustion of hydrocarbons, mainly diesel emissions.

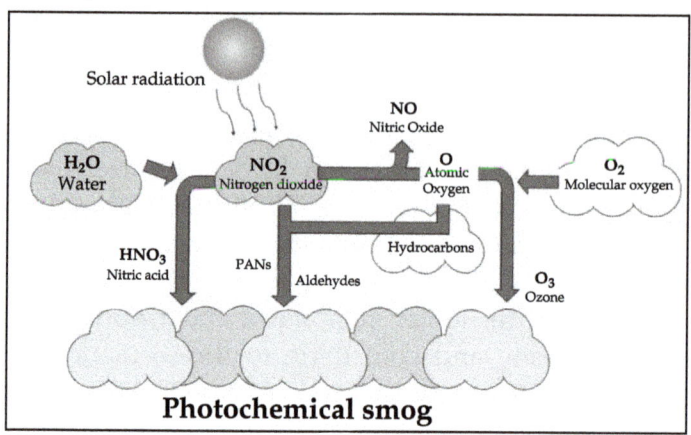

Acid precipitation in Mumbai

There have been many reports of acid rain in India. In the industrial areas of Mumbai, an acid rain of approximately pH 5.28 was recorded. The main reason is attributed to the increase in sulphate and nitrate ions. Air pollution is the chief cause of acid rain. The gaseous pollutants like sulphur dioxide (SO_2) and nitrogen oxides (NO & NO_2) produced by combustion of fossil fuels (coal, oil and natural gas) from smelters, power plants, automobile exhausts, forest fires, domestic fires etc. are the causative agents of acid rain. These oxides as primary pollutants are swept up into the atmosphere and can travel to long distances. In atmosphere sulphur dioxide is oxidized to sulphuric acid (H_2SO_4) while nitrogen oxides are oxidised to nitric acid (HNO_3). Sulphur dioxide present in air gets oxidised to sulphur trioxide by the oxygen of air. The sulphur trioxide combines with the water vapours present in air to form sulphuric acid. Nitrogen oxides present in the air combines with oxygen and water vapours to form nitric acid. Apart from Mumbai, Delhi, Nagpur, Pune, Bombay and Kolkata are the cities where the critical pH values are being recorded. Anti-pollution devices like scrubbers need to be used in the smoke-stacks of factories to prevent the release of sulphur dioxide and nitrogen oxides in the atmosphere. Frequent use of catalytic converters in the automobiles can also be helpful in checking the emissions of sulphur dioxide and nitrogen oxides in the atmosphere.

Impacts of air pollution

Air pollution is a major concern of new civilised world, which has a serious toxicological impact on human health and the environment. According to the

Air

World Health Organization, six major air pollutants include particle pollution, ground-level ozone, carbon monoxide, sulphur oxides, nitrogen oxides, and lead. Long and short-term exposure to air suspended toxicants have a different toxicological impact on humans including respiratory and cardiovascular diseases, neuropsychiatric complications, the eyes irritation, skin diseases, and long-term chronic diseases such as cancer.

Effects of air pollution

1. Pollution affects the economy in following ways :

a. **Health cost**—Exposure to pollutants is affecting the health of the residents. A lot of money is required to be spent on curing the diseases caused due to pollutants.

b. Pollution is responsible for damaging sculptures and buildings. Repairing and maintenance cost of damaged building is high.

c. Many tourist places are ruined because of pollution. This affects the income of those local people who are dependent on tourism.

Taj Trapezium is a classic example of effect on air pollution.

Taj Trapezium—Case study

Taj Mahal, the white marble structure was built by Mughal emperor Shah Jahan in the 17th century. It was declared as the world heritage by UNESCO

in 1983. But now the structure has developed a yellowish tinge as a result of increased pollution in that area. Taj Mahal is being exposed to sulphur dioxide and Suspended Particulate Matter (SPM). Mathura Oil Refinery which is situated close to that area releases its by-products in the Yamuna river. This has led to acid rain, which is also responsible for damaging the marbles of Taj Mahal. A Public Interest Litigation (PIL) was filed in 1984 to express concerns over the havoc caused by such industries. Later, the Supreme Court ordered more than 200 industries in that vicinity to adopt pollution control measures.

d. Pollution results in reduced crop yield, which is a huge loss to the agricultural industry.

2. Depletion in crop yield (Lowered agricultural productivity)–

Plant growth is affected in following ways —

(a) Pollutants interfere with enzyme systems;

(b) Pollutants change in cellular chemical constituents and physical structure;

(c) Continuous exposure of pollutants results in retardation of growth and reduced production because of metabolic changes;

(d) Acute and immediate plant tissue degeneration is caused.

(e) Continuous exposure may lead to mottling, bronzing or reddening of the leaf.

(f) In the lower atmosphere, ozone damages plants by preventing photosynthesis and obstructing stomata, restricting respiration and stunting plant growth.

3. Health problems—Long-term exposure to polluted air can have permanent health effects such as :

a. Accelerated aging of the lungs.
b. Loss of lung capacity and decreased lung function.
c. Development of diseases such as asthma, bronchitis, emphysema, and possibly cancer.
d. Shortened life span.
e. Tobacco smoke generates a wide range of harmful chemicals and is a major cause of ill health, as it is known to cause cancer, not only to the smoker but affecting passive smokers too.
f. Volatile compounds can cause irritation of the eye, nose and throat. In severe cases there may be headaches, nausea, and loss of coordination.

Air

In the longer run, some of them are suspected to cause damage to the liver and other parts of the body.

g. Exposure to formaldehyde causes irritation to the eyes, nose and may cause allergies in some people.

h. Prolonged exposure to lead can cause damage to the nervous system, digestive problems, and in some cases cause cancer. It is especially hazardous to small children.

i. Exposure to ozone gas makes our eyes itch, burn, and water and it has also been associated with increase in respiratory disorders such as asthma. It lowers our resistance to colds and pneumonia.

j. Suspended matter consists of dust, fumes, mist and smoke. The main chemical component of SPM that is of major concern is lead, others being nickel, arsenic, and those present in diesel exhaust. These particles when breathed in, lodge in the lung tissues and cause lung damage and respiratory problems.

Those most susceptible to severe health problems from air pollution are :

a. Individuals with heart disease, coronary artery disease or congestive heart failure
b. Individuals with lung diseases such as asthma, emphysema or chronic obstructive pulmonary disease (COPD)
c. Pregnant women
d. Outdoor workers
e. Older adults and the elderly
f. Children under age 14
g. Athletes who exercise vigorously outdoors

Common atmospheric pollution sources and their pollutants

Category	Source	Emitting Pollutants
Agriculture	Open burning	Suspended particulate matter, carbon monoxide, volatile organic compounds
Mining and quarrying	Coal mining; crude oil and gas production; stone quarrying	Suspended particulate matter, sulphur dioxide, oxides of nitrogen, volatile organic compounds
Power generation	Electricity; gas; steam	Suspended particulate matter, sulphur dioxide, oxides of nitrogen, carbon monoxide, volatile organic compounds, sulphur trioxide, lead
Transport	Combustion engines	Suspended particulate matter, sulphur dioxide, oxides of nitrogen, carbon monoxide, volatile organic compounds, lead.

| Community service | Municipal incinerators | Suspended particulate matter, sulphur dioxide, oxides of nitrogen, carbon monoxide, volatile organic compounds, lead. |

 SUMMARY

- Pollution is caused when contaminants are induced into the natural environment that cause adverse change.
- Human activities like urbanisation, industrialisation and other advancements in technologies have reaped us immense economic gain along with an easy and comfortable lifestyle.
- Air quality is defined as the degree to which the air in a particular place is pollution-free.
- Our daily use appliances like gas ranges, furnaces, gas water heaters, gas clothes dryers, wood or coal-burning stoves, and fireplaces which use fuels like CNG, LPG, fuel oil, kerosene, wood, or coal cause air pollution.
- Major sources of air pollution are domestic activities, industries, vehicles and natural disasters.
- Air pollutants are emitted from a range of both man-made and natural sources. Air pollutants can be released directly into the atmosphere (primary emissions) or can form as a result of chemical interaction involving precursor substances.
- There are complex links between air pollutant emissions and air quality. These include emission heights, chemical transformations, reactions to sunlight, additional natural and hemispheric contributions and the impact of weather and topography.
- According to the World Health Organization, six major air pollutants include particle pollution, ground-level ozone, carbon monoxide, sulphur oxides, nitrogen oxides, and lead.
- A variety of poisonous gases like oxides of nitrogen and sulphur, chlorine, carbon monoxide, carbon dioxide, volatile chemicals, dusts etc. are liberated into the atmosphere by industries and vehicles which cause acute air pollution.
- Industries must have devices for removal of potential pollutants before the industrial waste is let out to the environment.

 EXERCISE

A. **Define each of these terms :**
   1. Pollution, 2. Pollutants, 3. Air quality, 4. Thermal inversion, 5. Smog, 6. Cyclone

B. **Answer each of these questions in brief :**
   1. Which are the natural sources of aerosols ?

Air

2. Differentiate between smog and photochemical smog.
3. Differentiate between point pollution and non point pollution.
4. How does each of these factors lead to air pollution—
   a. Forest fire,   b. Earthquake   c. Tornado   d. Volcano
5. How does ozone impact human health ?
6. In what way is CFC hazardous to our environment ?

C. Answer each of these questions in detail—

1. How can you control domestic pollution ?
2. How does air pollution affect agriculture ?
3. How does air pollution affect economy of our country ?
4. Explain thermal inversion with an example.
5. Explain the direct and indirect effects of aerosols.
6. List out the causes of industrial pollution.

WORKSHEET

A. Write the full form of—
1. PAN
2. PAH
3. DMS
4. MIC
5. SPM

B. Justify each of these statements—
1. Aerosols prevent sun's warmth from reaching the earth.
2. Inversion layers are also called as stable air masses.
3. Los Angeles has the ideal geography for thermal inversions.
4. PAN is not normally oxidised.
5. Soot can form acid rain.
6. Ozone is a victim and culprit of air pollution.

C. Read the following excerpts and answer the questions that follow. (open-ended questions) :
1. Kerosene is a cooking fuel in many villages in India though it is not an ideal fuel.
   (a) What are the disadvantages of using kerosene as a fuel ?
   (b) Which type of fuel should be ideally used for domestic purposes ?
2. Vehicular pollution has grown at an alarming rate due to growing urbanisation in India. The air pollution from vehicles in urban areas, particularly in big cities, has become a serious problem.
   (a) Name the major pollutants emitted by vehicles.
   (b) List out few measures of preventing vehicular pollution.

D. Activity :
1. Make a chart comprising sources and effects of each type of air pollutant. Analyse the severity of each type of air pollutant.

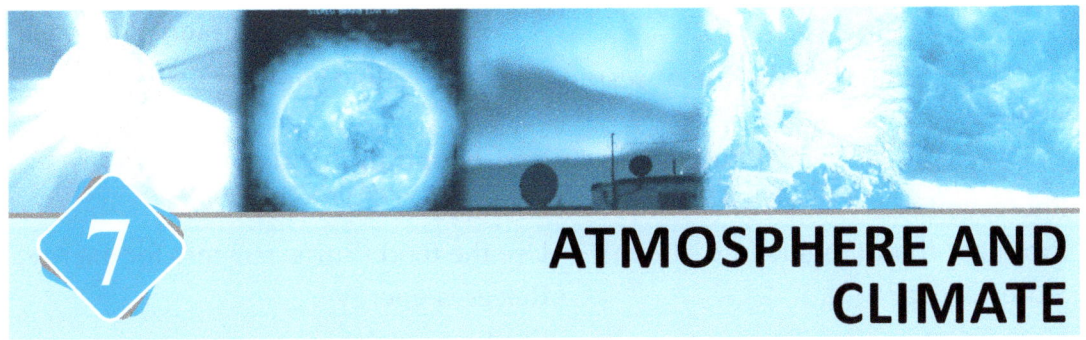

ATMOSPHERE AND CLIMATE

We all know that earth is a unique planet due to the presence of life. The air is one among the necessary conditions for the existence of life on this planet. The air is a mixture of several gases and it encompasses the earth from all sides. The air surrounding the earth is called the atmosphere. The earth's atmosphere is a layer of gases surrounding our planet and the gravity. The Earth has an atmosphere which is commonly called air. Air contains oxygen for breathing, nitrogen and small amount of other gases, like the greenhouse gases which keep the Earth naturally warm and suitable for life. There is no specific boundary between the atmosphere and outer space. It slowly becomes thinner and fades into the space. The atmosphere provides various functions, not least the ability to sustain life. The atmosphere protects us by filtering out deadly cosmic rays, powerful ultraviolet (UV) radiation from the Sun, and even meteors on collision course with Earth. Although traces of atmospheric gases have been detected well out into space, 99% of the mass of the atmosphere lies below about 25 to 30 km altitude, whilst 50% is concentrated in the lowest 5 km. The atmosphere which is the layer of gases that surrounds Earth above the air layer affects our climate, which is the pattern of variation in temperature, humidity, atmospheric pressure, wind, precipitation, ultraviolet light, and other climate variables that occur over long periods.

Balance between Photosynthesis and Respiration

Plants grow through photosynthesis, a process that uses the energy from sunlight to combine carbon dioxide from the air with water to make carbohydrates plus oxygen. The carbohydrates formed through photosynthesis feed not only the plants, but also almost all other organisms on the earth, including herbivores and carnivores. Solar energy, water availability, nutrients in the soil affect the rate of photosynthesis. The process of converting sugar and starch into energy through a series of biochemical steps is called Respiration. Respiration is the chemical process opposite of photosynthesis because it releases energy, using food and oxygen and produces carbondioxide. All carbohydrates that are gained in photosynthesis and subsequently used in respiration vary considerably.

The differences between respiration and photosynthesis are tabulated below–

Photosynthesis and Respiration

Photosynthesis	Respiration
Produces food (Sugars and starch)	Use the food (Burns suggars for energy)
Stores energy	Releases energy
Uses water	Produces water
Use CO_2	Produces CO_2
Releases O_2	Uses O_2
Occurs in hight	Occurs at all time
Only in cells antaining chloroplast	All cells but rates are tissue specific

During photosynthesis, plants take carbon from the atmosphere in the form of carbon dioxide to make the glucose. Plants also respire, giving carbon dioxide back to the atmosphere; but they take in much more carbon dioxide than they give out. Animals get their carbon from eating either plants (carbohydrates) or other animals (proteins and fats), which they then digest. They respire, giving off carbon dioxide into the air. The released carbon dioxide in the atmosphere is consumed by the plants during the photosynthesis. In this manner, the amount of carbon dioxide is balanced in the nature.

Layers of atmosphere

Composition of atmosphere varies from one place to another and also with varying height in the atmosphere. Nitrogen accounts for 78% of the atmosphere, oxygen 21% and argon 0.9%. Gases like carbon dioxide, nitrous oxides, methane, and ozone are trace gases that account for about a tenth of one percent of the atmosphere. Water vapour content varies from 0-4% of the atmosphere depending on the area. In the cold, dry arctic regions water vapour usually accounts for less than 1% of the atmosphere, while in humid, tropical regions water vapour can account for almost 4% of the atmosphere. The table given below shows the composition of atmosphere –

Constituent	Percent by Volume	Concentration in Parts Per Million (PPM)
Nitrogen (N_2)	78.084	780,840.0
Oxygen (O_2)	20.946	209,460.0
Argon (Ar)	0.934	9340.0
Carbon dioxide (CO_2)	0.036	360.0
Neon (Ne)	0.00182	18.2
Helium (He)	0.000524	5.24
Krypton (Kr)	0.000114	1.14
Hydrogen (H_2)	0.00005	0.5

Atmosphere and Climate

The atmosphere can be divided into five layers according to the diversity of temperature and density.

Troposphere

a. It is the lowermost layer of the atmosphere.
b. The height of this layer is about 18 km on the equator and 8 km on the poles.
c. The thickness of the troposphere is greatest at the equator because heat is transported to great heights by strong convectional currents.
d. The zone separating troposphere from the stratosphere is known as tropopause.

Stratosphere

a. Stratosphere is found just above the troposphere.
b. It extends up to a height of 50 km.
c. The temperature remains almost the same in the lower part of this layer up to the height of 20 km. After this, the temperature increases slowly with the increase in the height. The temperature increases due to the presence of ozone gas in the upper part of this layer.
d. Weather related incidents do not take place in this layer. The air blows horizontally here. Therefore, this layer is considered ideal for flying of aircraft.
e. The upper limit of the stratosphere is known as stratopause.
f. Stratosphere contains a layer of ozone gas. It contains a high concentration of ozone compared to other parts of the atmosphere.
g. It is the region of the stratosphere that absorbs most of the sun's ultraviolet radiations.

Mesosphere

a. It is the third layer of the atmosphere spreading over the stratosphere.
b. It extends up to a height of 80 km.
c. In this layer, the temperature starts decreasing with increasing altitude and reaches up to − 100°C at the height of 80 km.
d. Meteors or falling stars occur in this layer.
e. The upper limit of the mesosphere is known as mesopause.

Thermosphere—It is divided into two layers – Ionosphere and Exosphere.

(i) Ionosphere

a. This layer is located about 600 km above the surface.
b. It contains electrically charged particles known as ions, and hence, it is known as the ionosphere.

c. Radio waves transmitted from the earth are reflected back to the earth by this layer and due to this radio broadcasting has become possible.
d. The temperature here starts increasing with heights.

Exosphere

a. The exosphere is the uppermost layer of the atmosphere.
b. Gases are very sparse in this sphere due to the lack of gravitational force. Therefore, the density of air is very less here.

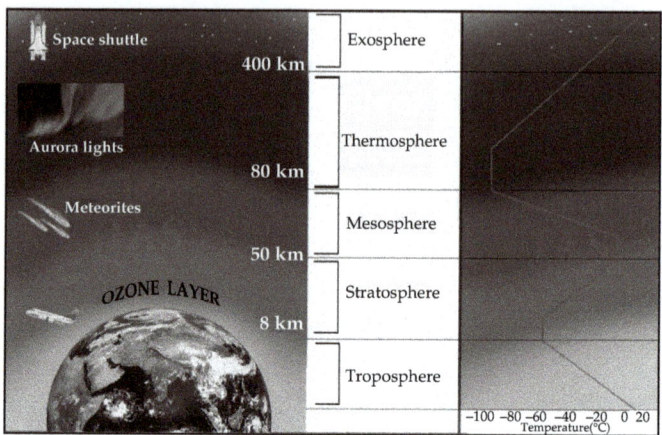

Intext Questions

1. List out the gases present in the atmosphere.
2. Name the layers of atmosphere.
3. Which are the trace gases present in the atmosphere ?
4. What is the importance of atmosphere to the biosphere ?
5. Why is the density of air less in exosphere ?

Fascinating Facts

1. If the area of our head is 10 cm x 10 cm, we carry air of weight 1000 kg on our head. But we are not crushed under this heavy weight, the internal pressure within our body cancels this pressure.
2. Moving jets leave white trails. The hot, humid exhaust (carbon dioxide, oxides of sulphur and nitrogen, unburned fuel, soot and metal particles, as well as water vapour) from jet engines mixes with the atmosphere, which at high altitude is of much lower vapour pressure and temperature than the exhaust gas. The water vapour contained in the jet exhaust condenses and may freeze.

Weather and climate

Weather is the day-to-day condition of the atmosphere. This includes temperature, rainfall and wind. Climate is the average weather conditions of a

Atmosphere and Climate

place, usually measured over one year. This includes temperature and rainfall. The climate of a place will be different when compared to another. The reasons for these differences can be quite complex. These factors are listed below –

1. Latitude—Latitude is the distance north or south from the equator and is expressed in degrees. The equator is located at 0° latitude. The most northerly latitude is the North Pole, at 90° north, whereas the most southerly latitude is the South Pole, at 90° south. Latitude strongly affects climate because the amount of solar energy an area of the Earth receives depends on its latitude. The temperatures drop in an area is due to the curvature of the earth. In areas closer to the poles, sunlight has a larger area of atmosphere to pass through and the sun is at a lower angle in the sky. As a result, more energy is lost and temperatures are cooler. Temperature range increases with distance from the equator. Also, temperature decreases as we move away from the equator. This is because the sunrays are dispersed over a larger area of land as we move away from the equator.

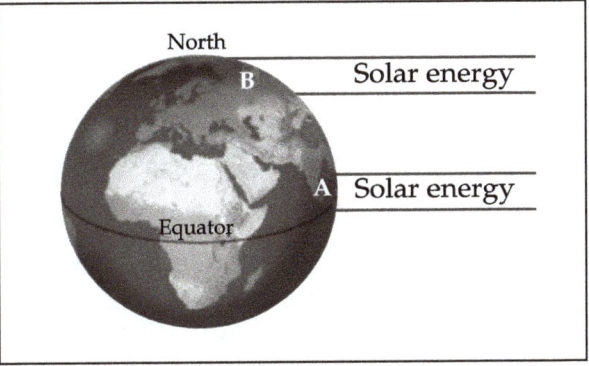

2. Atmospheric circulation pattern—Cold air sinks because it is denser than warm air. As the air sinks, it compresses and warms. Warm air rises. It expands and cools as it rises. Warm air holds more water vapour than cold air. Therefore, when warm air cools, the water vapour it contains may condense into liquid water to form rain, snow, or fog. Solar energy heats the ground, which warms the air above it. This warm air rises, and cooler air moves in to replace it. This movement of air within the atmosphere is called wind and because the Earth rotates, and because different latitudes receive different amounts of solar energy, a pattern of global atmospheric circulation results. This circulation pattern determines Earth's precipitation patterns.

3. Ocean circulation patterns—Oceanic circulation currents have a great effect on climate because water holds large amounts of heat. The movement of surface ocean currents is caused mostly by winds and the rotation of the Earth. These surface currents redistribute warm and cool masses of water around the world and in doing so, they affect the climate in many parts of the world.

4. Local geography—Topography such as mountains, valleys, canyons and plains impact climate. For example, large mountain ranges can influence precipitation patterns. Mountains force incoming air to rise; as it does, it cools and condenses, forming clouds and eventually rain or snow, which typically falls on the windward side of the mountains. Hence, areas on the windward side of high mountain ranges experience greater precipitation than areas on the leeward side because the mountains essentially drain the moisture from the air.

Other examples of topographical influence on climate include chilly nights in valleys due to downslope winds and the "heat island" effect in cities in which the concrete landscape contributes to elevated night time temperatures.

5. **Seasonal changes in climate**—The seasons result from the tilt of the Earth's axis, which is about 23.5° relative to the plane of its orbit. Because of this tilt the angle at which the sun's rays strike the Earth changes as the Earth moves around the sun. During summer the Northern Hemisphere, the tilts toward the sun and receives direct sunlight. The number of hours of daylight is greatest in the summer. Therefore, the amount of time available for the sun to heat the Earth becomes greater. During summer the Southern Hemisphere tilts away from the sun and receives less direct sunlight.

Greenhouse Earth

Greenhouse is a glass structure used for growing plants. In cool climates, greenhouses are useful for growing and propagating plants because they have an arrangement to allow sunlight to enter and prevent heat from escaping. The transparent covering of the greenhouse allows for the selective transmission of visible light while preventing the transmission of excess UV radiation. The film also maintains a microclimate inside of the greenhouse as it traps heat from solar radiation, thereby warming the air and producing the "greenhouse effect". Earth too behaves like a greenhouse.

Greenhouse effect

The greenhouse effect is a natural process that warms the Earth's surface. When the Sun's energy reaches the Earth's atmosphere, some of it is reflected back to space and the rest is absorbed and re-radiated by greenhouse gases. Greenhouse gases include water vapour, carbon dioxide, methane, nitrous oxide, ozone and some artificial chemicals such as chlorofluorocarbons (CFCs). The absorbed energy warms the atmosphere and the surface of the Earth. This process maintains the Earth's temperature at around 33 degrees Celsius warmer than it would otherwise be, allowing life on Earth to exist. However, currently we are facing enhanced greenhouse effect. Burning fossil fuels (coal, oil and natural gas), agriculture and land clearing are increasing the concentrations of greenhouse gases. This is the enhanced greenhouse effect, which is contributing to warming of the Earth.

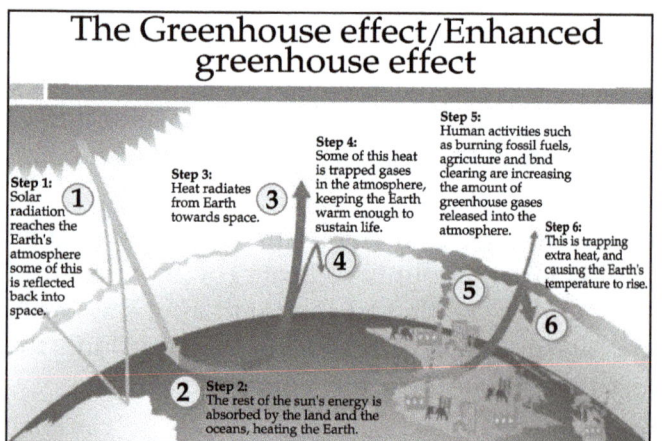

Atmosphere and Climate

The greenhouse effect can be defined as the heating up of the earth's atmosphere due to trapping of infrared rays by the carbon dioxide layer in the atmosphere. Solar energy absorbed at Earth's surface is radiated back into the atmosphere as heat. As the heat makes its way through the atmosphere and back out to space, greenhouse gases absorb much of it. Greenhouse gases are more complex than other gas molecules in the atmosphere, with a structure that can absorb heat. They radiate the heat back to the Earth's surface, to another greenhouse gas molecule, or out to space. Therefore, if the amount of greenhouse gases present in the earth's atmosphere is high then the earth's temperature too will keep getting higher; which is what has been happening lately adding to the greenhouse effect and warming up earth than it already is. The greenhouse effect occurs when greenhouse gases like carbon dioxide, methane, nitrous oxide and fluoride gases synergize with sun's energy. These gases are composed of more than three atoms and it is this atomic structure that enables them to trap the atmospheric heat which is absorbed by the earth's surface. Carbon dioxide in the atmosphere performs various important functions. The blanket of carbon dioxide allows the sunlight to come in freely but does not allow the infrared radiation reflected by the earth's surface. The rise in the temperature is directly related to the amount of carbon dioxide produced. Global warming is the average temperature of the Earth's near surface air and oceans. Now, take a look at some of the causes of global warming.

a. **The Greenhouse Effect**—Greenhouse gases like carbon dioxide, methane, water vapour, nitrous oxide, etc. reflect radiation that the earth emits and stops it from getting lost in space. Without the greenhouse gases, the earth would be too cold to support life. However, human activities are adding greenhouse gases to the atmosphere leading to an increase in the earth's temperature. The most important gas added to the atmosphere by humans is carbon dioxide which is less than 0.4% of the atmosphere. Carbon dioxide is released when humans burn fossil fuels such as oil, coal, and natural gas. In addition to this, we also add methane to the atmosphere by raising cattle and other farm animals.

b. **Deforestation**—The forests on earth, especially the rainforests, are like the planet's lungs. They produce a lot of the oxygen needed by, humans to breathe, and they capture much of the harmful carbon from the atmosphere. Cutting the trees down increases the carbon release which in turn contributes to rising global temperatures. Forests hold a major green area on the planet Earth. Plants and trees intake carbon dioxide and release oxygen, through the process of photosynthesis, which is required by humans and animals to survive. Large scale development has resulted in cutting down of trees and forests which has forced people to look for alternate places for living. When the wood is burnt, the stored carbon is converted back into carbon dioxide.

c. **Burning fossil fuels**—Fossil fuels like coal, oil and natural gas have become an integral part of our life. They are used on large basis to produce electricity and for transportation. When they are burnt, the carbon stored inside them is released which combines with oxygen in the air to create carbon dioxide. With the increase in the population, the number of vehicles has also increased and this has resulted in increase in pollution in the atmosphere. When these vehicles run, they release carbon dioxide, which is one of the main gases responsible for increase in greenhouse effect. Apart from that, electricity-related emissions are high because we are still dependent on coal for electricity generation which releases large amount of carbon dioxide into the atmosphere and is still the primary source of fuel for generating electricity. Although, renewable sources are catching up, but it may take a while before we can reduce our dependence on coal for electricity generation. Activities such as mining, releases the stored up carbon inside the earth into the atmosphere, which also contributes to the rising temperatures.

d. **Increase in Population**—Over the last few decades, there has been huge increase in the population. Now, this has resulted in increased demand for food, cloth and shelter. New manufacturing hubs have come up in cities and towns that release some harmful gases into the atmosphere which increases the greenhouse effect.

e. **Farming**—The base chemicals that are used to create pesticides can be harmful to the environment even before they are combined with other chemicals to create pesticides. For example, Nitrogen oxide is a gas that blocks sunlight and traps heat. This gas is released by Nitrogen-based fertilizers which release a significant unnatural amounts of nitrogen oxide into the atmosphere causing the greenhouse effect which results in further global warming. On the other hand, pesticides can attach themselves to dust particles and travel away from their intended destinations to other unintended places. This increases the likelihood of these chemicals mixing with other chemicals. Some pesticides produce volatile organic compounds that pollute the atmosphere when they react with other chemicals. This reaction produces tropospheric ozone. Ozone traps heat and further contributes to global warming. Agriculture is often the reason for deforestation and a change in land use, from natural ecosystems that take up and store carbon dioxide from the atmosphere, to farmland. Deforestation is also a reason for global warming. It is estimated that at least 14% of global greenhouse gas emissions comes directly from the farm sector.

f. **Industrial Waste and Landfills**—Industries which are involved in cement production, fertilizers, coal mining activities, oil extraction produce harmful greenhouse gases. Also, landfills filled with garbage

Atmosphere and Climate

produce carbon dioxide and methane gas contributing significantly to greenhouse effect.

Excessive global warming can have hazardous effects on our ecosystem. These effects are –

a. **Air pollution**—Rising temperatures also worsen air pollution by increasing ground level ozone, which is created when pollution from cars, factories, and other sources react to sunlight and heat.

b. **Species extinction**—As land and sea undergo rapid changes, the animals that inhabit them are destined to disappear if they do not adapt quickly enough. With changing seasonal behaviours and traditional migration patterns of animals also modify. Vertebrate species animals like fish, birds, mammals, amphibians, and reptiles are disappearing 114 times faster than they should be.

c. **More acidic oceans**—The earth's marine ecosystems are under pressure as a result of climate change. Oceans are becoming more acidic, due to large part absorption of some of our excess emissions. As this acidification accelerates, it poses a serious threat to underwater life, particularly creatures with calcium carbonate shells or skeletons, including molluscs, crabs, and corals.

d. **Increased melting of Ice Caps**—The world over, snow and ice is melting at a much faster pace than observed in the past. This is clearly seen in areas like Alps, Himalayas, Andes, Rockies, Alaska, and Africa. Antarctica has been losing about 134 billion metric tons of ice per year since 2002. During the past 30 years, more than a million square miles of sea ice has vanished, an area equivalent to the size of Norway, Denmark and Sweden combined.

e. **Rise in Sea Levels**—Global warming has affected the earth's oceans in two ways: warmer average temperatures cause ocean waters to expand (thermal expansion) and the accelerated melting of ice and have glaciers has increased the amount of water in the oceans. The rate of rising water levels is accelerating and is now at a pace which has been never seen before.

f. **Desertification**—Increasing temperatures are turning arid and semi-arid areas even more dry than before. The water cycle is also changing and rainfall patterns are shifting to make the already dry areas even drier. This is resulting in water shortages and causing great distress to over 2.5 million people in dry regions which are degrading into a desert.

g. **Hurricane & Cyclones**—Global warming also increases the frequency of strong cyclones. Every $1^O C$ increase in sea surface temperature results in 31% increase in the global frequency of category 4 and 5 storms per year.

h. The corals are directly threatened by the increasing atmospheric concentrations of carbon dioxide which is acidifying the water.

Intext Questions

1. How is wind formed ?
2. Name the greenhouse gas released during farming activities.
3. Why is earth compared to a greenhouse ?
4. How do mountain ranges influence the climate of an area ?
5. Why is the temperature of an area dependant on its distance from the equator ?

Ways to slow down the temperature change—

We have seen the alarming consequences of global warming. Therefore, it is critical to take necessary steps to curb global warming. A robust intervention of community, technology and governing bodies is essential for controlling global warming. This is because global warming is a result of human activities.

The ozone layer

Ozone is an 'allotrope' of oxygen. This gas makes up 21 per cent of the atmosphere. Ozone is formed from oxygen in a reversible reaction. Near the end of the last century, scientists discovered that ozone levels over the Antarctic were reduced. This discovery was unexpected. Scientists knew that reactive chlorine atoms could destroy ozone. They also knew that chemicals called chlorofluorocarbons (CFCs) break down in ultraviolet light to release reactive chlorine atoms. Scientists used these ideas to explain the low ozone levels. The ozone layer is the part of the upper atmosphere where ozone is found in the highest concentrations. The ozone there absorbs ultraviolet radiation, preventing most of it from reaching the ground. Ultraviolet radiation is found naturally in sunlight. Exposure to ultraviolet radiation can cause our skin to tan. It can also cause :

a. Sunburn
b. Skin cancer
c. Eye cataracts
d. Premature ageing of the skin.

However, various human activities can cause thinning of the ozone layer.

CFCs were once used widely in insulating foam and aerosol spray-cans. Once released, they gradually spread through the atmosphere, eventually reaching the ozone layer. Once there, they destroy ozone. CFCs have now been almost completely replaced by chemicals that do not cause this damage. Ozone depletion is caused by chemicals containing the elements chlorine and bromine, which are halogens. They are important components of a class of refrigerants called chlorofluorocarbons (CFCs) that were in heavy use in the mid 20th century.

Atmosphere and Climate

CFCs are inert and able to migrate to the upper atmosphere on wind currents, where the sun's ultraviolet energy breaks them apart. Chlorine and bromine atoms are highly reactive, and once freed from the CFC molecules, they react with the extra oxygen atom in ozone to produce the hypochlorite or hypobromite ions and molecular oxygen. These ions are still unstable, and they react with a second ozone molecule to produce more molecular oxygen and leave the halogen ion free to start the process over again. The most severe depletion of the ozone layer occurs over the South Pole in late winter and early spring. At that time, the ozone layer is reduced to as little as 100 Dobson units, or about the thickness of a dime. Since it was discovered, this "ozone hole" has grown larger in each successive Antarctic winter before it disappears in the summer.

In 1987, a group of 24 nations met in Montreal and negotiated the "Montreal Protocol on Substances that Deplete the Ozone Layer." They agreed to phase out the use of CFCs and other ozone-depleting chemicals by 1995. Since that time, the ozone hole has continued to grow, largely due to chemicals that were already in the atmosphere. On 21 September 2007, approximately 200 countries agreed to accelerate the elimination of hydrochlorofluorocarbons entirely by 2020 in a United Nations-sponsored Montreal summit. HCFCs (Hydrochloroflurocarbons) and PFCs (Perflurocarbons) were used as substitutes for CFCs. These are non-toxic and non-flammable. The hydrocarbons like iso-butane and propane are also used as alternatives to CFCs. They are low cost and widely available materials. In addition they have zero ozone depletion potential and very low global warming potential. They also have good energy efficiency. The hydrochlorofluorocarbons (HCFCs) are less stable in the lower atmosphere, enabling them to break down before reaching the ozone layer.

> **Fascinating Facts**
> 1. The molecules in CFCs destroy ozone molecules at a rate of 1:100,000 which make them very dangerous to the ozone layer.
> 2. The Golden Toad is the first species to go extinct due to climate change.

SUMMARY

- The air is a mixture of several gases and it encompasses the earth from all sides. The air surrounding the earth is called the atmosphere.
- The atmosphere protects us by filtering out deadly cosmic rays, powerful ultraviolet (UV) radiation from the Sun, and even meteors on collision course with Earth.
- Nitrogen accounts for 78% of the atmosphere, oxygen 21% and argon 0.9%. Gases like carbon dioxide, nitrous oxides, methane, and ozone are trace gases that account for about a tenth of one percent of the atmosphere.

- The atmosphere can be divided into six layers according to the diversity of temperature and density—troposphere, stratosphere, mesosphere, thermosphere, ionosphere and exosphere.
- Weather is the day-to-day condition of the atmosphere. This includes temperature, rainfall and wind.
- Climate is the average weather conditions of a place, usually measured over one year. This includes temperature and rainfall.
- The greenhouse effect is a natural process that warms the Earth's surface. When the Sun's energy reaches the Earth's atmosphere, some of it is reflected back to space and the rest is absorbed and re-radiated by greenhouse gases.
- Greenhouse gases include water vapour, carbon dioxide, methane, nitrous oxide, ozone and some artificial chemicals such as chlorofluorocarbons (CFCs).
- Agriculture is often the reason for deforestation and a change in land use, from natural ecosystems that take up and store carbon dioxide from the atmosphere, to farmland.
- Ozone is an 'allotrope' of oxygen.
- The ozone layer is the part of the upper atmosphere where ozone is found in the highest concentrations.
- The ozone there absorbs ultraviolet radiation, preventing most of it from reaching the ground.
- In 1987, a group of 24 nations met in Montreal and negotiated the "Montreal Protocol on Substances that Deplete the Ozone Layer." They agreed to phase out the use of CFCs and other ozone-depleting chemicals by 1995.

EXERCISE

A. Define each of these terms :

1. Atmosphere, 2. Climate, 3. Greenhouse gases, 4. Weather, 5. Latitude, 6. Wind, 7. Topography, 8. Tropopause, 9. Mesopause, 10. Green house effect

B. Answer each of these in brief :

1. Name the green house gases.
2. What is the difference between weather and climate ?
3. How does humidity differ in arctic region and tropical region ?
4. In what way global warming is a threat to coral reefs ?
5. Write the uses of CFC.
6. How does green house effect cause global warming ?

C. Answer each of these in detail—

1. Describe each of these layers of atmosphere –

    a. Troposphere, b. Stratosphere, c. Mesosphere, d. Thermosphere, e. Exosphere.

Atmosphere and Climate

2. Differentiate between photosynthesis and respiration.
3. How do each of these factors affect climate ?
   a. Latitude   b. Atmosphere circulation pattern   c. Oceanic circulation
   d. Seasonal change   e. Local geography
4. How does global warming result in –
   a. Desertification   b. Melting of ice caps   c. Species extinction   d. Air pollution
5. Enlist the harmful effects of UV rays on human beings.
6. How does CFC react with ozone ?
7. Which substance was prescribed as a substitute for CFC ? Why ?

WORKSHEET

A. Multiple Choice Questions :

1. Earth's atmosphere is divided into layers on basis of
   (a) weight
   (b) pressure
   (c) temperature
   (d) energy

2. Lowest layer of atmosphere is called
   (a) troposphere
   (b) stratosphere
   (c) mesosphere
   (d) thermosphere

3. We live in which layer of the atmosphere. This is also where weather occurs.
   (a) troposphere
   (b) stratosphere
   (c) mesosphere
   (d) thermosphere

4. As you get higher off of the ground what happens to air pressure ?
   (a) It decreases
   (b) It increases
   (c) Air pressure is always the same
   (d) There is no air pressure in the atmosphere

5. Which of the following is NOT true of Ozone ?
   (a) It contains 3 oxygen atoms
   (b) It makes up a layer in our atmosphere found in the stratosphere
   (c) It is just like regular oxygen
   (d) It protects from UV radiations

B. Justify these statements :

1. Respiration and photosynthesis are reverse processes.
2. Polar areas are colder compared to equatorial areas.
3. The seasons result from the tilt of the Earth's axis.
4. Acidic oceans are a threat to molluscs and corals.
5. Ground-level ozone is hazardous.

Atmosphere and Climate

C. **Read the following excerpts and answer the questions that follow. (open-ended questions) :**

1. A layer of atmosphere is very crucial for working of mass communication technologies.
   (a) Identify the layer.
   (b) Explain, why is this layer critical for mass communication ?
2. Mount Emei is the highest of the Four Sacred Mountains of Buddhism and receives the most rainfall in China.
   (a) Why do mountain regions receive high rainfall ?
3. Nursery greenhouses in India are specialised in growing containerised seedlings may be it for vegetables, fruits and herbs.
   (a) Why are plants grown in green house ?

D. **Activities :**

1. Make a list of factors that makes atmosphere function properly on Earth. Compare these factors with other planets.
2. Make a list of environmental problems caused due to population explosion.

8

SOIL AND LAND

Earth is a terrestrial planet which supports life. It has a solid crust. Weathering of rocks forming the surface of earth provides the soil layer. Soils are natural unconsolidated materials on the surface of the earth and are composed of solid, liquid and gas. Land is the part of the earth's surface that is not covered by water. It is the earth's surface occupied by continents and islands. Approximately, 25% of our planet consists of land. Soil is the upper layer of earth in which plants grow. It is the material found on the surface of the earth which is composed of organic and inorganic material including air and water. The vast majority of human activity throughout history has occurred in land areas that support agriculture, habitat, and various natural resources. Soils form a narrow interface between the atmosphere and the lithosphere and possess elements of both water, a gaseous phase and mineral matter, together with a diverse range of organisms and materials of biological origin. Soils are essential for life, in the sense that they provide the medium for plant growth, habitat for many insects and other organisms, act as a filtration system for surface water, carbon store and maintenance of atmospheric gases. It would be impossible to initiate the food chain without soil. Only 25% of the earth's surface is made

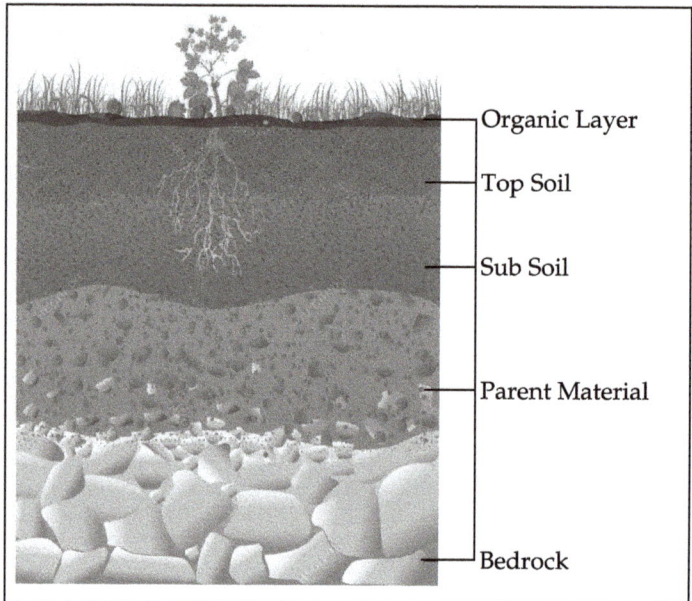

- Organic Layer
- Top Soil
- Sub Soil
- Parent Material
- Bedrock

> **Fascinating Fact**
>
> Soil is home to a quarter of all known species on the Earth.
> Soil is at the bottom of the food chain, yet it is the corner stone of life on earth.

Soil and Land

up of soil and only 10 percent of that soil can be used to grow food. Therefore, it is crucial to maintain the quality of soil. Owing to various human activities, the quality of soil is degrading. Soil degradation can be defined as a process by which one or more of the potential ecological functions of the soil are harmed.

8.0. DEFORESTATION

Trees are one of the most important aspects of the planet we live in. Trees are vitally important to the environment, animals and of course for us humans. They are important for the climate of the Earth, as they act as filters of carbon dioxide. Forests are known as habitats and shelters to millions of species. However, the trees on our planet are being depleted at a very fast rate. Deforestation is the permanent destruction of forests in order to make the land available for other uses. Several million square kilometres of forest are cut down every year. The destruction of the forests is occurring due to various reasons, one of the main reasons being the short-term economic benefits. These causes are listed below –

(a) Fuel crisis—Trees are cut down in developing countries to be used as firewood or turned into charcoal, which are used for cooking and heating purposes. Since humans began to harness fire, wood has been used as a primary fuel and it is still a major source of energy for people from developing countries. Though wood fuel may not be a major cause of deforestation on a global scale compared to other drivers of deforestation, it can still have a serious effect at local level.

> **Fascinating Fact**
>
> In just one tablespoon of soil, you will find more than seven Billon organisms – that's more than the amount of people on the planet!

(b) Infrastructure development and Competition for land—The cutting down of trees for timber that is used for building materials, furniture and paper products have a major impact on forest life. Forests are cleared to accommodate expanding urban areas. Large-scale deforestation is done with an intent of building infrastructure such as roads, railways and bridges for transportation, energy projects such as dams and irrigation. The road expansions also leads to illegal logging, where the people take benefits of doubt and slash down trees without obtaining permission from authorities. This results in loss of forest area and massive deforestation. Apart from infrastructural needs, land is required for human settlements, gardens, amusement parks, malls, hospitals, schools and other such amenities. When population increases, more land is required for construction of these amenities.

(c) Land exploited for cash and food crops—Forests are also cut down to clear land for growing crops, build farms, ranches and other food growing lands. The conversion of forests into agricultural land is a big reason for deforestation. Due to overgrowing demand for food products, many trees are chopped down for crops and for cattle grazing. Over 40% of the forests are cleared to obtain land and meet the needs of agriculture and wood. Space and soil is required to grow commercially important crops or cash crops. Tress are cut down to make space and soil available for growing cash crops. Industrial agriculture and subsistence agriculture together is the second most substantial driver of deforestation after animal agriculture.

(d) Population pressures—It is obvious that the rise in population invariably results in a rise in deforestation and so far these two variables have not been mutually exclusive. Deforestation is taking place at a faster rate to cater the explosive growth in population. Due to rapid increase in human population in developing countries, it has become necessary that the vast areas of forests should be cleaned and farmed so that the needs of the growing population can be met.

> **Fascinating Fact**
>
> 0.01% of the Earth's water is held in soil.

According to a report by the United Nations Framework Convention on Climate Change :

1. Deforestation attributed to agriculture is approximately 80 percent
2. Deforestation attributed to logging is approximately 14 percent
3. Deforestation attributed to firewood is approximately 5 percent
4. Remaining deforestation is utilised for other purposes

All these human activities which cause deforestation tend to rise with the rise of population.

(e) Increasing demand for timber—One of the primary causes of deforestation is the production of timber. There is a lot of demand for timber and so deforestation increases. It is a source of raw material which is used for the production of paper and also for construction. Logging for timber is the process of cutting and processing trees to meet the demand of the world's markets for furniture, construction, and other wooden products. Non-timber forest products should be preferred. (NTFPs) are biological resources other than timber that can be harvested from forest for subsistence and/or for trade.

Soil and Land

(f) Grazing Land and its link with deforestation—Forests in major parts of the world have already been cleared for livestock ranching, or cattle farming. Cattle ranchers have burned huge tracts of rainforests converting them into pastures for the cattle. They clear vast swaths of forest lands for cattle grazing. Later, when the land prices increase, they sell the land and make profit. This kind of deforestation is very common in developing countries. Forests have decayed due to grazing  of animals in the normal density forests of hot and subtropical and dry and semi-arid regions. It is known that in the developing and undeveloped countries of these areas, milch animals feed on bushes, and plants, scattered on the ground and in open forests. They also trample upon the land with their hooves so that plants do not bloom there. In most countries, large herds of sheep have completely wiped out the grass. Huge herds of animals require food and forests are cleared out to make way for grazing lands for these cattle. Forest areas make up a significant portion of lands used for livestock grazing. Overgrazing leads to soil erosion. The nutritious top soil is washed away, making the soil less nutritious. Soil erosion leads to depletion of soil quality. The fertility of soil is affected. Overgrazing leads to speedy depletion of forest plants. The time taken to replenish these plants is much slower than the depletion speed. The microbes, forest animals or insects dependent on such plants will be affected. Overgrazing leads to depletion of forest plants which eventually affects the forest food chain and food web. Thereby, disturbing the forest ecosystem.

> **Fascinating Fact**
>
> Recycling a tonne of paper spares 17 trees, and recycling half the world's paper would free 20 million acres of forest land.

(g) Soybean Production—The biggest driver of deforestation under crop production is soybean production. Only a small percentage of soy is used for human consumption whereas 70% to 75% of it is used as feed for animal farms. Soy is used as a primary source of protein in livestock feed for cows, chickens, pigs, as well as for farmed fish.

(h) Palm Oil—It is the most widely consumed vegetable oil on the planet and found in everything from our foods, cosmetics, cleaning products to fuels, thus one of the world's leading deforestation drivers. It is a source of huge profits for multinational corporations, and biggest palm oil producers are Malaysia and Indonesia.

Besides cutting trees as building materials, the slash-and-burn technique is used where any wild or forested land is to be cleared and any remaining vegetation is burned for short-term agriculture. Once the land is infertile they move into a new plot which causes further deforestation.

> **? Intext Questions**
> 1. Name the layers of soil.
> 2. What is the difference between soil and land?
> 3. List down the uses of palm oil.
> 4. Why is soy used as a feed for animal farms?

The effects of deforestation are—

(a) Climate change—It is well-known that global warming is being caused largely due to emissions of greenhouse gases like carbon dioxide into the atmosphere. However, what is not known quite as well is that deforestation has a direct association with carbon dioxide emissions into the atmosphere. Trees act as a major storage depot for carbon, since they absorb carbon dioxide from the atmosphere, which is then used to produce carbohydrates, fats and proteins that make up trees. When deforestation occurs, many of the trees are burnt or they are allowed to rot, which results in releasing the carbon that is stored in them as carbon dioxide. This, in turn, leads to greater concentrations of carbon dioxide in the atmosphere.

(b) Effect of deforestation on atmosphere—The effect of deforestation can be seen in the following:

(i) Loss of biodiversity—The unique biodiversity of various geographical areas is being lost on a scale that is quite unprecedented. Due to massive felling of trees, about 50 to 100 species of animals are being lost each day. The outcome of which is extinction of animals and plants on a massive scale. They not only lose their habitat and protective cover, but they are pushed to extinction. Many beautiful creatures, both plants and animals have vanished from the face of the earth.

(ii) Flooding and drought—One of the vital functions of forests is to absorb and store great amounts of water quickly when there are heavy rains. When forests are cut down, this regulation of the flow of water is disrupted, which leads to alternating periods of flood and then

Soil and Land

drought in the affected area. Thus, leading to disruption of human settlements and loss of life in thousands.

(iii) Greenhouse emissions—Gases such as methane and carbon dioxide trap heat in Earth's atmosphere, leading to change in climate. Trees absorb the carbon dioxide and release oxygen and water into the atmosphere and this contributes to the global warming. Cutting carbon dioxide adds to the environment and then this lack of the trees creates an absorption deficit. Deforestation leads to the emission of greenhouse gas.

> **Fascinating Fact**
>
> Up to 28,000 species are expected to become extinct by the next quarter of the century due to deforestation.

(c) Soil erosion—Cutting down on trees leads to clearance of forests and thus soil erosion occurs. Exposure of the soil to the sun's heat dries up the moisture inside the soil. Nutrients evaporate and it affects the bacteria that help to break down organic matter. Due to this, rain washes the soil surfaces and erosion takes place. Large amounts of soil wash into local streams and rivers and cause damage to hydroelectric structures and irrigation infrastructure.

8.1. SOIL EROSION AND DESERTIFICATION

Soil is the foundation of life and of civilization on this planet. Soil formation is a long and slow process. It is estimated that an inch of soil takes 500 to 1000 years to form. Soil is being lost at rates much faster than it can reasonably be sustained or built. One of the major reasons for soil degradation is soil erosion. Soil erosion is a process that involves the wearing away of the topsoil. The process involves the loosening of the soil particles, blowing or washing away of the soil particles, and either ends up in the valley and faraway lands or washed away to the oceans

> **Fascinating Fact**
>
> Almost half of world's timber and up to 70% of paper is consumed by Europe, United States and Japan alone.

by rivers and streams. Soil erosion is a natural process which has increasingly been worsened by human activities such as agriculture and deforestation. Desertification is a type of land degradation in which a relatively dry area of land becomes increasingly arid, typically losing its bodies of water as well as vegetation and wildlife.

Types of Erosion

1. Sheet erosion (water) is almost invisible. Lighter coloured soils are a sign that over the years erosion has taken its toll.

2. Wind erosion is highly visible. Although it is a problem, water erosion is generally much more severe.

3. Rill erosion occurs during heavy rains, when small rills form over an entire hillside, making farming difficult.

4. Gully erosion makes gullies, some of them huge, impossible to cross with farm machinery.

5. Ephemeral erosion occurs in natural depressions. It differs from gully erosion in that the area can be crossed by farm equipment.

Causes and consequences of soil erosion and desertification

1. Removal of vegetation –The physical characteristics of the land can also contribute to soil erosion. For example, land with a high hill slope will perpetuate the process of rainwater or runoff saturation in the area, particularly due to the faster movement of the water down a slope. The plants are anchored to the soil. Their roots hold on the soil. Such a network of vegetation and their root system prevent the soil erosion. If the vegetation is cleared, the loose soil particle is vulnerable for erosion.

2. Overgrazing, Overstocking and Tillage Practices—The transformation of natural ecosystems to pasture lands has largely contributed to increased rates of soil erosion and the loss of soil nutrients and the top soil. Overstocking and overgrazing has led to reduced ground cover and break down of the soil particles, giving room for erosion and accelerating the erosive effects by wind and rain. This reduces soil quality and agricultural productivity. Agricultural tillage depending on the machinery used also breaks down the soil particles, making the soils vulnerable to erosion by water. Up and down field tillage practices as well create pathways for surface water runoff and can speed up the soil erosion process. Animal grazing is a huge problem for many areas that are starting to become desert biomes. If there are too many animals that are overgrazing in certain spots, it makes it difficult for the plants to grow back.

3. Over-culture –It is when the land is being continuously under cultivation and is not allowed to lie fallow between crops. This constant farming of the land reduces the soil's ability to produce valuable humus for soil fertility as it is constantly being ploughed or stripped for crop growth. The soil becomes drier and less fertile. While humus is primarily needed for the addition of nutrients and minerals, it is also a valuable source of air and water needed by soil to keep it moist and aerated. With less humus, the soil dries out and is open for

Soil and Land

wind and rain erosion. Usually overcropping occurs in areas where there is a demand for crops either for market or a large local population.

4. Clearance of slopes—A sloped plane is cut into a series of flat surfaces or platforms, which resemble steps. It is an effective method to control erosion and surface run-off. The speed of the running or flowing water is interrupted when it flows through steps. When such slopes are cleared, the speed of moving water increases. Thus, soil erosion increases.

5. Drought—Drought can cause soil erosion due to the effects of wind and flooding. Moreover, the drying out of soil causes cracks which reduces the volume of the soil. In regions with frequent or extensive dry periods, the soil and vegetation can suffer severe damage from which they will not be able to recover. In such cases, the process of desertification starts. Drought brings a general lack of rainfall, which leads to death and decay of organic matter within the soil in the region. The organic matter no longer keeps the composure it otherwise would have, and its surface area lessens due to drying. Not only does organic matter suffer a surface level deterioration, but the clay within soils do as well. When clay lose water as a result of drought and evaporation, they also lose a separating factor which abates them from becoming a single, nearly uniform, mass. This leads to another drastic lessening of surface area.

6. Heavy rainfall—Greater duration and intensity of rainstorm means greater potential for soil erosion. Rainstorm produces four major types of soil erosion including rill erosion, gully erosion, sheet erosion, and splash erosion. These types of erosions are caused by the impacts of raindrops on the soil surface that break down and disperse the soil particles, which are then washed away by the stormwater runoff. Over time, repeated rainfall can lead to significant amounts of soil loss. Rapidly moving stormwater, flash floods, and flooding may also occur because of excess surface water run-off, thus, causing extreme local erosion by plucking bed rocks, forming rock cut-basins, creating potholes, and washing away the loosened soil particles.

7. Bad farming practices—Some farmers do not know how to use the land effectively. They may essentially strip the land of everything that it has, before moving on to another plot of land. By stripping the soil of its nutrients, desertification becomes more and more of a reality for the area that is being used for farming. When land is worked through crops or other agricultural processes, it reduces the overall structure of the soil, in addition to reducing the levels of organic matter, making it more susceptible to the effects of rain and water. Tilling in particular, can be a major contributor to erosion because it often breaks up and softens the structure of soil, farming practices that reduce this activity tend to have far less issues with soil erosion.

Consequences of soil erosion are –

1. The loss of topsoil decreases the productivity of soils and negatively affects our capability to grow crops on them. When topsoil erodes away, nutrient

and organic material is lost and only compacted clayish soils with poor structure remain behind. Due to the unfavourable conditions, plants grown on these soils strive and often do not produce sufficient yields.

2. Overexploited lands in dry regions are extremely vulnerable to soil erosion. Soil erosion itself seriously impairs the quality of soil and its natural recovery rate, but it is not the worst problem that can occur. In many cases, erosion is the first step that starts the irreversible transformation of the landscape into the barren desert.

3. The soil erosion also affects the waterways. It leads to deposition of silt in the water courses and in the paths through which water flows. The eroded soil might contain fertilizers, pesticides and other harmful chemicals which will degrade the quality of the water in these rivers and streams.

4. Air pollution is caused due to soil erosion. The soil particles carried in the air lead to dust. The air might also contain chemicals from agricultural lands. This soil dust in the air often leads to respiratory problems and skin infections in humans.

Erosion control techniques

(i) Building bunds—Bunds are embankments or a causeway. There are two types of bunds *i.e.,* the contour bunds and the semi-circular bunds. Contour bunds are built using stones down the slope. Semi-circular bunds are made by digging small pits. By building bunds along the contour lines, water runoff is slowed down, which leads to increased water infiltration and enhanced soil moisture. Bunds are usually constructed either with soil or stones.

(ii) Removing or patching gullies—Gullies are a ravine formed by the action of water. Excessive clearing, inappropriate land use and overgrazing are all factors leading to the formation of gully. Proper land management and use strategy is must to control such scenarios. Gully erosion occurs when water is channelled across unprotected land and washes away the soil along the drainage lines. Such gullies should be patched. Alternatively, installation of pipelines or planting grass can also prevent gully erosion.

(iii) Windbreakers—A windbreak is a plantation usually made up of one or more rows of trees or shrubs planted in such a manner as to provide shelter from the wind and to protect soil from erosion. They are commonly planted in hedgerows around the edges of fields on farms. These are rows of trees and shrubs that are planted along the edges of agricultural fields, to shield the fields against winds. Windbreakers not only significantly reduce wind erosion but also enhance air quality and aesthetic appearance of the fields. Big trees have strong and dense network roots. Hence, they hold soil tightly and reduce soil erosion caused by flowing water.

(iv) Usage of organic manure—Organic manures are natural fertilizers which are obtained from sources like animal excreta, plant waste, crop residues,

Soil and Land

etc. Manures increase soil fertility by adding various macro-nutrients and micro-nutrients like Nitrogen, Potassium, Phosphorous, Zinc, etc. Manures easily decompose under the soil. Unlike chemical fertilizers, manures do not affect the microbes and worms residing in the soil.

> **? Intext Questions**
> 1. Name few bad farming practices that lead to loosening of soil.
> 2. Explain the types of soil erosion.
> 3. How is deforestation and soil erosion inter-related ?

Addition of organic manure contributes to improved soil structure, resulting in improved water infiltration and greater water-holding capacity. Thus, soil erosion is reduced.

8.2. LAND POLLUTION

Land pollution is the degradation of earth's land surfaces often caused by human activities and its misuse. There are many causes and consequences of land pollution.

1. Salinization—Soil salinization occurs when water-soluble salts accumulate in the soil to a level that impacts the agricultural production, environmental health, and economics. The accumulation of salts in the soil can occur through natural processes such as physical or chemical weathering and transport from parent material, geological deposits or groundwater. It can also occur due to parent rock constituents, such as carbonate minerals and/or feldspars or as a result of the one-time submergence of  soils under seawater. Sea level rises and also induces seepage into areas lying below sea level. In arid areas, saline soils are formed due to evapotranspiration and lack of rainfall to flush the soils. Finally, wind in coastal areas can blow moderate amounts of salts inland. Human activities can cause salinization through the use of salt-rich irrigation water, which can be exacerbated by overexploitation of coastal groundwater aquifers causing seawater intrusion, or due to other inappropriate irrigation practices, and/or poor drainage conditions. The excessive use of water for irrigation in dry climates, with heavy soils, causes salt accumulation because they are not washed out by rainfall. The process occurs in cultivated areas where irrigation is associated with high evaporation rates and a clay texture of the soil. The practice of waterlogging without adequate drainage has also become a serious cause of soil salinization. Waterlogged soils prevent leaching of the salts imported by the irrigation water.

2. Fertilizers—Fertilizers are commercially produced plant nutrients. Fertilizers should be applied carefully in terms of proper dose, time, and observing pre—and post-application precautions for their complete utilisation. Sometimes

fertilizers get washed away due to excessive irrigation and are not fully absorbed by the plants. This excessive fertilizer then leads to water pollution. Continuous use of fertilizers in an area can destroy soil fertility because the organic matter in the soil is not replenished and micro-organisms in the soil are harmed by the fertilizers used. The presence of a number of acids in the soil, such as hydrochloric and sulphuric acids, creates a damaging effect on soil referred to as soil friability. The different acids in the soil dissolve the soil crumbs which help to hold together the rock particles. Soil crumbs result from the combination of humus, or decomposed natural material such as dead leaves, with clay. These mineral-rich soil crumbs are essential to soil drainage and greatly improve air circulation in the soil. As the chemicals in the chemical fertilizers destroy soil crumbs, the result is a highly compacted soil with reduced drainage and air circulation. In place of fertilizers, use of manure should be encouraged. Manure is nutrient rich organic matter which is used as organic fertilizer in agriculture. Manure is the substances that adds nutrients to the soil. The nutrients may be in the form of animal waste, plant waste. Addition of manure to the soil makes the soil fertile by adding organic matter and nutrients like nitrogen. Addition of manure to garden soil or in agricultural fields improves the soil structure and adds nutrients to the soil. It also helps to hold moisture in the soil and enhances micro-organism activity. In fact using manure in agriculture is one of the oldest methods of fertilization.

3. Pesticides—The extensive use of pesticides in agricultural production can degrade and damage the community of microorganisms living in the soil, particularly when these chemicals are overused or misused. Pesticides are detrimental for the environment and produce considerable damage to ecosystems. Insecticides and herbicides may be harmful for non-target species. Pesticides pollute air, water and soil. Carried by the wind, pesticide suspensions contaminate other areas. Pesticides affect considerably natural biological equilibrium. Pesticides diminish biodiversity, reduce nitrogen fixation, contribute

Soil and Land

to the disappearance of pollinators, threaten fish, and destroy bird and animal habitats. Pets may also become affected by strong pesticides.

4. Toxic waste—Industrial wastes that pollute land include paints, chemicals, plastics, and metals among other industrial manufacturing by-products and residues. The major industrial waste products are generated from power plants, oil refineries, construction works, pharmaceuticals, and agricultural product producers. Energy producing power plants release chemical wastes that are disposed in landfills. Examples include nuclear, coal, and fossil fuel driven energy production processes. Oil refinery processes also produce petroleum hydrocarbon by-products that end up as waste and construction sites generate metal, wood, and plastic wastes whereas agricultural industries release scores of chemical wastes that find their way into landfills. Power plants combust fossil fuels and biomass while other industrial manufacturers such as pharmaceuticals, oil refineries, and agricultural product producers utilise a series of raw materials with a lot of chemical residues and by-products. As much as the bulk of industrial waste products disposals are regulated, at times, they find way to the landfills or end up disposed on land somewhere. Wastewater and liquids from industrial, agricultural farms and manufacturing processes also contain all kinds of chemicals that at times contaminate lands when they are not disposed off correctly.

5. Nuclear waste—This includes waste from nuclear power stations that is disposed off underground. Rays from this kind of waste can cause lung or skin cancer. This can have hazardous effect on the health of humans and wildlife. Every exposure to radiation increases the risk of damage to tissues, cells, DNA and other vital molecules. Each exposure potentially can cause programmed cell death, genetic mutations, cancers, leukaemia, birth defects, and reproductive, immune and endocrine system disorders. There is no safe threshold to exposure to radiation.

6. Domestic waste—Solid wastes include the magnitude of rubbish from schools, home, hospitals, market, work, restaurants, public places and so on. The bulk of these wastes typically winds up in the landfills. Examples of the solid wastes include things like bottles, cans, plastics containers, food, glass, wood, paper, used and grounded cars, broken furniture, obsolete electronic goods, hospitals waste and so on. Some of these waste products are biodegradable, *i.e.*, they are capable of decomposing into organic matter. Examples include waste products produced from vegetations such as food remains and paper. There are others that are not biodegradable like plastics, broken car and electronic parts, glass, and metals. Since the majority of solid wastes cannot readily decay, they heap up in the landfills where they remain for thousands of years. As a result, they cause significant damage to the land and people within the surrounding.

The pollution of land has calamitous consequences especially concerning the survival of animals and humans and the quality of soil and water. Environmental protection agencies indicate that the effects can even be more devastating if wastes in landfills are not separated into reusable, recyclable, or organic waste. Since the advent of industrialization, human activities have gradually destroyed and degraded land, causing diseases to humans and animals and reducing the capacity to support ecosystem and various life forms. Land pollution has many long lasting effects. The effects of land pollution are as follows—

1. Effect on Human Health

Miscellaneous wastes contain dangerous chemicals, pesticides, and metals that have adverse effects on humans. Plastic waste, for instance, might contain acrylic, polyvinyl chloride, polycarbonate, and phthalates that are associated with cancers, skin diseases, respiratory disorders, and birth defects for pregnant women. Chemical components such as cadmium, asbestos, mercury, cyanide, arsenic, and chromium commonly found in pharmaceutical, pesticides, and fertilizer. Industrial wastes also have devastating effects on human health. They have cancer causing elements and can also lead to lung and kidney disease as well as liver damage.

2. Increase in Landfill Sites

When land is contaminated with solid agricultural and industrial waste, it leads to increase in landfill sites across the city. Landfills also become breeding grounds for mice, rodents, flies, and birds that can transmit diseases. These landfills are contaminated with such kind of toxic chemicals that they can reach the human body via vegetables and foods that are grown in polluted lands. They can also seep into water bodies  used for consumption purposes or could be inhaled by humans from polluted dust. Apart from that, these huge pile of wastes spoils the aesthetic value of the city.

3. Air Pollution

Landfills and dump sites generate appalling smells and odour in the areas in which they are located. In cities and towns located near huge dump sites and landfill areas, residents have experienced high scores of pungent smell. Apart from the bad smell, landfills are always burning which contributes to air pollution.

Soil and Land

4. Water Pollution

Land pollution can spread in all directions so that it results in an adverse impact on the immediate environments. On this basis, it can contaminate water and significantly reduce its quality. It happens when the chemicals and other toxic substances from the landfills and solid wastes are mostly carried into waterways by surface rainwater run-off. When the polluted water gets collected on the surface of soil, it is slowly absorbed. The contaminated water thus reaches the ground water. At the same time, leaching takes place which makes the toxic elements and chemicals to infiltrate into aquifers and water tables. Also, the contaminated water evaporates and falls back as precipitation with the impurities, advancing the cycle of pollution and contamination.

Soil is one of the world's most important natural resources. Together with air and water it is the basis for life on planet earth. It has many important functions which are essential for life. Not only does it play major part in allowing us to feed the world's population, but it also plays a major role in the recycling of air, water, nutrients, and maintaining a number of natural cycles, thereby ensuring that there will be a basis for life in generations to come. Without soil, the world's population neither would nor could survive.

SUMMARY

- Land is the part of the earth surface that is not covered by water. It is the earth surface occupied by Continents and Islands. Approximately 25% of our planet consists of land.
- Soil is the upper layer of earth in which plants grow.
- Deforestation is the permanent destruction of forests in order to make the land available for other uses.
- The destruction of the forests is occurring due to various reasons, one of the main reasons being the short-term economic benefits.
- The causes of deforestation are infrastructure development, creation of pasture land, fuel crisis, natural calamities, etc.
- The effects of deforestation are loss of biodiversity, drought, floods, climate change, soil erosion, etc.
- Soil erosion is a process that involves the wearing away of the topsoil. The process involves the loosening of the soil particles, blowing or washing away of the soil particles, and either ends up in the valley and faraway lands or washed away to the oceans by rivers and streams.
- Desertification is a type of land degradation in which a relatively dry area of land becomes increasingly arid, typically losing its bodies of water as well as vegetation and wildlife.
- Heavy rainfall, drought, overgrazing, over tillage, bad farming practices, clearance of slopes are few factors that cause soil erosion.

- Land pollution is the degradation of earth's land surfaces often caused by human activities and its misuse.
- Some common causes of land pollution are fertilizers, pesticides, waste accumulation (nuclear, toxic, domestic, solid).

 EXERCISE

A. Define each of these terms :

1. Soil erosion 2. Deforestation   3. Primary fuel   4. Climate change 5. Soil degradation

B. Answer each of these questions in brief :

1. Which method of tillage induces soil erosion ?
2. What are the disadvantages of fertilizers and pesticides ?
3. Give an account of any two commercially important crops that are grown on large scale.
4. Why are timber in great demand ?
5. How does nuclear radiation affect human beings ?
6. Which factors causes soil salinization ?
7. Which natural calamities lead to soil erosion ?

C. Answer these questions in detail—

1. Explain how each of these factors cause deforestation –
   (a) Infrastructure development
   (b) Agriculture
   (c) Fuel crisis
   (d) Creation grazing land
   (e) Overpopulation
2. Explain the types of soil erosion.
3. How does land pollution affect human health ?
4. Write four points to justify that soil is an important resource.
5. How does deforestation result in—
   (a) Loss of biodiversity
   (b) Drought
   (c) Flood
   (d) Climate change
   (e) Global warming
   (f) Soil erosion

Soil and Land

WORKSHEET

A. Multiple Choice Questions :

1. Which one of the following is not a factor of soil formation ?
   (a) Time
   (b) Soil texture
   (c) Organic matter
   (d) Temperature
2. Which of the following is not a threat commonly faced by soils ?
   (a) Soil erosion
   (b) Percolation
   (c) Deforestation
   (d) Climate change
3. A continuous area of land surrounded by ocean is called_____
   (a) Seashore
   (b) Beach
   (c) Landmass
   (d) Wetland
4. The thin layer of grainy substance covering the surface of the earth is called as_____
   (a) Mineral
   (b) Soil
   (c) Sand
   (d) Chemical fertilizers
5. Land capable of being ploughed and used to grow crops is called as_____
   (a) Domestic land
   (b) Arable land
   (c) Un-arable land
   (d) Dry land

B. Justify the following statements :

1. Deforestation is one of the reason of landslide.
2. Water erosion is significant in the regions of heavy rainfall and steep slopes.
3. Air pollution is seen as a result of land pollution.
4. Agriculture is the victim as well as culprit of environmental degradation.

C. Read the following excerpts and answer the questions that follow. (open-ended questions) :

1. Exploring non-timber options in our daily life is the need of an hour.
   In what way are non-timber products used in daily life ?
2. According to a report by the United Nations Framework Convention on Climate Change deforestation attributed to logging is approximately 14%. What is wood logging ? List out the other impacts of logging on environment apart from deforestation.

D. Activity :

1. Find out what are the measures and initiatives taken by United Nations in order to curb deforestation and land degradation.

9

PEOPLE

Food, clothing and shelter are the basic needs of man. Apart from these basic needs, we desire for some other amenities too. Possessions like house, furniture, vehicle, decor items, etc. are a part of our daily lifestyle. In addition to possession, we also wish to take services like education, healthcare, recreation, entertainment, etc. Most of the times, our economic status is measured by assets we have. Poverty is the state of one who lacks a usual or socially acceptable amount of money or material possessions. Poverty is said to exist when people lack the means to satisfy their basic needs. Poverty has been associated, for example, with poor health, low levels of education or skills, an inability or an unwillingness to work, high rates of disruptive or disorderly behaviour, and improvidence. The UN definition of poverty is "Fundamentally, poverty is a denial of choices and opportunities, a violation of human dignity. It means lack of basic capacity to participate effectively in society. It means not having enough to feed and clothe a family, not having a school or clinic to go to, not having the land on which to grow one's food or a job to earn one's living, not having access to credit. It means insecurity, powerlessness and exclusion of individuals, households and communities. It means susceptibility to violence, and it often implies living on marginal or fragile environments, without access to clean water or sanitation". While these attributes have often been found to exist with poverty, their inclusion in a definition of poverty would tend to obscure the relation between them and the inability to provide for one's basic needs.

For several thousand years, the world has been experiencing increased urbanisation. Urbanisation has got a few negative aspects as well like creation of slums, reduced quality of life, lack of resources, etc. Poverty is also one such effect of inequality caused by urbanisation. Following are the causes of poverty –

1. Overpopulation
2. Unemployment
3. Increase in prices of commodities
4. Economy of the country or nation
5. Lack of opportunity
6. Lack of education

People

9.0. RELATIVE AND ABSOLUTE POVERTY

Poverty is an economic state where people experiencing certain commodities that are considered essential for the lives of human beings. The two main types of poverty are—Relative poverty and Absolute poverty. **Absolute poverty** is a condition where household income is below a necessary level to maintain basic living standards (food, shelter, clothing). **Relative poverty** is a condition where household income is below median incomes. Relative poverty is defined in relation to the overall distribution of income or consumption in a country. The difference between relative and absolute poverty are tabulated below-

Criteria	Absolute poverty	Relative poverty
Biological needs	Absolute poverty focuses more on the biological needs.	Relative poverty does not consider biological needs.
Income levels	In absolute poverty, income levels are an important criterion.	Relative poverty does not consider income levels.
Country dependence	Absolute poverty does not vary from country to country.	Relative poverty varies between developed and developing countries.
Poverty alleviation	Different international bodies and government of various countries have developed policies and measures to ensure that absolute poverty is eradicated around the world.	There are no measures and policies implemented to alleviate relative poverty.

The distribution of Income in an economy is represented by a Lorenz Curve and the degree of income inequality is measured through the Gini Coefficient. The Lorenz Curve depicts the proportion of income earned by any given percentage of the population. An example of Lorenz curve is show alongside–

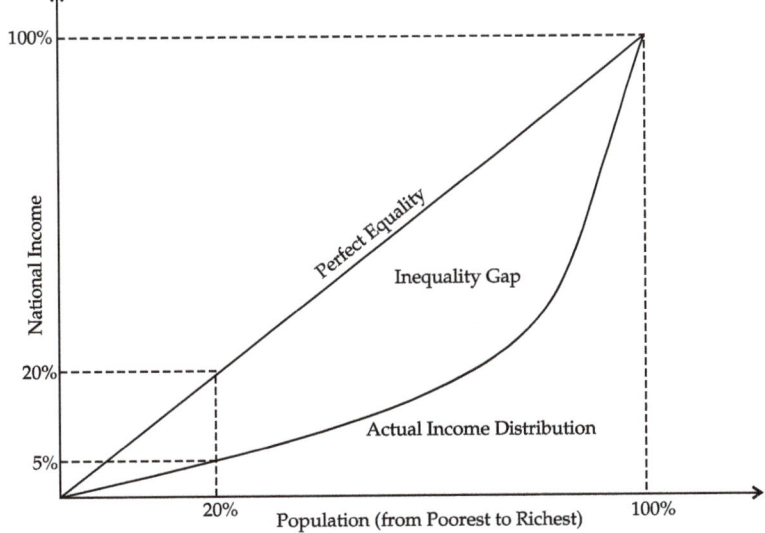

In the graph it is clearly visible that 20% of population earn only 5% of the national income. In an ideal condition i.e., perfect equality, 20% of the population should have earned 20 % of the national income.

The Gini Coefficient, which is derived from the Lorenz Curve, can be used as an indicator of economic development in a country. The Gini Coefficient measures the degree of income equality in a population. The Gini Coefficient can vary from 0 (perfect equality) to 1 (perfect inequality). A Gini Coefficient of zero means that everyone has the same income, while a Coefficient of 1 represents a single individual receiving all the income.

> **? Intext Questions**
> 1. Which are the basic needs of man ?
> 2. How does UN define poverty ?
> 3. Name the two categories of poverty.

9.1. WORLD POVERTY

The proportion of people in developing countries living in extreme economic poverty as defined by the World Bank is living on less than $1.25 per day. The number of people in this category has fallen substantially. Poverty has declined considerably in some of the Southeast Asian countries and China due to rapid technological advancements and economic growth. Number of poor people in China has come down markedly. However, in the countries of South Asia (India, Pakistan, Sri Lanka, Nepal, Bangladesh, Bhutan) the decline has not been as rapid. In Sub-Saharan Africa, poverty in fact declined from 51 % in 1981 to 47 % in 2008. In Latin America, the ratio of poverty remained the same. It has declined from 11% in 1981 to 6.4 per cent in 2008. Poverty has also reappeared in some of the former socialist countries like Russia, where officially it was non-existent earlier.

MPI (Multi Dimensional Poverty Index) is an international measure of poverty which covers more than 100 developing countries. MPI is released every year after collecting the income data and carrying out analysis on the same. These studies are done by United Nations in collaboration with OPHI (Oxford Poverty and Human development Initiative).

Poverty indicator

Income and level of consumption are the usual indicators of poverty. But many social scientists view poverty from many other parameters; like illiteracy, lack of general resistance due to malnutrition, lack of access to safe drinking water and sanitation, etc. Refer to the table given ahead—

People

Dimensions of Poverty	Indicator	Deprived if living in the household where...
Health	Nutrition	An adult under 70 years of age or a child is undernourished.
	Child mortality	Any child has died in the family in the five-year period preceding the survey.
Education	Years of schooling	No household member aged 10 years or older has completed six years of schooling.
	School attendance	Any school-aged child is not attending school up to the age at which he/she would complete class 8.
Standard of living	Cooking Fuel	The houlehold cooks with dung, wood, charcoal or coal.
	Sanitation	The houlsehold's sanitation facility is not improved (according to SDG guidelines) or it is imporved but shared with other households.
	Drinking Water	The household does not have access to improved drinking water (according to SDG guidelines) or safe drinking water is at least 30-minute walk from home, round trip.
	Electricity	The household has no electricity.
	Housing	Housing materials for at least one of roof, walls and floor are inadequate; the floor is of natural materials and/or the roof and or walls are of natural or rudimentary materials.
	Assets	The household does not own more than one of these assets—radio, TV, telephone, computer, animal cart, bicycle, motorbike or refrigerator and does not own a car or truck.

1. Per-capita income—Per-capita income is a measure of the amount of money earned per person in a certain area. It can apply to the average per-person income for a city, region or country, and is used as a means of evaluating the living conditions and quality of life in different areas. It can be calculated for a country by dividing the country's national income by its population. The most common use of per capita income is to ascertain an area's wealth or lack of wealth.

2. Housing—Poverty and low incomes prevent people from accessing potential housing options. Poverty increases the risk of homelessness. One third of the world's population lives in a slum. Poverty forces millions of people to become homeless or to live in degrading conditions, in town and country.

Lack of earnings prevents poor people from securing minimum comfort such as electricity, water supply, sanitisation, drainage facilities, etc.

3. Levels of disease and nutrition—Poverty and poor health worldwide are indistinguishably linked. Poverty increases the chances of poor health by the following means—

   a. People face ill-health because the kind of environments they live in make them sick. As discussed, the housing of poor people lacks hygiene, decent shelter and adequate sanitation. Such living conditions can give rise to various diseases like cholera, diarrhoea, cancer, etc.

   b. Infectious and neglected tropical diseases kill and weaken millions of the poorest and most vulnerable people each year. This is because they do not have access or cannot afford medicines and appropriate treatment and health services to cure such diseases.

   c. Poor people cannot afford nutritious food. In some cases, it is difficult to reach market due to lack of transportation, and insufficient financial resources. Absence of different nutrients in our daily diet often leads to malnutrition and other deficiency diseases. World Health Organisation defines malnutrition as to deficiencies, excesses or imbalances in a person's intake of energy and/or nutrients. Night blindness, kwashiorkor, marasmus, rickets, beriberi, scurvy are few examples of deficiency diseases.

Poverty figures given by UN are—

   a. 783 million people live below the international poverty line of US$1.90 a day.

   b. In 2016, almost 10 per cent of the world's workers and their families lived on less than US$1.90 per person per day.

   c. Most people living below the poverty line belong to two regions: Southern Asia and sub-Saharan Africa.

   d. High poverty rates are often found in small, fragile and conflict-affected countries.

   e. As of 2016, only 45% of the world's population was effectively covered by at least one social protection cash benefit.

Intext Questions

1. Which are the developing countries in South Asia ?
2. Which organisation does the MPI studies ?
3. List out all the indicators of poverty.

Fascinating Fact

On 22 December 1992, UN declared 17 October as the International Day for the Eradication of Poverty.

9.2. POVERTY IN DEVELOPED AND DEVELOPING COUNTRIES

Human development is often gauzed in terms of economic development or progress in technology. A common method used to measure poverty is based on the income or consumption level. This minimum level is called a poverty line. A person is considered poor if his or her income or consumption level falls below a given "minimum level" necessary to fulfil basic needs. What is necessary to satisfy basic needs is different at different times and in different countries. Therefore, poverty line may vary with time and place. Each country uses an imaginary line that is considered appropriate for its existing level of development and its accepted minimum social norms. For example, in a developed country, person not having his/her own vehicle may be considered poor while in a developing country like India having an own vehicle is still a luxury. The nations are classified as developed, developing and under-developed based on economic and technological status. The developed nations have exploited a huge amount of natural resources in the process of achieving the current economic and technological status. As the development progressed rich countries got even richer while poor nations did not show much progress. An imbalance was evident. This form of development hampered environment and nature.

A nation being developed can imply to following things—

a. An improvement in living standards and access to all basic needs such that a person has enough food, water, shelter, clothing, health, education, etc.

b. A stable political, social and economic environment, with associated political, social and economic freedoms, such as (though not limited to) equitable ownership of land and property.

c. The ability to make free and informed choices that are not forced.

d. Be able to participate in a democratic environment with the ability to have a say in one's own future.

Poverty in developed countries

Usually in wealthy countries, poverty is not absolute. The poor in these nations do not experience famine, starvation, or homelessness. In fact, many poor people in the developed world work full time and earn more money per week than those in the developing would earn per year. Therefore, the poverty in developed country is of the relative type, which means that people are poor if their income is below a certain fraction of the income of the person in the middle of the income distribution.

Poverty in developing countries

In developing countries, poor section of the society leads a lifestyle that denies and deprives one from opportunities and comforts. In other words, this is a challenge faced by people living in harsh conditions due to lack of money. Thus, it is clearly evident that poverty deprives poor people of decent lifestyle, proper medical care, and quality education system. Apart from this, poverty is a life full of challenging experiences, inconsistency, and unreliable sources of sustaining ones livelihood.

The causes of poverty in developing countries are –

1. Developing countries are unable to reap adequate economic benefit through globalisation. For example- developing countries sell the raw materials to developed countries at a lower price. Developed countries manufacture the goods using those raw materials. Obviously, the prices of finished goods are much higher than the raw materials. Poorer countries can be forced to sell their stuff cheap owing to their need to sell it.

2. In the developing countries there is a lack of technical expertise. This leads to lower amount of Intellectual Property being generated in these countries and subsequently their dependence on developed countries for using high end technology.

3. It is difficult for countries with bigger populations to provide services too. So huge numbers of people are deprived of basic amenities leaving them out of the economic work force. The economy of developing nations is not able to effectively handle such huge population due to their lower GDP, thus, increasing the rate of poverty.

4. Many developing countries carry significant debt loads due to loans from developed nations and international financial institutions.

5. Natural disasters like earthquake, flood or drought impact the monetary conditions of the developing countries. Due to the fact that the countries are still developing when compared to developed countries, an earthquake or a flood would have a much greater impact due to their lack of education about what to do in an emergency and lack of preparation for such disasters occurring.

9.3. RURAL POVERTY VERSUS URBAN POVERTY

Urban poverty is usually defined in two ways: as an absolute standard based on a minimum amount of income needed to sustain a healthy and minimally comfortable life, and as a relative standard that is set based on average of the standard of living in a nation. Rural poverty refers to poverty in rural areas, including factors of rural society, rural economy, and rural political systems that give rise to the poverty found there. The basic differences between rural and urban poverty are as listed below-

Nature of job—The rural poor work mainly as landless agricultural labourers, cultivators with very small land holdings, landless labourers who are engaged in a variety of non-agricultural jobs and tenant cultivators with small land holdings. On the other hand, the urban poor are largely the overflow of the rural poor who had migrated to urban areas in search of alternative employment and livelihood, labourers who do a variety of casual jobs and the self-employed who sell a variety of things on roadsides and are engaged in various activities.

Less job opportunities—In rural areas, most people are cultivators as there are no other job opportunities but urban areas would have other available job

People

opportunities. The urban poor have more job opportunities but, being mostly unskilled workers, they will have to compete for these jobs with the many other migrants. Urban areas being more populated means that they have a lot more competition for any work that they may decide to take up.

Basic amenities—The rural poor also have very little access to transport, healthcare and in some cases even electricity, especially if the area that they are living in is very backward. The urban poor on the other hand are mostly migrants who have come to the place looking for opportunities. While such places may have electricity and healthcare, there is a much higher chance for them to be unable to actually afford any amenities. The rural poor lives in kutcha house whereas urban poor lives in pucca house with proper sanitation facilities.

Social evils—Villagers are generally filled with backward mindsets and social evils hence, discrimination on all counts may be faced a lot more severely. Wrong practices like child marriage, discrimination on widows, discrimination on females, female foeticides, etc. are still practised severely in many rural areas. Each of these practices impact the health and well-being of the residents of that particular area. Females are not given opportunity to educate themselves or work to earn money. They are often restricted to household and domestic work. Thus, the burden of earning solely becomes the man's responsibility. Due to lack of education and awareness, they are not efficient to plan and manage the money earnt. Many rural people are unaware of various government schemes which were introduced to help below poverty line people. Practices like child marriage, female foeticide, early pregnancy, lack of family planning severely impacts the health of rural people.

The studies done by World Bank on India's poverty profile can be presented as follows—

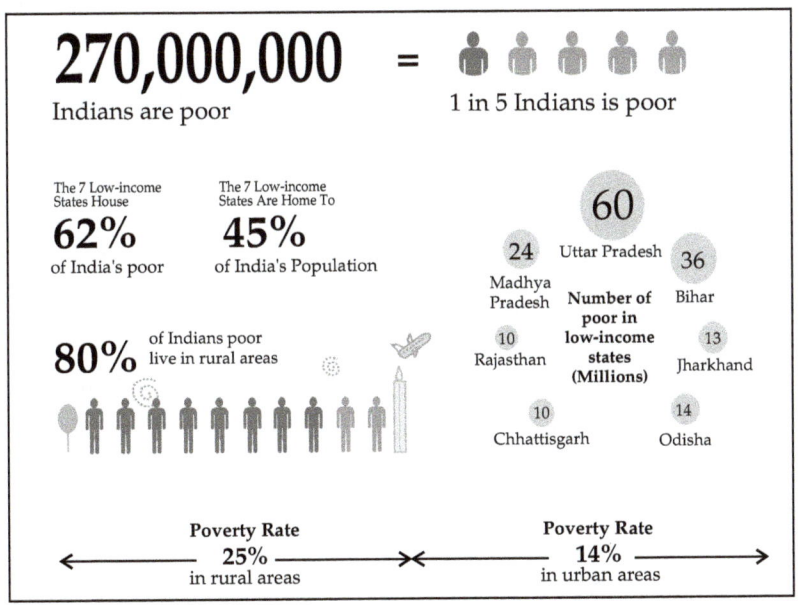

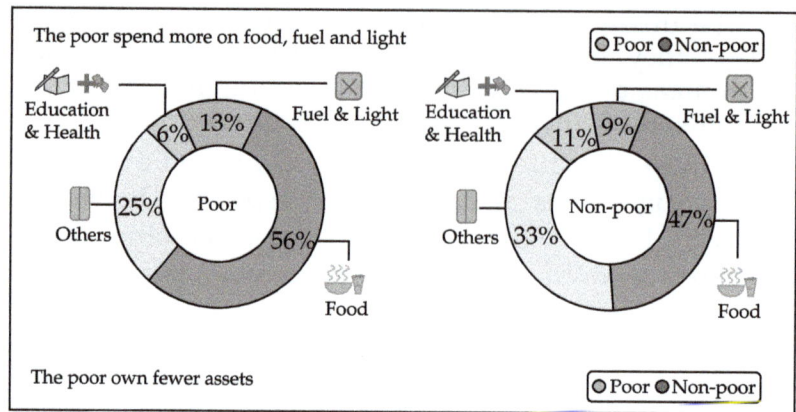

? Intext Questions

1. On what basis are the countries classified as developed, developing and under-developed nations ?
2. List out a few social evils that contribute to poverty.

💡 Fascinating Fact

Almost three-fifths of the world's extreme poor are concentrated in just five countries: Bangladesh, China, the Democratic Republic of Congo, India, and Nigeria.

9.4. THE IMPLICATIONS OF POVERTY TRAP FOR THE ENVIRONMENT IN DEVELOPING COUNTRIES

Poverty, Environment and Development

A poverty trap refers to a situation in which people get stuck in a cyclical pattern of poverty. The effects of poverty create more poverty. Apart from lack of money following factors also cause poverty—

a. **Poor work opportunities**—In population dense areas, it is difficult for people to even find jobs, let alone jobs that pay well.

b. **Inability to pay for education**—Without money, people cannot pay for the education they need to get a better job.

c. **Violence**—Many poverty-stricken areas are so stuck in a poverty trap that people fight for food, which creates very dangerous and violent areas. Violence can inhibit education, industry, and an individual's ability to excel.

d. **Expense of goods and services**—In poor areas, certain products and services, including food and medical care, can be unaffordable for large portions of the population. People who are hungry, sick, or cannot afford transportation cannot work.

e. **Lack of industry growth**—In extremely poor areas, even if there is room to build buildings for large industries, the corruption of government, the price of power, and the lack of skilled labour can deter business and industry growth.

f. **Poor sanitation**—Poor sanitation, or tainted resources (like bacteria tainted water), can lead to disease, which spreads quickly and can be difficult to control in countries that are already lacking essential resources.

g. **Lack of medical care**—Due to the lack of money or resources, people do not get the medical care they need and die due to starvation, malnutrition, and inability to get the medical insurance or supplies that are necessary.

h. **Per-capita income**—Per capita income (PCI) or average income measures the average income earned per person in a given area (city, region, country, etc.) in a specified year. It is calculated by dividing the area's total income by its total population.

Effects of poverty on environment

Poverty impacts the environment negatively. The definition of poverty is being unable to meet one's basic needs. Such needs include food, water, shelter, healthcare and education. The focus of such people is on obtaining the basic needs for short-term survival. Many of these people are forced to deplete or degrade forests, rivers, fields and soil. These groups do not have the privilege to be concerned about environmental impact. Sanitization is a good example in this concept. Poor people cannot afford to build bathrooms and toilets. Thus, they use rivers and outdoor fields for sanitisation purposes. This pollutes rivers and fields. In addition, this sector of people cannot afford birth control facilities and also lack awareness about population issues. Therefore, their population increases and as we know increase in population effects the carrying capacity of our nature. Every human being consumes their share of resources from the environment, and with so many births originating from poor communities, the burdens placed on the environment grow heavier and heavier each day. While mankind, in general, places stress on the environment, poverty in particular has played a major role in environmental degradation across the world.

Despite of many definitions, one thing is certain; poverty is a complex societal issue. No matter how poverty is defined, it can be agreed that it is an issue that requires everyone's attention. It is important that all members of our society work together to provide the opportunities for all our members to reach their full potential.

SUMMARY

- Poverty is the state of one who lacks a usual or socially acceptable amount of money or material possessions.
- The two main types of poverty are Relative poverty and Absolute poverty.
- Absolute poverty is a condition where household income is below a necessary level to maintain basic living standards (food, shelter, clothing).
- Relative poverty is a condition where household income is below median incomes. Relative poverty is defined in relation to the overall distribution of income or consumption in a country.
- The Gini Coefficient, which is derived from the Lorenz Curve, can be used as an indicator of economic development in a country.
- A common method used to measure poverty is based on the income or consumption level. This minimum level is called a poverty line.
- A person is considered poor if his or her income or consumption level falls below a given "minimum level" necessary to fulfil basic needs.
- The poverty in developed country is of the relative type.
- A poverty trap refers to a situation in which people get stuck in a cyclical pattern of poverty.
- Poverty has significant implications on the environment.

EXERCISE

A. Define the following terms :

1. Poverty 2. Absolute poverty 3. Relative poverty 4. Per-capita income 5. Poverty trap 6. Urban poverty 7. Rural poverty

B. Answer each of these questions in brief :

1. List out the negative impacts of urbanisation.
2. What information is obtained from Lorenz Curve and Gini Coefficient?
3. How does the World Bank catagorise extreme poverty in developing nations ?
4. What is MPI ?
5. How is per-capita income calculated ?

C. Answer each of these questions in detail—

1. Differentiate between relative and absolute poverty.
2. On what basis would you say a particular country is a developed nation ?
3. Explain each of these as an indicator of poverty-
   (a) Per capita income

People

    (b) Housing

    (c) Level of disease and nutrition

4. Explain the causes of poverty in developing countries.
5. Differentiate between urban and rural poverty with respect to the nature of job, job opportunities and basic amenties.
6. How are social evils and poverty linked to each other ?
7. How does poverty affect the environment ?
8. Enlist the effects of poverty trap.

WORKSHEET

A. Choose the most appropriate alternative for each of these statements :
1. Which of the following is a method to measure relative poverty ?
   (a) Gini coefficient
   (b) Lorenz curve
   (c) Both (a) and (b)
   (d) Poverty line
2. Poverty as defined by the World bank implies to the living below
   (a) $ 1.25 per day
   (b) $ 125 per day
   (c) $ 0.125 per day
   (d) $ 1250 per month
3. According to critical alternative views, what is poverty ?
   (a) A monetary condition brought about by people's own laziness.
   (b) A monetary condition where people do not have enough to satisfy basic needs.
   (c) A monetary and non-monetary condition where people lack access to community regulated common resources, opportunities, and income.
   (d) All of the options given are correct.
4. What could be the main cause of poverty in India ?
   (a) High income inequalities
   (b) Less job opportunities
   (c) High growth in population
   (d) All of these

B. Justify the following statements :
1. Poverty line may vary with time and place.
2. Usually in wealthy countries, poverty is not absolute.
3. Violence induces poverty.
4. Natural disasters affect the developing countries more than developed countries.

C. Read the following excerpts and answer the questions that follow. (open-ended questions) :
1. According to the World Bank, Poverty gap at $1.90 a day (2011 PPP) (%) in India was 4.30 as of 2011. Its highest value over the past 34 years was 20.15 in 1977, while its lowest value was 4.30 in 2011.

People

(a) What do you understand by the term poverty gap ?

(b) What could be the main reasons for poverty gap in India ?

D. Activities :

Collect information about the World bank and make a report on the same. Your report should have following information—

(a) What are the main goals of World bank ?

(b) What is the contribution of the World Bank in achieving the SDG (Sustainable Development Goals) ?

(c) Pick any instances where the World Bank has helped India in development.

10

URBANISATION

Migration is one of the distinguishing features of human beings that has been occurring since the very beginning of man's appearance in this universe. Human mobility was even present in the primitive times and people used to migrate in search of abundant food and in search of a safe living environment and protection from physical dangers. In modern age, migration has gained importance with the ushering of the era of industrialisation and urbanisation. Since the 19th century a rapid growth in technology and thus economy is seen. Such a development has induced urbanisation. Urbanisation has become a common feature and outcome of economic development. Urbanisation refers to the population shift from rural to urban areas and the ways in which society adapts to the changes. It is basically the process by which towns and cities are formed and become larger as more people begin living and working in central areas. More than half of the world's population lives in urban areas. Due to the ongoing urbanisation and growth of the world's population, there will be about 2.5 billion more people added to the urban population by 2050, mainly in Africa and Asia. Urbanisation is a process whereby populations move from rural to urban area, enabling cities and towns to grow. It can also be termed as the progressive increase of the number of people living in towns and cities. It is highly influenced by the notion that cities and towns have achieved better economic, political, and social mileages compared to the rural areas.

> **Fascinating Fact**
>
> By 2050, about 70% of the world's population is expected to live in urban areas.

The movement of people towards cities has accelerated in the past 40 years, particularly in the less-developed regions, and the share of the global population living in urban areas has increased from one third in 1960 to 47% (2.8 billion people) in 1999. The world's urban population is now growing by 60 million persons per year, about three times the increase in the rural population. Increased urbanisation results about equally from births in urban areas and from the continuous movement of people from the rural surrounding. These forces are also feeding the sprawl of urban areas as formerly rural peri-urban settlements become incorporated into nearby cities and as secondary cities, linked by commerce to larger urban centres, grow larger. The proportion of people in

Urbanisation

developing countries who live in cities has almost doubled since 1960 (from less than 22% to more than 40%), while in more developed regions the urban share has grown from 61% to 76%. There is a significant association between this population movement from rural to urban areas and declines in average family size. Asia and Africa remain the least urbanised of the developing regions (less than 38% each). Latin America and the Caribbean is more than 75% urban, a level almost equal to those in Europe, Northern America and Japan (all are between 75 and 79%). Urbanisation is projected to continue well into the next century. By 2030, it is expected that nearly 5 billion (61%) of the world's 8.1 billion people will live in cities.

10.0. PULL AND PUSH FACTORS

Urbanisation is the shift from a rural to an urban society, bringing a large concentration of people into towns and cities. This process usually occurs when a nation is still developing. The trend towards urbanization is a worldwide phenomenon. The main cause of global urbanisation is the new economic opportunities it brings to people and governments; however, it has both positive and negative effects on society.

Causes of Urbanisation

1. Industrialization

Industrialisation is a trend representing a shift from the old agricultural economies to novel non-agricultural economy, which creates a modernised society. Through industrial revolution, more people have been attracted to move from rural to urban areas on the account of improved employment opportunities. Industrialisation has increased employment opportunities by giving people the chance to work in modern sectors in job categories that aid to stir economic developments.

> **Fascinating Fact**
>
> Today, there are 13 mega cities in Asia, 4 in Latin America, and 2 each in Africa, Europe and Northern America.

2. Commercialisation

Commerce and trade play a major role in urbanisation. The distribution of goods and services and commercial transactions in the modern era has developed modern marketing institutions and exchange methods that have tremendously given rise to the growth of towns and cities. Commercialisation and trade comes with the general perception that the towns and cities offer better commercial opportunities and return as compared to the rural areas.

3. Social benefits and services

There are numerous social benefits attributed to life in the cities and towns. Examples include better educational facilities, better living standards, better sanitation and housing, better health care, better recreation facilities, and better social life in general. On this account, more and more people are prompted to migrate into cities and towns to obtain the wide variety of social benefits and services which are unavailable in the rural areas.

4. Employment opportunities

In cities and towns, there are ample job opportunities that continually draw people from the rural areas to seek better livelihood. Therefore, the majority of people frequently migrate into urban areas to access well paying jobs as urban areas have countless employment opportunities in all developmental sectors such as public health, education, transport, sports and recreation, industries, and business enterprises. Services and industries generate and increase higher value-added jobs, and this leads to more employment opportunities.

5. Modernisation and changes in the mode of living

Modernisation plays a very important role in the process of urbanisation. As urban areas become more technology savvy together with highly sophisticated communication, infrastructure, medical facilities, dressing code, enlightenment, liberalization, and other social amenities availability, people believe they can lead a happy life in cities. In urban areas, people also embrace changes in the modes of living namely residential habits, attitudes, dressing, food, and beliefs. As a result, people migrate to cities and the cities grow by absorbing the growing number of people day after day.

6. Rural urban transformation

As localities become more fruitful and prosperous due to the discovery of minerals, resource exploitation, or agricultural activities, cities start emerging as the rural areas transform to urbanism. The increase in productivity leads to economic growth and higher value-added employment opportunities. This brings about the need to develop better infrastructure, better education institutions, better health facilities, better transportation networks, establishment of banking institutions, better governance, and better housing. As this takes place, rural communities start to adopt the urban culture and ultimately become urban centres that continue to grow as more people move to such locations in search of a better life.

> **Fascinating Fact**
>
> Cities contribute to up to 70 per cent of the total greenhouse gas emissions.

People migrate for many different reasons. These reasons can be classified as economic, social, political or environmental :

a. **Economic migration**—moving to find work or follow a particular career path.

b. **Social migration**—moving somewhere for a better quality of life or to be closer to family or friends.

Urbanisation

   c. **Political migration**—moving to escape political persecution or war.
   d. **Environmental migration**—causes of migration include natural disasters such as flooding, cyclones etc.

> **Intext Questions**
> 1. Rapid growth in technology has induced urbanisation. Why ?
> 2. Why do you think migration of people to urban areas is more evident in developing nations ?
> 3. How does modern and fancy life in city influence people to migrate ?

Migration is broadly understood as a permanent or semi-permanent change of residence. In other words, migration may be defined as a form of relocation diffusion (the spread of people, ideas, innovations, behaviours, from one place to another), involving permanent moves to new locations. The reasons that people migrate are determined by push and pull factors, which are forces that either induce people to move to a new location, or oblige them to leave old residences. These could be economic, political, cultural, and environmental.

Push factors are conditions that can force people to leave their homes and are related to the country from which a person migrates. Push factors include non-availability of enough livelihood opportunities, poverty, rapid population growth that surpasses available resources. Pull factors are exactly the opposite of push factors.

Push factors are the reasons why people leave an area. They include :

   a. lack of services
   b. lack of safety
   c. high crime
   d. crop failure
   e. drought
   f. flooding
   g. poverty
   h. war

Pull factors are the reasons why people move to a particular area. They include :

   a. higher employment
   b. more wealth
   c. better services
   d. good climate
   e. safer, less crime
   f. political stability

g. more fertile land

h. lower risk from natural hazards

Migration usually happens as a result of a combination of these push and pull factors.

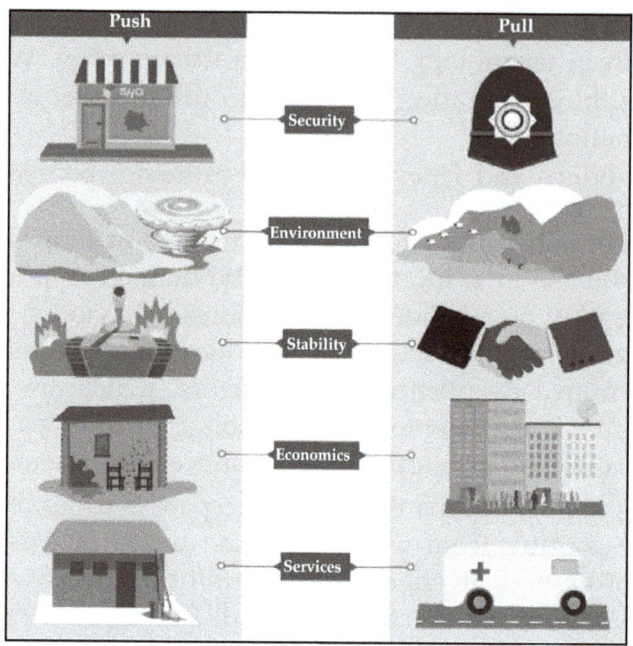

10.1. MANIFESTATIONS OF URBANISATION

Urbanisation is closely linked to modernisation, industrialisation and the sociological process of rationalisation. But the picture of urbanisation is not so much glorious as it apparently seems. Modern cities have grown in a haphazard and unplanned manner. Cities in developing countries become overpopulated and overcrowded. The process of rapid urbanisation poses serious challenge to towns and cities, which are struggling to provide and maintain the already inadequate level of urban services. Besides air and water pollution, the cities are facing growing volume of wastes. Following effects can be seen in overpopulated cities—

1. Growth of slums—Urban slums are settlements, neighbourhood, or city regions that cannot provide the basic living conditions necessary for its inhabitants, or slum dwellers, to live in a safe and healthy environment. Slum houses are devoid of permanent houses, sufficient living space, access to safe water, adequate sanitation and security. Urbanisation is one of factors leading to slum creation in the cities. Due to urbanisation, a greater demand for housing is created. With rapid increase in urban population, the capacity to

> **Fascinating Fact**
>
> Almost 180,000 people are added to the urban population each day.

Urbanisation

cope with the diverse demands for infrastructural provision to meet economic and social needs is hampered. Not only strategic planning and intervention are major issues in agenda to manage rapid urbanisation, but city governments are not effectively linking the economic development trajectory to implications for urban growth and, hence, housing needs. The fast urbanisation in combination with industrialisation has resulted in the enlargement of slums. The explosion of slums occurs due to many factors, such as, the lack of developed land for housing, the high prices of land beyond the reach of urban poor, a large influx of rural migrants to the cities in search of jobs.

2. Growth of informal sector—The informal sector, informal economy, or grey economy is the part of an economy that is neither taxed nor monitored by any form of government. The wages or salary offered by the informal sectors are usually low and unstructured. In addition to low wages, the employees working in informal sectors have to face following difficulties—

(a) Little or no job security.

(b) Unprotected by labour laws.

(c) Odd working hours.

(d) No pension, insurance or health insurance scheme.

Due to mass increased population in the cities, competition for the existing jobs is also enormous. Thus, people end up working in informal sectors.

3. Pressure on civic amenities—Civic amenities include facilities provided by the government to public like water supply, electricity, transport services, health services, waste disposal, etc. The growing urban centres and the process of urbanisation have brought in many issues to the front; from governance and management of these areas to the provision of basic civic services. Consequently, it resulted in heavy pressure on civic amenities. Urbanisation poses major challenge to transport system. Transport problem increases and becomes more complex as the town grows in dimension. Water is also one of the most essential elements of nature to maintain life and right from the beginning of urban civilisation. However, supply of water will start falling short of demand as the cities grow in size and number. Urban centres in India are almost consistently affected with inadequate sewage facilities. Most cities do not have proper arrangements for treating the sewerage waste and it is drained into a nearly river. Urbanisation pushed Indian cities to grow in number and size and as a result people have to face the problem of trash disposal which is in alarming stage. Enormous quantities of garbage produced by Indian cities cause a serious health problem. Most cities do not have proper arrangements for garbage disposal and the existing landfills are full to the edge. Thus, there is a lot of pressure on the government to take a control over providing these civic amenities to the residents of the cities.

4. Degradation of human resources—As we know the crime rates are high in urbans areas. Crime in the city can create a sense of insecurity in its inhabitants.

This unsafe feeling in city streets separates residential areas into higher-income and lower-income groups, which reduces the sense of community and forms areas with dissimilar incomes, costs and security levels. The lifestyle of urban residents is way busy than the rural people. Fast lifestyle, heavy work load, pressure of competition, tension of job insecurity could be the reasons for many uneasiness like depression, stress and anxiety. Disturbed mental condition affects the general health. Unhealthy body is not very productive. Therefore, this is a vicious circle. Insecurity leads to mental disturbance, mental disturbance affects health, health affects productivity and due to failure in performing unhappiness is caused.

5. Growing sense of despair—Large-scale migration to urban centres has, in many cases, led to social fragmentation and profound feelings of isolation and despair. People migrate to urban areas in order to improve the quality of their life in terms of gaining better facilities and/or financial conditions. However, these residents face other issues like stress, health issues due to poor environment quality, work pressure, busy life, etc. these factors lead to sense of despair. Many people realise that they are missing peace, family bonding and emotional support from friends and family in their lives. Growing sense of despair is one of the outcome of living in such conditions. Research shows that the number of people suffering from depression, anxiety and stress are much more in urban areas compared to rural areas. The migrants and rural poor who are responsible for urbanization tend to settle in the slums. They also face discrimination to various social, political and economic reasons.

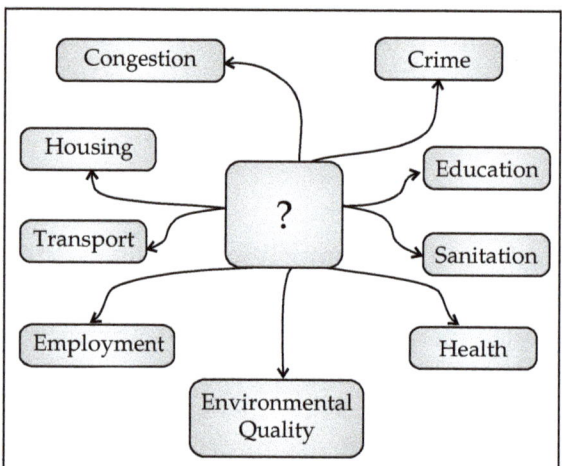

The diagram given above shows negative as well positive impacts of a certain types of change. Do you think you can identify one main cause of these impacts ?

? Intext Questions

1. List out the difficulties faced by employees working in informal sector.
2. What is the difference between permanent and temporary migration ?
3. Why do most of the urban residents lead a busy compared to rural residents ?
4. The number of people suffering from depression, anxiety and stress are much more in urban areas compared to rural areas. Why ?

Urbanisation

10.2. SOCIAL, ECONOMIC AND ENVIRONMENTAL ISSUES OF URBANISATION

Urban populations interact with their environment. Urban people change their environment through their consumption of food, energy, water, and land. And in turn, the polluted urban environment affects the health and quality of life of the urban population. Poor air and water quality, insufficient water availability, waste disposal problems, and high energy consumption are exacerbated by the increasing population density and demands of urban environments. Strong city planning will be essential in managing these and other difficulties as the world's urban areas swell.

1. Problems of housing

Urbanisation attracts people to cities and towns which leads to high population increase. With the increase in the number of people living in urban centres, there is continous scarcity of houses. This is due to insufficient expansion space for housing and public utilities, poverty, unemployment, and costly building materials which can only be afforded by few individuals. Due to continuous pressure of population living in urban centres, there is a continuous scarcity of houses. This is mainly due to insufficient expansion space for housing and public utilities, poverty, unemployment and also costly building materials that can be afforded only by few rich individuals.

2. Congestion

Overcrowding leads to a constant problem of scarcity of houses in urban areas. The major factors for housing problems are lack of building materials and financial resources, insufficient expansion of public utilities into sub-urban areas, poverty and unemployment of urban immigrants, strong caste and family ties and lack of enough transportation to suburban areas where most of the available land for new construction is to be found.

 **Fascinating Fact**

In the 1800s, only 2% of the world's population was urbanised.

Overcrowding is a consistent result of overpopulation in urban areas. It is obviously expected that cities are increasing their size due to massive movement of people from undeveloped areas but it squeezed in a small space due to overcrowding.

3. Pollution

Due to urbanisation, there is environmental degradation especially in the quality of water, air and noise. The domestic waste, industrial effluents and other wastes that are dumped directly to the river, degrade the water quality. Another after-effect of rapid urbanisation is the air pollution which has also increased due to emanation from motor vehicles, industrial development and use of non-environmental friendly fuel sources. As the number of people increases in urban areas then the demand of food, clothes and other materials increases due to which more industries come up to supply their needs. More people use more fuel which adds to more pollution. The noise pollution is produced from the various human actions which also degrade the environment and ultimately affect the human health. In addition, lots of artificial lights in the form of sky glow, glare, light trespass, street lights, advertising boards are installed in the city areas. This causes light pollution.

4. Loss of agricultural land

The cultivated land across India has fragmented significantly resulting in change in land use. The agricultural land has continued to shrink due to rapid urbanisation. Steep increase in urban population is seen which impacts the environment and results in the loss of arable land. Expansion of urban landscape has affected the food production in multiple ways; age-old farming land has been altered, traditional practice of farming from farmers and family farms have decreased due to migration to urban areas. Agriculture is crucial in terms of employment and food security. In the growing population it's important to conserve and protect the potential farmlands.

5. Provision of services

In our daily life, we require services like transport, health care, education, banking, etc. Due to overpopulation there is always a congestion and crowd at all these places. Therefore, city dwellers are to make good use of these services. In cities the number of transport facilities (bus, trains, metros, auto-rickshaw), hospitals, clinics, schools, colleges, universities, banks are exponentially high compared to villages and small towns. Yet, availing these services is easier, simpler and less time-consuming in small towns.

6. Overcrowding

Overcrowding is a situation whereby a huge number of people live in a small space. This form of congestion in urban areas is consistent because of overpopulation and it is an aspect that increases day by day as more people and immigrants move into cities and towns in search of better life. Most people from rural or undeveloped areas always have the urge of migrating into the city that normally leads to congestion of people within a small area.

7. Unemployment

The problem of joblessness is highest in urban areas and it is even higher among the educated people. It is estimated that more than half of unemployed youths around the globe live in metropolitan cities. And, as much as income in urban areas is high, the costs of living make the incomes to seem horribly low. The increasing relocation of people from rural or developing areas to urban areas is the leading cause of urban unemployment.

Urbanisation

8. Development of slums

The cost of living in urban areas is very high. When this is combined with random and unexpected growth as well as unemployment, there is the spread of unlawful resident settlements represented by slums and squatters. The growth of slums and squatters in urban areas is even further exacerbated by fast-paced industrialisation, lack of developed land for housing, large influx of rural immigrants to the cities in search of better life, and the elevated prices of land beyond the reach of the urban poor.

9. Water and sanitation problems

Due to overpopulation and rapid population increase in most urban centres, it is common to find there are inadequate sewage facilities. Municipalities and local governments are faced with serious resource crisis in the management of sewage facilities. As a result, sanitation becomes poor and sewages flow chaotically, and they are drained into neighbouring streams, rivers, lakes, or seas. Eventually, communicable diseases such as typhoid, dysentery, plague and diarrhoea spread very fast leading to suffering and even deaths. Overcrowding also highly contributes to water scarcity as supply falls short of demand.

10. Poor health and spread of diseases

The social and economic living conditions in congested urban areas affect access and utilisation of public health care services. Slum areas in particular experience poor sanitation and insufficient water supply which generally make slum populations susceptible to communicable diseases. The environmental problems such as urban pollution also cause many health problems namely allergies, asthma, infertility, food poisoning, cancer and even premature deaths.

11. Traffic congestion

When more people move to towns and cities, one of the major challenges posed is in the transport system. More people means increased number of vehicles which leads to traffic congestion and vehicular pollution. Many people in urban areas drive to work and this creates a severe traffic problem, especially during the rush hours. Also as the cities grow in dimension, people will move to shop and access other social needs or wants which often cause traffic congestion and blockage.

12. Urban crime

Issues of lack of resources, overcrowding, unemployment, poverty and lack of social services and education habitually lead to many social problems including violence, drug abuse and crime. Most of the crimes such as murder, rape, kidnapping, riots, assault, theft, robbery and hijacking are reported to be more prominent in the urban vicinities. Besides, poverty related crimes are the highest in fast-growing urban regions. These acts of urban crime normally upset the tranquility of cities or towns.

While the process of urbanisation occurs at a global scale, it is more evident in the developing cities. Moving forward, the government should consider the impacts towards the social and environmental aspect. A sustainable city should be built. Building a sustainable city requires proper planning and immense strategy. But it ensures a better living place for everyone.

SUMMARY

- Urbanisation refers to the population shift from rural to urban areas and the ways in which society adapts to the changes.
- Migration is broadly understood as a permanent or semi-permanent change of residence.
- The reasons that people migrate are determined by push and pull factors, which are forces that either induce people to move to a new location, or oblige them to leave old residences.
- Push factors are conditions that can force people to leave their homes and are related to the country from which a person migrates. The pull factors attract people to a certain location.
- The effects of urbanisation are—growing slum, growth of informal sector, pressure on civic amenities and growing sense of despair.
- Urbanisation is also responsible for economic, environmental and social issues in the city.
- Modernisation plays a very important role in the process of urbanisation.
- The informal sector, informal economy, or grey economy is the part of an economy that is neither taxed nor monitored by any form of government.
- Overcrowding leads to a constant problem of scarcity of houses in urban areas.
- The acts of urban crime normally upset tranquility of cities or towns.

EXERCISE

A. Define each of these terms :
1. Urbanisation
2. Migration
3. Overcrowding
4. Pollution

B. Answer these questions in brief :
1. What is relocation diffusion ?
2. What are slums ?
3. Why do people work in informal sectors ?

Urbanisation

4. List out some important civic amenities.
5. What do you understand by the term 'sustainable city' ?
6. Enlist the points of difference between the pull and push factors.
7. What is the difference between population growth and population change ?

C. Answer each of these in detail :

1. How has urbanisation affected each of the following ?
   (a) Growing slums
   (b) Growth of informal sector
   (c) Growing sense of despair
   (d) Pressure of civic amenities
   (e) Loss of agricultural land
   (f) Pollution
   (g) Overcrowding
2. Explain the categories of motives leading to migration in terms economy, political, environmental and social factors.

WORKSHEET

A. Choose the most appropriate option from the following :

1. All of the following are reasons for urbanisation except:
   a. Rent is more affordable in urban areas
   b. Urban areas have better healthcare and educational facilities
   c. There are more jobs available in urban areas
   d. There are more opportunities for entertainment in urban areas
2. A person moves to another country to study for a few years and then returns home. This is an example of :
   a. Short-term migration
   b. Long-term migration
   c. Rural to urban migration
   d. Annual migration
3. Which of the following statements about urban areas is NOT true ?
   a. There is traffic congestion
   b. Public utilities are not readily available
   c. There are higher crime rates
   d. Slums often develop in and around urban areas

B. Justify these statements :

1. Urbanisation has remarkably increased after 19th century.
2. Garbage disposal is a major problem in cities.
3. Research shows that the number of people suffering from depression, anxiety and stress are much more in urban areas compared to rural areas.
4. Air quality of villages is better than that of urban area.
5. Expansion of urban landscape has affected the food production in multiple ways.

C. Read the following excerpts and answer the questions that follow. (open-ended questions) :

1. Life in the city can be taxing. City dwellers often face higher rates of crime, pollution, social isolation. Why do you think social isolation is faced by city dwellers ? Also comment on social isolation and despair in rural residents.
2. Make a comparative chart showing the positive and negative impacts of urbanisation.

Urbanisation

D. Activity :

1. Interview your family members, neighbours and/or teachers and make a report on their experience about migration. Your report should consist of following information—
   (a) Reasons for migration
   (b) Challenges faced during initial period
   (c) Benefits reaped due to migration.

11. AGRICULTURE

Food is one of the primary needs of human beings. In order to provide food for a large population, regular production, proper management and distribution of food is necessary. Food enriches us with nutrients like proteins, carbohydrates, fats, vitamins and minerals, all of which we require for body development, growth and health. The major sources of food for us are both plants and animals. We obtain most of this food from agriculture and animal husbandry. Till 10,000 B.C. man was a nomad. He kept wandering in groups from place to place in search of food and shelter. He ate raw fruits and vegetables and started hunting for animals for food. After many years, he was able to cultivate land and produce food crops. Thus, the term, 'Agriculture' came into existence. Each type of crop has its own criteria. Climate, soil, irrigation pattern, type of fertilizer or manure are a few of them. Agriculture is the cultivation of land and breeding of animals and plants to provide food, fibre, medicinal plants and other products to sustain and enhance life. The word agriculture is derived from a Latin word- 'ager' or 'agri' meaning soil, and 'culture' meaning cultivation of the soil. In modern terms, agriculture comprises "the art and science of cultivating the soil, growing crops and rearing livestock." Large scale crop production is a very challenging task. It requires a lot of efforts, investment and strategic planning. Continuous efforts are being made to ensure food security. This becomes a challenging task when the population is so huge. Also, simply increasing grain production for storage in warehouses cannot solve the problem of malnutrition and hunger. People should have money to purchase food. Food security depends on both availability of food and access to it. The majority of our population depends on agriculture for their livelihood. Increasing the incomes of people working in agriculture is therefore necessary to combat the problem of hunger. Scientific management practices should be undertaken to obtain high yields from farms. Farming can be broadly classified into two categories, *i.e.*, subsistence farming and commercial farming. Subsistence Farming is the farming which is done for consumption of the farm owners, can be either Primitive or Intensive. Here the only aim is to fulfil the needs of the farmer and his family. When farmers grow crops and rear animals for economic activity, it becomes Commercial Farming.

Agriculture

11.0. UNSUSTAINABLE PATTERNS OF MODERN INDUSTRIALISED AGRICULTURE

Industrial agriculture refers to a process of mechanising the growing, harvesting, and processing of food. The goal of industrialised agriculture is to increase crop yield. Crop yield is defined as the amount of food that is produced for each unit of land. Crops and livestock made through this type of agriculture are produced to feed the masses and the products are sold worldwide. In order to increase the crop yield, a certain set of farming methods are used. These farming methods include use of mechanised tools, irrigation systems, pesticides, fertilizers, monoculture. However, these methods may enable maximum yield, but are unsustainable methods.

(i) Monoculture farming—It is the raising of a single crop within a specified area. This is in contrast to the traditional method of farming, which relied on multiple crops being planted within a specific area. Monoculture farming eliminates biological controls provided by mixed crop gardening and it also causes soil degradation. In a traditional farm, different plant species require different levels of nutrients and many also replace depleted nutrients. Traditional crops are grown by local farmers. These seeds are highly adapted to the local climatic and geographical conditions. But they do not give enough yield to feed to the entire population of the nation. The advantages and disadvantages of monocultures well known as traditional farming are listed below—

Advantages of monoculture

a. **Large scale crop yield**—By continuously growing only one crop, a farmer can develop the best farm practice to achieve high yields. Crops grown are adopted on certain environmental conditions, such as drought, saline soils, or high temperatures, helps maintain a sustainable yield.

b. **Minimised cost**—By cultivating the same species, the farmers can optimise their operations. As the growing requirements, planting, maintenance and harvesting will be the same across the farmed land, greater yield can be obtained at a lower cost.

c. **High efficiency**—Crops that are best suited for the land can be planted so that soil and climate specificities such as winds, droughts or a short growing season, do not impact the yield as much. This helps to maximise the efficiency of farming processes.

d. **Simplicity**—A monoculture field is a very simple system. Soil preparation, irrigation and chemical inputs can all be focused on the needs and preferences of a single plant species. This allows the field to be heavily specialised towards producing maximum yields for a specific crop. Pests and diseases can be treated without considering the effects of the treatment on any other plants. The uniformity of a monoculture field is especially important in harvesting, since the desirable parts of a plant can be easily collected using straightforward techniques which would often be highly destructive to other crops sharing the same field.

Disadvantages of monoculture

a. **High use of pesticides**—Monoculture encourages increase usage of pesticides to boost the crop yield. Impacts of overuse of pesticides on environment is significant.

b. **Susceptibility to pests**—Monoculture promotes pest infestation. As there is no biodiversity to mitigate these effects, and the pests can so easily obtain food and multiply, the pests can infest an entire monoculture.

c. **Environmental pollution**—As we know, the objective of monoculture is to achieve high yield and reap high profits in the market. Thus, various measures are implemented to boost the crop yield. Such methods may have effect on environment in the form of pollution, acid rain, global warming and contamination.

d. **Loss of biodiversity**—Farmers are interested in growing commercially important crops. Thus, cultivation of traditional and indigenous crop varieties is ignored. Therefore, loss of biodiversity is one of the effects of monoculture. Loss of biodiversity is not only with respect to crops, but also the organisms dependent on them. The diversity of pollination insects, soil bacteria, symbiont organisms and herbivores which are dependant on those crops are also lost.

e. **Disappearance of traditional crop varieties**—Since the rise of modern agriculture, many farmers have been replacing traditional local crop varieties with a smaller number of newly developed or foreign ones, and have adopted the practice of monocropping on a large scale. As a result, significant loss in agricultural biodiversity is seen. Since traditional crop varieties have been selected and cultivated by local farmers over generations, they are usually well adapted to local environmental conditions. The production output of traditional crop varieties is rather stable and they are highly risk-resilient. They are also less dependent on external inputs. Moreover, traditional crop varieties meet local tastes and food preferences and are also connected with local culture and traditional customs.

Intext Questions

1. Name the two main categories of farming.
2. What makes monoculture field a simple system?
3. Why is monoculture agriculture less expensive than the traditional agriculture?
4. Why should we conserve traditional crops?

Agriculture

Pollution caused due to agriculture : Use of pesticides and inorganic fertilizers

Plants require nutrients for their growth and development. These nutrients can be classified as micronutrients and macronutrients. The macronutrients are obtained from air and water. The micronutrients are the minerals which are absorbed from the soil. Fertilizers and manures are added to the soil to add the nutritive value to the soil. Fertilizers are commercially produced plant nutrients. Fertilizers supply nitrogen, phosphorus and potassium. They ensure good vegetative growth (leaves, branches and flowers), giving rise to healthy plants. Manure is prepared by the decomposition of animal excreta and plant waste. Manure helps in enriching soil with nutrients and organic matter and increasing soil fertility. Fertilizers should be applied carefully in terms of proper dose, time, and observing pre and post-application precautions for their complete utilisation. The excess fertilizers are not fully absorbed by the plants and get washed away due to excessive irrigation. Further it flows into the nearby water source like a lake, river or pond, then leads to water pollution. The continuous use of fertilizers in an area can destroy soil fertility because the organic matter in the soil is not replenished and microorganisms in the soil are harmed by the fertilizers used. On the other hand, manure enriches the soil with nutrients and organic matter and increasing soil fertility. The bulk of organic matter in manure helps in improving the soil structure. This involves increasing the water holding capacity in sandy soils. In clayey soils, the large quantities of organic matter help in drainage and in avoiding water logging. In addition to soil pollution, biomagnification is also caused due to excessive use of fertilisers and pesticides.

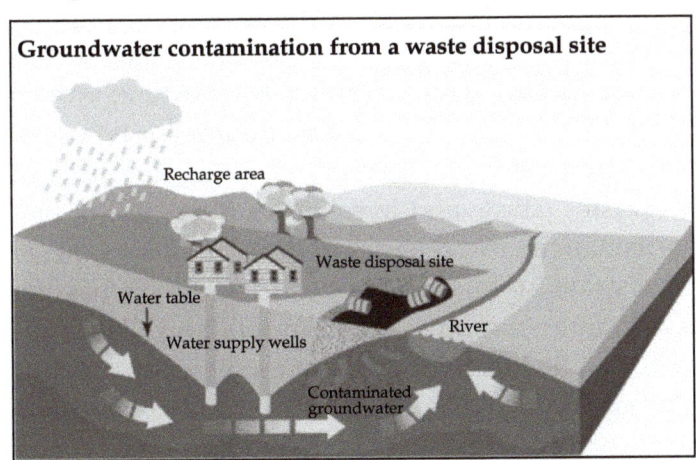

Groundwater contamination from a waste disposal site

The accelerated use of agricultural chemicals over the past 20 to 30 years has profitably increased production but has also had an adverse impact on ground water quality in many of the major agricultural areas of the world. The pollution of ground water, related to nitrogen fertilizers and pesticides, from widespread, routine land application, as well as point sources has become a serious concern. Excess fertilizers that are not absorbed by the plants, stay in the soil. When it rains, the unabsorbed fertilizers are washed away and get accumulated in the nearby water bodies. The nutrients from the fertilizers like nitrogen, potassium and phosphorus cause many adverse effects. Runoff of pesticide leads to contamination of surface water and biota. Some pesticides and fertilizers may also leach into groundwater.

Biomagnification is the process in which toxins are concentrated in an organism as larger animals continue to eat smaller animals. This process moves toxins up the food chain to larger organisms and is of particular concern with regards to concentrating dangerous toxins in larger species. Thus, the farmer has to think about the short-term and long-term benefits before choosing the fertilizing agents. The concept of organic farming is quite popular nowadays. Organic farming is a farming system with minimal or no use of chemicals as fertilizers, herbicides, pesticides etc. and with a maximum input of organic manures, recycled farm wastes (straw and livestock excreta), use of bio-agents such as culture of blue green algae in preparation of biofertilizers, neem leaves or turmeric specifically in grain storage as bio-pesticides, with healthy cropping systems [mixed cropping, inter-cropping and crop rotation]. The crops grown in this method have proven to be healthier as there are no contaminants in it. However, organic farming has its own advantages and disadvantages.

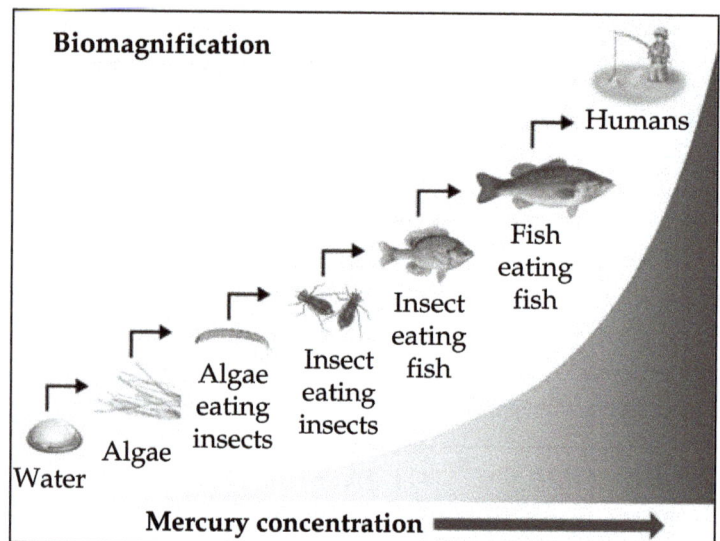

Advantages

1. It creates higher natural levels of resistance to pests and disease.
2. This farming process supports a healthier soil and supports pollinators.
3. Organic food is pure and devoid of chemicals in the form of pesticides, fertilizers and hormones which are artificially injected.
4. The working environment for organic farmers is healthier.

Agriculture

5. Organic farmers can often create their own fertilizers at their farming location.
6. It can be implemented in almost any geographic location or growing season.

Disadvantages

1. There are no subsidies offered for most organic farmers.
2. It requires more work to produce goods that are ready for sale.
3. Organic farmers must have specific knowledge about localised growing systems.
4. There are unique marketing challenges in place for organic goods.
5. It usually costs more to be competitive with organic farming.
6. Organic crops generally spoil faster.

> **Fascinating Fact**
> Organic farming typically requires 2.5 times more labour than conventional farming.

(ii) Irrigation—Water source is generally classified into two groups: surface water and groundwater. Groundwater is located underground in large aquifers and must be pumped out of the ground after drilling a deep well. Surface water is found in lakes, rivers and streams and is drawn into the public water supply by an intake. For irrigation purposes, we depend on both the sources of water.

Majority of the successful yield depends on the rainfall. Irrigation is the application of controlled amounts of water to plants at needed intervals. Irrigation helps to grow agricultural crops, maintain landscapes, and revegetate disturbed soils in dry areas and during periods of less than average rainfall. Some common types of irrigation are as follows—

1. Wells—Wells are of two types *i.e.*, dug wells and tube wells. In dug wells, the water is drawn using a strata while in tube wells, the water is lifted by pumps.

2. Canals—Canals receive water from river and then it is distributed to nearby fields.

3. River lift system—In this method, water is directly taken from the river. Lift irrigation schemes are either individually owned or owned by a group of farmers in a cooperative mode. This system is adopted when canal flow is insufficient or irregular due to inadequate reservoir release.

4. Tanks—Tanks are small water reservoirs. The water stored is used for different purposes like irrigation, domestic use, industrial use, etc. Tanks can be made up of ceramic, cement or plastic. It can be also of different sizes and volumes.

5. Sprinklers—Sprinkler irrigation is a method of applying irrigation water which is similar to rainfall. Water is distributed through a system of pipes usually by pumping. It is then sprayed into the air and irrigated entire soil surface through spray heads so that it breaks up into small water drops which fall to the ground.

6. Drip irrigation—A network of pipe is laid near the roots of the crops. Small nozzles are fixed along the length of this network of pipes. Water flows from these nozzles.

The water source for all these irrigation methods is either groundwater or nearby water body like river or lake. Though irrigation has a very crucial purpose in agriculture, it has impacted the environment. The environmental effects of irrigation are prominently seen in soil and water. Some of the impacts are listed below—

a. Reduction in downstream river flow

b. Increased evaporation in the river area

c. Water logging

e. Soil salination

e. Disturbance in the aquatic ecosystem

f. When more groundwater is pumped from wells than replenished, storage of water in the aquifer is being mined and the use of that water is no longer sustainable.

Intext Questions

1. Why should we use proper protective clothes and accessories while applying fertilizers or pesticides to the crops?
2. What is the difference between tube well and dug well?
3. Name any three healthy cropping systems.
4. Write one advantage of river-lift irrigation system.

It may be noted that, using irrigation facility judiciously is very important. Often, water is not used cautiously. Lots of water is wasted in the farms and fields due to faulty irrigation methods or just ignorance. Such a wastage of water is responsible for the environmental impacts that are listed above.

11.1. ENVIRONMENTAL DAMAGE DUE TO LARGE FARM UNITS

Agriculture is essential for producing food. It is an important source of livelihood because it is the process of producing food, feed, fibre and many other desired products by the cultivation of certain plants and the raising of domesticated animals (livestock). Modern agriculture is an evolving approach to agricultural innovations and farming practices that help farmers increase efficiency and reduce the number of natural resources like water, land, and energy necessary to meet the world's food, fuel, and fibre needs. Modern agriculture improved our affordability of food, increases the food supply, ensured the food

Agriculture

safety, increases the sustainability and also produces more biofuels. But at the same time it has shown a few negative impacts on the environment—

1. Pollution—In order to enhance agricultural production quantity and quality, several chemicals in the form of fertilizers and pesticides to the soil are used in farming. These chemicals end up as pollutants in water run-off from the soil. This run-off can adversely affect more people and animal wildlife. Large scale agriculture accompanied by intensive use of chemicals in the form of pesticides and fertilizers is one of major causes of surface and groundwater pollution.

2. Soil Degradation—In all ecosystems, the biodiversity held in soil is massive. Healthy soils are vital to creating ample food production. Although agriculture is not the sole cause of soil degradation, poor farming practices are known to cause a considerable decline in the quality of soil. This mainly results from pesticide contamination, water logging and salting. Soil erosion leads to loss of soil fertility and structure. Excessive water supply and wind removes the top fertile layer of the farm. Loss of nutrient rich soil not only reduces productivity, but also results in silting of water bodies and streams and induces release of soil carbon from particulate organic material.

3. Deforestation—Forests are crucial to us as they produce vital oxygen and provide homes for people and wildlife. Many of the world's most threatened and endangered animals live in forests, and we too rely on benefits forests offer, including food, fresh water, clothing, traditional medicine and shelter. But forests around the world are under threat from deforestation, jeopardizing these benefits. One of the reasons for deforestation is agriculture. Deforestation enhances the effects of climate change. Destruction of habitat amongst species also leads to fragmentation and depletion. Extensive deforestation affects the water cycle, which results in interferences with precipitation. 70% of the world's plants and animals that live in forests are losing their habitats due to deforestation, ultimately leading to species extinction.

4. Eutrophication—When the water runoff with chemical fertilizers reaches to the nearby water body small water plants grow in excess known as Algal Bloom. These chemicals act as nutrients for the algae to flourish. The algae form a cover on the surface of water. It prevents or stops intermixing of atmospheric oxygen to dissolved oxygen in water. The water plants and animals start dying due to lack of oxygen. The dead parts will deposit at the bottom of the water body. Once these algae and other aquatic organisms die, they serve as food for decomposers. A lot of oxygen in the water body gets used up. The process continues and cause threat to the waterbody. The process is known as Eutrophication.

5. Global warming—The base chemicals that are used to create pesticides can be harmful to the environment even before they are combined with other chemicals to create pesticides. For example, Nitrogen oxide is a gas that blocks sunlight and traps heat. This gas is released by Nitrogen-based fertilizers which release a significant unnatural amounts of nitrogen oxide into the atmosphere causing the greenhouse effect which results in further global warming. On the other hand, pesticides can attach themselves to dust particles and travel away from their intended destinations to other unintended places. This increases the likelyhood of these chemicals mixing with other chemicals. Some pesticides produce volatile organic compounds that pollute the atmosphere when they react with other chemicals. This reaction produces tropospheric ozone. Ozone traps heat and further contributes to global warming. Agriculture is often the reason for deforestation and a change in land use, from natural ecosystems that take up and store carbon dioxide from the atmosphere, to farmland. Deforestation is also a reason for global warming. It is estimated that at least 14% of global greenhouse gas emissions come directly from the farm sector.

6. Climate change—Countries are increasingly recognising the contributions of agriculture to climate change. The agriculture sector was the second largest emitter in 2011. It is estimated around 75% of global deforestation comes from agriculture, mostly in developing countries. As we know, following are the impacts of global warming—

a. Heat waves

b. Drought

Agriculture

   c. Melting of ice caps
   d. Floods
   e. Rising sea levels
   f. Rise in temperature of oceans and other water bodies
   g. Acidifying of oceans

11.2. FOOD MOUNTAINS IN DEVELOPED COUNTRIES

Surplus and Waste

Surplus food is the agricultural produce or a quantity of food grown by a nation or area in excess than its needs. On the other hand, waste food is the food that is not intended to be consumed by the consumer due to various reasons. The amount of surplus food and waste food generated are result of faulty planning and execution.

Achieving adequate food security is arguably a necessary first step towards the alleviation of poverty and hunger and sustainable economic growth. According to the Food and Agriculture Organization of the United Nation, "Food security exists when all people, at all times, have physical, social, and economic access to sufficient, safe, and nutritious food that meets their dietary needs and food preferences for an active and healthy life. Food insecurity exists when people do not have adequate physical, social, or economic access to food as defined above." Population explosion, climate change, depletion of natural resources and imbalance in food distribution are major causes which affect food security. The United Nations Food and Agriculture Organization estimates that about 795 million people of the 7.3 billion people in the world, were suffering from chronic undernourishment in the year 2014 to 2016. Out of 795 million, a big majority of around 780 million people population is from developing and underdeveloped countries. This clearly depicts imbalance in food distribution or supply. It would be ironical to observe that as millions are not provided with adequate amounts of food while others have so much that obesity becomes an issue. Around 1.02 billion people are suffering from chronic hunger, while obesity rates are constantly rising in developed countries. Food security is an assembly of food availability, food access and food use. Food waste or food loss is food that is discarded or lost uneaten. The causes of food waste or loss are numerous and occur at the stages of producing, processing, retailing and consuming. The reasons for food wastage are enlisted below—

   a. In food processing industry, overcooking, production trials, packaging defects, trial runs, and wrong sizes and weights are some of the aspects resulting in imperfection and the eventual rejection of the foods.
   b. Most restaurants, hotels and the food service industry alike have a tendency of over-preparing or producing food.

c. Inappropriate or inadequate food storage facilities leads to food spoilage. The spoilt food has to be disposed.

d. Sometimes people buy lots of food without appropriately making plans on when and how the food will be prepared for consumption.

Food is an important commodity. It is irrational to waste it. Food is obtained from nature (plants or animals). By wasting food, we are actually wasting an important natural resource. Following are the consequences of food wastage :

a. **Biodiversity loss**—In order to maximise agricultural yields, farmers have increasingly invaded wild areas in search for more fertile lands which has led to loss of biodiversity. The reason for this is that practices such as slash and burn, deforestation, and conversion of wild areas into farm lands have destroyed the natural habitats for birds, fish, mammals and amphibians. Agricultural practices such as monocropping have also compounded biodiversity loss.

b. **Wastage of fertile lands**—According to research, the produced but unconsumed food accounts for approximately 1.4 billion hectares of land, constituting almost 1/3 of the planet's agricultural land.

c. **Wastage of water**—The volume of water used in agricultural food production is immense. Therefore, if 30% of all the food produced goes to waste, then it means that more than 30 percent of freshwater used in the production and processing of food also goes to waste.

e. **Carbon emission**—The fuel burnt in processing these food products are also wasted.

e. In addition to the environmental impacts, food wastage also results in direct economic costs.

> **Fascinating Fact**
>
> People in developing countries often spend 60-80% of their income on food.
> 75% of the world's food is generated from only 12 plants and 5 animal species.
> Grains make up 45% of the world's diet.

The major solution to control food wastage is to plan our requirement. Foremost, precedence should be centred on balancing food production with demand to reduce the problem of food wastage. The first thing is to cut back on the use of natural resources in food production. In hotels, restaurants and the food service industry, risk management tools can be applied.

Intext Questions

1. On which factors do food security depend ?
2. How does deforestation lead to loss of biodiversity ?
3. How does agriculture lead to global warming ?

Agriculture

11.3. GREEN REVOLUTION

The Green Revolution is a set of research and technology transfer initiatives that increased agricultural production worldwide, particularly in the developing world. This technology came into implementation in the year 1950. The initiatives resulted in the adoption of new technologies, including high-yielding varieties (HYVs) of cereals, in association with chemical fertilizers and agro-chemicals, and with controlled water-supply (usually involving irrigation) and new methods of cultivation, including mechanization. The three basic elements of green revolution are—

1. Continuing expansion of farming
2. Double-cropping in the existing farmland
3. Using seeds with improved genetics

The Green Revolution was a technology package comprising material components of improved high yielding varieties of two staple cereals (rice and wheat), irrigation or controlled water supply and improved moisture utilization, fertilizers, and pesticides, and associated management skills.

Benefits of Green Revolution

In 1961, India was on the brink of mass famine. Punjab was selected by the Indian government to be the first site to try the new crops because of its reliable water supply and a history of agricultural success. India began its own Green Revolution program of plant breeding, irrigation development and financing of agrochemicals. The Green Revolution resulted in a grain output of about 131 million tonnes in the year 1978-79. This

established India as one of the world's biggest agricultural producers. The crop area under high yielding varieties of wheat and rice grew considerably during the Green Revolution. The Green Revolution also created plenty of jobs not only for agricultural workers but also for industrial workers by the creation of related facilities such as factories and hydroelectric power stations. Benefits of Green Revolution are detailed below—

1. Helps to carry out agricultural process on a large scale.

2. It is possible to grow any kind of crop in any kind of field.

3. The fields are never fallow, thus ensuring optimum utilisation of land resources.

4. Irrigation facilities are improved.

5. The community or country becomes self-sufficient in food grains.

6. Use of advanced machinery.

7. Prevents starvation in many developing countries.

8. Production cost is reduced.

Shortcomings of Green Revolution

In spite of this, India's agricultural output sometimes falls short of demand even today. India has failed to extend the concept of high yield value seeds to all crops or all regions. In terms of crops, it remains largely confined to foodgrains only, not to all kinds of agricultural produce.

The Green Revolution has created some problems mainly to adverse impacts on the environment. The increasing use of agrochemical-based pest and weed control in some crops has affected the surrounding environment as well as human health. Increase in the area under irrigation has led to rise in the salinity of the land. Although high yielding varieties had their plus points, it has led to significant genetic erosion. Only the states of Punjab, Haryana, the eastern plains of river Ganges in West Bengal showed the best results of the Green Revolution. But results were less impressive in other parts of India.

Shortcomings of green revolution are—

1. Presence of some dangerous forms of pests.
2. New forms of weeds may grow.
3. No measures are taken to increase the fertility of the soil.
4. It leads to land and soil degradation.
5. Affects agricultural biodiversity.
6. Affects biodiversity.
7. Highly reliant on non-renewable resources of energy like fossil fuels.
8. Use of fertilizers and pesticides in high amounts.
9. Using new agricultural methods may not be feasible for small scale farmers.
10. Bigger investments on machinery and transport is required.
11. Over dependence on artificial fertilizers, pesticides, machinery affects the environment.

Fascinating Fact

Farmers will have to grow 70 percent more food than what is currently produced to feed the world's growing population by 2050.

Women make up 30 percent of today's farmers.

40% of today's global population works in agriculture, making it the single largest employer in the world.

Agriculture

It is crucial to understand that saving food does not only mean saving money. By preventing food wastage, we are indirectly protecting our environment. We have understood that agriculture and related processes are indispensable. But if the agricultural practices are unplanned and designed by considering only the crop yield and commercial profits, it leads to environmental hazards like acid rain, pollution, disturbed ecological cycle, etc. Along with adapting sustainable agricultural practices, it should be also ensured that food distribution among all sectors of people happens properly. Food security is indeed a challenge for all the nations especially the developing and underdeveloped ones.

SUMMARY

- Food is one of the primary needs of human beings.
- In order to provide food for a large population, regular production, proper management and distribution of food is necessary.
- Food enriches us with nutrients like proteins, carbohydrates, fats, vitamins and minerals, all of which we require for body development, growth and health.
- Industrial agriculture refers to a process of mechanising the growing, harvesting and processing of food.
- Monoculture farming is the raising of a single crop within a specified area.
- Fertilizers are commercially produced plant nutrients. Fertilizers supply nitrogen, phosphorus and potassium.
- Biomagnification is the process in which toxins are concentrated in an organism as larger animals continue to eat smaller animals.
- Organic farming is a farming system with minimal or no use of chemicals as fertilizers, herbicides, pesticides etc. and with a maximum input of organic manures, recycled farm wastes (straw and livestock excreta), use of bio-agents such as culture of blue green algae in preparation of biofertilizers, neem leaves or turmeric specifically in grain storage as bio-pesticides, with healthy cropping systems [mixed cropping, inter-cropping and crop rotation].
- Food waste or food loss is food that is discarded or lost uneaten. The causes of food waste or loss are numerous and occur at the stages of producing, processing, retailing and consuming.
- Pollution, soil degradation, eutrophication, biomagnification, soil erosion are some environmental problems caused as a result of agricultural activities.
- Heat waves, drought, melting of ice caps, floods, rising of sea levels, rise in temperature of water bodies and acidifying of oceans are the climate change effects seen as a result of agricultural activities.
- The Green Revolution is a set of research and technology transfer initiatives that increased agricultural production worldwide, particularly in the developing world.

- Food security exists when all people, at all times, have physical, social and economic access to sufficient, safe, and nutritious food that meets their dietary needs and food preferences for an active and healthy life.

EXERCISE

A. Define each of these terms :
1. Agriculture
2. Industrial agriculture
3. Monoculture
4. Crop yield
5. Biomagnification
6. Eutrophication
7. Irrigation
8. Deforestation
9. Green revolution
10. Organic farming

B. Answer each of these questions in brief :
1. How did the term 'agriculture' originate ?
2. Which are the two main categories of farming ?
3. Which are the main nutrients present in the fertilisers ?
4. What are bio-fertilisers made up of?
5. Why are bio-fertilisers better than chemical fertilisers ?
6. Differentiate between—
   a. Subsistence farming and Commercial farming
   b. Fertilizer and Manure
7. Explain any two methods of irrigation that ensure minimal wastage of water.
8. Which are the three basic elements of green revolution ?
9. What is food security ?

C. Answer each of these in detail :
1. How does agricultural activities pollute the environment ?
2. List out the benefits of monoculture.
3. In what way is monoculture harmful to the environment ?
4. Write any five advantages of organic farming.
5. Enlist the reasons as to why organic farming is not practised on a large scale ?
6. In what way is eutrophication harmful to the aquatic plants and animals ?
7. Write any six impacts of climate change.
8. How would you differentiate between surplus and waste ?
9. Wasting food is equivalent to wasting ecosystem services. Justify this statement.
10. Why did green revolution fail in India ?
11. What are the possible benefits of green revolution ?
12. Trace the points of similarities between the concept of monoculture and green revolution.

Agriculture

WORKSHEET

A. Fill in the blanks :
1. _____ farming is the raising of a single crop within a specified area.
2. _____ is the application of controlled amounts of water to plants at needed intervals.
3. _____ irrigation is a method of applying irrigation water which is similar to rainfall.
4. _____ was the first state where green revolution was implemented.

B. Write one example of each of these :
1. Bio-agent
2. Bio-pesticide

C. Justify these statements :
1. Agricultural activities produce ozone.
2. Drip irrigation and sprinklers ensure minimum wastage of water.
3. We should use manure on clayey soil.
4. The farmer who sprays pesticide must always wear protective clothes.
5. Monoculture results in loss of traditional crops.
6. Fruits and vegetable from organic farm are relatively expensive.
7. Drip irrigation should be used where rate of evaporation is high.

D. Read the following excerpts and answer the questions that follow. (open-ended questions) :
1. The Green Revolution was started in India in 1950. The Prime Minister Late Shri Lal Bahadur Shastri, who gave the slogan of **"Jai Jawan, Jai Kisan"** encouraged this concept. However, it has benefited only some limited farmers. Make a list of challenges faced during implementation of Green Revolution in India.
2. It is said that the percentage of people suffering from obesity is almost equal to the percentage of people suffering from malnutrition and hunger. Discuss this statement with valid points.
3. Ram Singh is a farmer who grows wheat in his field. He does not sell the wheat in market but uses for his and his family's consumption. What kind of farming is seen in this case ?

E. Activity
1. Think of ways to minimise food wastage in your school and home. Spread this message in your surroundings. Enact your ideas in the form of a small skit.